"Anyone who has ever walked into a grocery store or who has ever cooked food from a grocery store or who has ever eaten food from a grocery store must read *Grocery*. It is food journalism at its best and I'm so freakin' jealous I didn't write it."
—Alton Brown, author of *EveryDayCook*

- -

Praise for GROCERY

- -

"As fascinating as it is instructive, Ruhlman's book digs deep into the world of how we shop and how we eat. It's a marvelous, smart, revealing work."
—Susan Orlean, author of *Rin Tin Tin: The Life and the Legend* and *The Orchid Thief*

"Mr. Ruhlman's skillful portrait of Heinen's might make you want to catch a flight to Cleveland—and as soon as possible."
—*Wall Street Journal*

"Deeply reported."
—*Time*

"This fascinating look at the ins and outs of the grocery store offers something for everyone."
—*Library Journal*, starred review

"Grocery not only covers insights on how we produce, distribute, and buy food, but seeks ways of understanding our changing relationship with what we eat and how we get it."
—*All Things Considered*, NPR

"[An] engaging exploration of the ways American eating habits have changed over the past half century."
—*Entertainment Weekly*

"Idiosyncratic . . . engaging . . . Ruhlman is a congenial guide and a friendly interviewer."
—*Christian Science Monitor*

"A mix of reporting, ranting, and social commentary through the lens of your local supermarket. It'll change the way you shop for food."
—Kitchn.com

GROCERY

ALSO BY MICHAEL RUHLMAN

NONFICTION

Ratio: The Simple Codes Behind the Craft of Everyday Cooking

The Elements of Cooking: Translating the Chef's Craft for Every Kitchen

The Reach of a Chef: Professional Cooks in the Age of Celebrity

The Soul of a Chef: The Journey Toward Perfection

The Making of a Chef: Mastering Heat at the Culinary Institute of America

COOKBOOKS

Ruhlman's How to Sauté: Foolproof Techniques and Recipes for the Home Cook

Ruhlman's How to Braise: Foolproof Techniques and Recipes for the Home Cook

Ruhlman's How to Roast: Foolproof Techniques and Recipes for the Home Cook

Egg: A Culinary Exploration of the World's Most Versatile Ingredient

The Book of Schmaltz: Love Song to a Forgotten Fat

Ruhlman's Twenty: 20 Techniques, 100 Recipes, A Cook's Manifesto

Salumi: The Craft of Italian Dry Curing (with Brian Polcyn)

Charcuterie: The Craft of Salting, Smoking, and Curing (with Brian Polcyn)

Bouchon Bakery (with Thomas Keller and Sebastien Rouxel)

Ad Hoc at Home (with Thomas Keller)

Under Pressure: Cooking Sous Vide (with Thomas Keller)

Bouchon (with Thomas Keller)

The French Laundry Cookbook (with Thomas Keller)

A Return to Cooking (with Eric Ripert)

Michael Symon's Live to Cook (with Michael Symon)

GROCERY

THE BUYING AND SELLING
OF FOOD IN AMERICA

Michael Ruhlman

ABRAMS PRESS, NEW YORK

ABRAMS The Art of Books
195 Broadway, New York, NY 10007
abramsbooks.com

For Miss Scarlett

And in memory of fathers we've lost

"I think it could plausibly be argued that changes of diet are more important than changes of dynasty or even of religion. The Great War, for instance, could never have happened if tinned food had not been invented. . . . Yet it is curious how seldom the all-importance of food is recognized. You see statues everywhere to politicians, poets, bishops, but none to cooks or bacon-curers or market-gardeners."

—George Orwell, *The Road to Wigan Pier*

"It seems to me that our three basic needs, for food and security and love, are so mixed and mingled and entwined that we cannot straightly think of one without the others. So it happens that when I write of hunger, I am really writing about love and the hunger for it, and warmth and the love of it and the hunger for it . . . and then the warmth and richness and fine reality of hunger satisfied . . . and it is all one."

—M. F. K. Fisher, *The Art of Eating*

"The destiny of nations depends on how they nourish themselves."

—Jean Anthelme Brillat-Savarin

CONTENTS

PART IV: THE PERIMETER

PART V: WHERE WE ARE HEADED

GROCERY

INTRODUCTION:
THE INVISIBLE BEHEMOTH ON MAIN STREET

Grocery stores are where we purchase most of our food—$650 billion annually at thirty-eight thousand of them in America, $1 trillion if you count all retail food sales[1]—yet most people know almost nothing about how they operate or where the food they sell comes from. We do, however, count on their always being here. While food issues drive some of the most compelling stories in the news (after national and international crises)—everything from the gluten-free fad, the pros and cons of genetically modified foods, questions about food's possible impact on increasing gastrointestinal illnesses, food fanaticism, food recalls, anxiety about food expiration dates, eating disorders, the paleo diet, our $1 billion-per-day health care crisis—we remain more confused than ever by conflicting information we receive about the food we eat.

Some of this confusion can be explored and clarified by looking inside a grocery store.

The American supermarket is like no other retail store, and we use it like no other retail store, venturing out to buy groceries on average twice a week, every week, all year long, to feed ourselves. A family's biggest expense, after housing and transportation, is groceries (about 10 percent of its income). A small portion of the population grows some of their own food, but almost no one, or no family, fails to go to a grocery store each week. It's the only store most Americans *have to* spend money in. Those who can't get to one tend to be sicker than those who can, according to researchers who study urban and rural food deserts, places where there are no convenient grocery stores.

Grocery stores are more than just places to buy food. They are in a broader sense a reflection of our culture. During the Cold War, for instance, supermarkets were a powerful symbol. "With their dizzying

---

1 Figures from Food Marketing Institute and US Bureau of Labor Statistics.

array of processed foods, [supermarkets] came to be regarded as quintessential symbols of the triumph of American capitalism," writes Harvey Levenstein in *Paradox of Plenty: A Social History of Eating in Modern America*. During the impromptu 1959 Kitchen Debate in Moscow, then vice president Richard Nixon pointed to the astonishing variety of goods available to Americans as evidence of capitalism's superiority, pooh-poohed by Soviet premier Nikita Khrushchev. The next year, however, when Khrushchev and his pals visited a San Francisco supermarket, "the expression on their faces was something to behold," writes Levenstein, quoting Henry Cabot Lodge, one of the hosts.

Because they are a reflection, even symbol, of our culture, and thus a gauge of who we are, supermarkets illuminate what we care about, what we fear, what we desire. They offer a view of our demographic makeup, including how much money we have and how big the country is, not to mention how much it is changing. The grocery store describes the effects of global warming on farms from Washington down through California, the state of our oceans, and the health of our land. It is a showcase for the latest food production innovations, which is critical given the world's escalating population. And the grocery store is at the center of broader issues of how the food we eat affects our bodies and our body politic.

All these issues, and countless others, come into focus when viewed through the American supermarket, food's last stop before it enters our homes. Though we aren't often reflective or thoughtful about grocery stores, they are in truth a barometer of our country's collective state of mind. Yet relatively little has been written about them, how they work, and what they mean.

Why this lack of attention? Perhaps because on the surface, grocery stores seem banal. Perhaps because they are so ubiquitous. I don't know. There's a scene in the extraordinary film *The Hurt Locker*, in which an American serviceman, a bomb diffuser, is home after a tour in Afghanistan, and is grocery shopping with his wife and young child. The fluorescent lighting in the supermarket aisles makes even the brightly colored boxes and packaging seem flat; we sense that the character, played by Jeremy Renner, will not be able to exist in this colorful but dead consumer landscape—a landscape embodied by the grocery store. Sure enough, he is soon back in Afghanistan, suiting up to dismantle a car bomb.

We tend to use grocery stores without thinking about them, or if we do think about them, it's with mild annoyance, the thought of shopping itself a chore. What we rarely reflect on is what a luxury it is to be able to buy an extraordinary variety and quantity of food whenever we want every day of the year.

I'm often asked about the reason for our country's growing obsession with food—the emergence of "the foodie," the 1993 creation of a twenty-four-hour TV channel devoted to food, chefs becoming celebrities, new cooking appliance fetishes, and ever-fancier kitchens that see less and less actual cooking. My response is that when something you need to survive starts making you confused and sick, you become obsessive about it. We don't tend to think much about air, but if we suddenly didn't have any, it would be pretty much all we'd be able to think about. The same might be said about grocery stores—if they suddenly vanished, if our only option for sustenance was the Cheesecake Factory or a CVS pharmacy, we'd think about them a lot.

Part of the reason we don't think about them is that food, on a daily basis, isn't a concern in this country. We have a lot of food—more than what we need, in fact. It's available every hour of every day. Just walk into any supermarket in America, an industry that responds aggressively to what America wants to buy, and you enter a landscape composed of tens of thousands of square feet of inexpensive food, food that's critical first to our comfort and ultimately to our health and happiness. And yet there's something wrong here, and we know it, though we can't we quite get at what it is.

Here's what this book is not: It is not a history of grocery stores, though their transformation from trading posts to country stores to stores selling packaged food to everything-under-one-roof supermarkets is part of the story. It's not an aisle-by-aisle tour of each of the ten main departments of a grocery store (produce, grocery, seafood, meat, floral, bakery, frozen/dairy, deli, prepared foods, wine and beer). Nor do I report on the industrial system we've developed to feed our hunger for beef and pork, the methods and impact of overfishing our oceans, or even the ways the major food manufacturing companies (Kraft, Kellogg, PepsiCo, Nestlé, etc.) create, market, and profit from the food that seems to be making us sick. And this is not a nutritional guide to what is on the shelves and how it affects our health, though food choices and health are central to my story. These issues have been widely covered in other books and in the media.[2]

This book is instead what I would call a reported reflection on the grocery store in America, and an expression of my own love, anger, opinions, and concerns over what is in them, how it got there, and what it all means. I've been writing about food and cooking since 1996, when I snuck into the Culinary Institute of America to write about what the most prominent cooking school said you had to know in order to be a chef. In the intervening two decades, food issues have become some of the most pressing and confusing of our time. Because these issues are so numerous and disparate, I've had to be selective about what I choose to write about, and about these subjects I do not attempt to conceal my opinions.

One fact about the business that became apparent during the writing is that grocery stores are constantly changing, a moving target. Big news in the grocery game came in August 2017 when Amazon bought Whole Foods. Most insiders saw any number of possible changes, but how the purchase will affect grocery shopping is not known. Furthermore, Whole Foods accounts for only 2 percent of groceries sold in the United States. So Amazon may not change what we eat, but it will likely change the way we get it.

Craig Giammona, a grocery industry reporter for Bloomberg News, believes that Amazon's entry into the grocery market will make it harder for family-owned chains to survive. "It's a massive player, with

----

2 See Michael Pollan's *The Omnivore's Dilemma* for beef (and more), Ted Genoways's *The Chain* for pork, and Paul Greenberg's *Four Fish* for seafood. Michael Moss's *Salt Sugar Fat* investigates food manufacturing giants. Dan Barber contrasts industrial agriculture with potential models for growing food sustainably in *The Third Plate*. Marion Nestle explores every department in the grocery store, examining food from a nutritionist's vantage point, in *What to Eat*.

a unique supply chain and delivery prowess, entering a market that is already extremely competitive with tiny margins. And, if we look at how they've done in other industries, we know they're willing to take losses, or at least run margin neutral, which is a very scary proposition for the competitors.

"I don't think brick and mortar stores are going anywhere anytime soon," Craig went on. "But it's going to get tougher. More and more stuff—paper towels, soap, condiments, soup, chips—will be delivered, and the question is how stores manage to continue drawing customers in."

"Whole Foods is a good company that is solidly profitable," Jeff Heinen told me after the sale. "There is very little about it that is broken. Amazon will leverage the existing strengths and use their strengths to change the food industry faster than most companies are going to be comfortable with. It will be a tumultuous next few years for the food industry. We're going to have to change much more quickly than we had originally thought."

So, acknowledging the fact that issues emanating from the grocery stores are all but endless and that the grocery store is a continuously evolving creation, I cover the food that interests me, the people who are most outspoken in the grocery business, and follow the stories that matter to me, whether it's on a vast ranch in a national park in Idaho or on a tour of the grocery store with my physician. In researching this book, I visited farms, stores, and produce auctions; I joined grocers at food shows and interviewed the cheese makers they buy from; I toured a fish auction in Honolulu, one of the major fish auctions in the country; I bagged groceries, got to know the people who ran the stores and who worked in them, and generally hung out in the supermarket. In short, as a lover of food, a cook, and a person who cares about the future of food in America, I wrote a book that, using a small family grocery chain in my hometown of Cleveland as my inroad, is the book that I wanted most to read. Ultimately it is a story that's never been written: an appreciation of, and wonder at, the American grocery store and the complex and fascinating business of retailing food to a country of 320 million people.

But it is also, as you'll see, a deeply personal subject, and I try to tell that story as well. Happily, I grew up in a household that loved food and cooking, the place where, surely, my love of food and my fascination with grocery stores began. Having written about the food world for twenty years now, I've come to care about food more than I ever thought possible—about how we grow it, raise it, catch it, kill it, package it, distribute it, buy it, cook it, and dispose of what we don't want. Our food (and the cooking of it, or lack thereof) is more important than most people realize, and we fail to understand this at our peril.

PART I

HOW WE GOT HERE

1.

MY FATHER'S GROCERY STORE JONES

Rip Ruhlman loved to eat, almost more than anything else. We'd be tucking in to the evening's meal when he'd ask, with excitement in his eyes, "What should we have for dinner tomorrow?" Used to drive Mom crazy. And because he loved to eat, my father loved grocery stores.

In my youth, two grocery stores operated less than a mile in either direction from our house in Shaker Heights, a suburb of Cleveland: Heinen's on Chagrin Boulevard and Fazio's on Van Aken Boulevard. Both were family-owned, open six days a week. Union laws forced them to close on weekdays at six p.m., the time my father stepped off the train from work, so Saturdays were the only time he could satisfy his grocery store jones. Mom went back to work once I started kindergarten, and I don't recall her ever setting foot in a grocery store through the rest of their twenty-two-year marriage.[3] That was my father's territory. And to my father, grocery stores were the land of opportunity.

Look at all this food! All the flavors! All the frozen appetizers! Such opportunity for pleasure! So many new items to try! Kiwi! What's that? The snack aisle! Diet Pepsi! Orange Crush!

A whole range of processed food appeared in the early 1960s, just as my parents started their marriage and had me, their only child, and items such as these were always on his list: Space Food Sticks, Cap'n Crunch, Tang (a synthetic form of orange juice), and Carnation Instant Breakfast. Milk and eggs, of course. Always pretzel rods for the jar in the den by the television set, which had knobs for changing the channel and adjusting the volume. Nuts, how he loved peanuts! An endless supply

---

3 "We bought a *lot* of frozen dinners," she recalls now about her shopping days. Asked about the produce department in March, she said, "Iceberg lettuce, carrots, apples, grapefruit, oranges, bananas, and the occasional pineapple. That was it. You only saw blueberries in the summer."

at the grocery store. Along the back aisle, the meat cases, oh Lord, the opportunities for ecstasy: veal and sausages and pork! Rack of lamb! And of course the beautifully marbled rib steaks (his favorite cut). The white button mushrooms in produce that he could sauté in butter and slather on top of that steak, which he'd lovingly grilled over charcoal (bought at the grocery store), which was lit with lighter fluid (bought at the grocery store), and into which he nestled Vidalia onions (grown as early as the 1930s, but new in Cleveland grocery stores in the 1970s) wrapped in foil with a pat of butter, and which would become charred and tender and sweet after an hour in the coals. Steak and a baked potato with a Vidalia onion was a beloved staple dinner of my youth. And always a salad. Heads of iceberg lettuce (this and a few sturdier greens were about the only salad options available through the long winters) were stacked into pyramids in the produce department. Five or six different bottled dressings were available to pour on that lettuce (back then, our choice was Wish-Bone Italian).

He bought pounds of Granny Smith apples, one of about five varieties to choose from, which were a part of his apple-a-day, broom-of-the-system regimen. He would proudly eat the entire apple, seeds and all. And carrots, bags and bags of carrots all year long. He loved carrots so much he ate them throughout the day. Dad routinely reached inside his suit jacket, mid-conversation in the hallway of the ad agency where he had become creative director, took a bite of a carrot, and returned it to his jacket pocket. To the bewilderment of new hires at the agency.

He would gladly deposit a few Rock Cornish game hens (a cross between Cornish game birds and the White Plymouth Rock, introduced in 1955) into the metal shopping cart, with its one wobbly wheel, and eventually a box of Uncle Ben's wild rice for my mother, who loved to roast the hens stuffed with it. If he and Mom were entertaining, he'd also grab a package of the mysteriously named "chipped beef," a package of boneless, skinless chicken breasts, a can of Campbell's cream of mushroom soup, and a bottle of "cooking sherry" for my mom's "party chicken" recipe. (Combine all in a casserole dish, more or less, and bake till the chicken is rock solid; serve with boxed wine or a Gallo "Chablis."

The party-chicken dinner would be followed, long into the laughter-filled Saturday night, by Rusty Nails and Stingers and cigarettes in the living room, a fire crackling on the hearth.)

And the holidays—grocery shopping times ten! Dad stuffed the cart with giant Hershey chocolate bars and cartons of Whoppers to fill my Christmas stocking. He ordered from the supermarket the turkey for Thanksgiving and the rib roast for Christmas (but not the green beans, Campbell's soup, and canned onion rings for the traditional green bean casserole, which was the domain of Aunt Barbara, who shopped at the Heinen's on Green Road). At Easter he picked up a leg of lamb, butterflied by the helpful butcher, and garlic he would sliver and stud the lamb with, and black pepper and dried rosemary for seasoning. I would not see or even recognize the existence of a fresh herb until I was an adult living in New York City. Before then, if a recipe called for an herb other than curly parsley,[4] it meant opening a small jar, usually containing something once green but now grayish, and held in a wall-mounted rack (a 1962 wedding gift to my parents, every jar but the tarragon untouched since the rack was mounted).

The tarragon—*that* was well used, for the béarnaise sauce to spoon over the filet mignon that Dad had wrapped in bacon and grilled. Béarnaise sauce—Mom's purview, composed mainly of butter whipped into egg yolks, flavored with minced shallot and dried tarragon—was my family's version of holy water. Dad and I watched Mom making Julia Child's recipe, or rather *spectated*, because she brought the making of béarnaise to the level of entertainment: The more butter, the better, but add too much and the sauce would break, the thick emulsion collapsing into soup; no one understood why. Mom insisted on giving the sauce a sporting chance to break and so always added more butter, to our alarm and excitement. *Bam! Gasp!* Cooking *could* be entertainment. The sauce was seasoned with tarragon vinegar, which for all we knew was distilled from the tarragon plant itself or simply dispensed from metal kegs that

---

4 Curly parsley was the only fresh herb I saw at the grocery store at the time, so I didn't consider it an herb; it was just a garnish on restaurant plates. Mom told me to eat it to freshen my breath.

had arrived from the tarragon vinegar factory somewhere outside Oakland. In other words, we had no idea at the time how or where vinegar was made or what it was. In those days, we had little inkling how most of our basic pantry items were created. None of us could have explained that vinegar was fermented from alcohol or that the quality of that vinegar was directly related to the quality of the alcohol. All we knew for certain was that tarragon vinegar came from the shelf of a grocery store.

The butter that went into that béarnaise sauce must be mentioned. Oh, how Dad loved butter—as much as he wanted awaited him on the supermarket dairy shelf. Any conduit for its entry into his mouth sufficed: boiled artichokes, snails, lobster, bread, it didn't matter. The man felt a kind of ecstasy when ounces and ounces sluiced down his gullet, nutritionists be damned. At the time, butter was considered bad for you. As were eggs. In the 1960s and 1970s, nutritionists, and in 1977 the US government, warned us that all fat was bad for you (thus the popularity of margarine and the creation of dubious concoctions such as I Can't Believe It's Not Butter!).[5] And eggs, regarded for thousands of years as a nutritious staple of the human diet, were determined to be heart attacks in a shell, the evidence of human history notwithstanding.

But my father wasn't going to let a nutritionist or a magazine article tell him he couldn't have eggs. "Malarkey," he would say. Dad was the one who showed me how to make a broken-yolk fried-egg sandwich basted with butter and eaten on Wonder Bread generously smeared with Hellmann's mayonnaise and served with a glass of milk. All available thanks to the grocery store—and *only* the grocery store at that time— one long block from our house in either direction. You couldn't buy this stuff anywhere else. "We're out of *butter*? I'll run to the grocery store and get another pound," he'd announce. "And another dozen eggs." It almost seemed he loved to have forgotten an item on his long lists—another excuse to be in the grocery store.

5 Researchers have recently discovered evidence that this advice was heavily influenced by the sugar industry, which sought to deflect attention from the impact of sugar on our health. See "How the Sugar Industry Shifted Blame to Fat," *New York Times*, September 12, 2016.

Chicken legs were a go-to staple of weeknight dinners—chicken had become increasingly prevalent in the 1970s, though it wouldn't overtake beef as America's preferred protein until about 2012—baked with honey and orange juice, served with frozen green beans thawed on the stovetop and a box of Minute Rice (the par-cooked invention of the 1940s).

The grocers' union mandate that Cleveland supermarket hours must end at six p.m. on weekday nights prevented working families from food shopping Monday through Friday. (Mom had become a buyer for Higbee's department store on Euclid Avenue and thus was something of an outcast among married women in our provincial suburb, so she couldn't shop during the week when most married women shopped. This was the beginning of a cultural shift, the rise of the working woman, that would help transform our food supply and arguably the quality of the food we served our families.) Hunter-gathering by necessity happened on Saturdays in Cleveland. So, in the 1960s and '70s, Saturdays at the grocery store meant lines and lines of shoppers, their carts overflowing, clogging the aisles all the way to the meat department at the back of the store. As a boy, I would join Dad and ride in the cart till it became too full and then push the second cartful when the first overflowed with the week's food. And then we'd load up the car—an invention that proved to be critical to the growth of the supermarket—for the short haul to our suburban colonial to stuff the refrigerator and the back pantry[6] with our booty.

Before the grocery shopping even began, my father spent at least an hour on Saturday morning at the ledge demarcating the kitchen from the breakfast nook, hand pressed to his forehead, the other hand pressing pen to paper. Here he created the shopping list, a week's worth of food, on one of his ubiquitous legal pads. He peppered me with

....

6 On the wall next to our pantry, by the back door, was a door about one square foot that opened, from both outside and in, to a small compartment that the milkman in previous decades would fill on schedule; here the milk kept cool in summer and didn't freeze in winter, and you didn't have to leave your house to get it. Milk, America's first convenience food, delivered by truck to your door, was an anachronism until recently.

questions about what I wanted, the Quisp cereal or Frosted Flakes, the Pepsi Light, the Tab for my mom, and what for dinner? What did I want to eat? "You can have *anything*"—oh, the bounty! This was how our world worked.

Throughout my life the supermarket had it all. Endless food to feed our family of three and the countless friends my parents loved to cook for.

After my parents' divorce in the mid-1980s, Dad lived alone in our house; by this time, the grocery store provided a variety of Lean Cuisine entrées and other frozen specialties, which he loved for their convenience, portion size, and calorie count. Long gone, at least from our household, were the Swanson's TV dinners in their sectioned aluminum trays and Stouffer's potpies that took thirty minutes in a preheated oven. The microwave oven, introduced in the late 1960s, had become a kitchen necessity by the 1980s—another invention that changed the way many American families ate.

My father stocked the kitchen with chickens and baked potatoes and, as time went on, fresh green beans. I would roast that chicken for us when I, a young adult, returned from New York City to re-gather myself and try to find my way in the world. By then, the mid-1980s, we ate in the dining room—a reflection, I like to think, of our growing appreciation of sharing a well-prepared meal—rather than in the overly lit breakfast nook where we ate when I was young and where, throughout my childhood, I found Dad in the morning. Without fail, he would be drinking a mug of black instant coffee and smoking a Lucky Strike (both grocery store purchases, of course) before it was time for him to catch the train to the Terminal Tower downtown and make the fifteen-minute walk to his office at 1010 Euclid Avenue.

This was how we ate. We took it for granted.

Millennia ago, before grocery stores, finding enough food to eat was the single daily business at hand. When civilizations took root, in part because we learned to cultivate food and create food surpluses, the business of the family was to put up food, to preserve it to keep the family from starving during the winter, because the grocery store (not to mention the car to get to it and haul the goods back) did not exist.

Instead, families farmed (and even most non-farmer families grew and raised some of their food through the 1940s), and they dry-cured pork loin and shoulder and belly and back fat, poached and cooled duck in its own fat in a way that would preserve it for years, and preserved fruit to eat throughout the winter.

But there, on Norwood Road in suburban Cleveland, Ohio, I watched my dad struggle not with spearing a wild hog in the brush, or cutting a slab of pork belly hanging in the kitchen, but rather writing a list of items to pull off a shelf or remove from a case in the grocery store, our community's shared pantry. This was the food that would keep our family alive and thriving—all available with a convenience unmatched in human history. We had gone from tribes hunting food, gathering it, preserving it, joining in the work of it, protecting it, and then sharing it in larger and larger communities to, thousands of years later, isolated families on suburban streets gathering our food from a single forty-thousand-square-foot store once a week and bringing it back home to eat by ourselves.

The grocery store had become our food surplus, that fundamental mechanism that allowed *Homo sapiens* to stay in one place and to form communities.

Most of these stores at the time were family-owned, except for the A&P, which in the first half of the twentieth century was loathed, as much as Walmart would one day be, for decimating Main Street, USA. The A&P grew to the size it did (the biggest retailer in the world at one point) by increasing volume to drive prices down. Most of the family-owned supermarkets in Cleveland had only a couple of options to increase their volume. They could open more stores, but without a central distribution center, a warehouse, they would essentially be creating stand-alone businesses rather than efficient chains. Most didn't have such a center. So instead they merged with other family-owned stores—the Rini's with the Rego's in Cleveland, for instance. But by the 1980s, an era of widespread mergers and acquisitions, they were forced to sell out to large multinational companies. Fisher Foods, begun in Cleveland in 1907 by the Fisher brothers, merged with the Fazio family, then merged again with the Stop-N-Shop chains (Rini's, Rego's, Russo's) to form Riser Foods; too much debt and other issues forced them to sell to Giant Eagle. The locally owned Pick-N-Pay became Finast, then sold to the Dutch conglomerate Ahold. By this point only behemoths could offer economies of scale, and the resulting low prices, to lure the customer looking for ever-cheaper food.

And another major cultural shift had begun that threatened grocery stores: More types of retail businesses began to sell food. Convenience stores had been around for decades in some areas of the country, but they began to mushroom in the latter part of the twentieth century and would eventually offer produce along with a tank of gas; drugstores began to sell milk, eggs, and other foods; and eventually, by the 1990s, Costco (1976) and Sam's Club (Walmart's 1983 creation) had a nationwide presence. All these places were beginning to sell food, of varying quality and costs, that was once the sole provenance of the supermarket.

The final marker of the food retail conversion from grocery store to supermarket to our modern, fragmented food retail system came in 1988, when, like the big kid doing a cannonball into a crowded swimming pool, Walmart entered the grocery business with its first Supercenters, which added groceries to their other nonfood offerings. Walmart instantly became the world's biggest grocer. Of its total net sales of $482 billion last year, Walmart stores in the United States accounted for $298 billion. According to its 2016 10-K filing with the SEC, 56 percent of those sales, $167 billion, came from selling groceries. Add Sam's Club grocery sales to that and Walmart's total sales of groceries last year were $202 billion. The nation's largest supermarket chain, Kroger, with its 2,600-odd stores, is a distant second with sales of roughly $110 billion.

Walmart's grocery revenue, its sales of lettuce and frozen dinners and eggs, beats those of other industry giants, such as General Motors or AT&T. Walmart alone took more than one quarter of all the dollars we spent on groceries. Inevitably, more discount retail stores, such as

Target, set up grocery sections in their stores. Everyone, it seemed, was getting into the food business.

Key players in this fragmentation were the niche grocery stores that had begun rapidly expanding in the 1990s, such as Whole Foods Market (opened in 1980, now doing $15 billion in annual sales) and Trader Joe's (1967, about $9 billion today), followed by newcomers such as Sprouts Farmers Market and Fresh Thyme Farmers Market, hoping to cut in on sales at Whole Foods (dubbed "Whole Paycheck" by some for their comparatively high prices).

All these big-box stores and niche markets promised to offer something the traditional grocery store did not. Whole Foods and the like had a wide range of organic foods (but you couldn't find Cheerios there); Trader Joe's carried a range of specialty and exotic packaged and frozen goods sold cheap; Costco offered a tenth of what you could find in a grocery store but promised great savings. And big traditional grocers would soon try to move into the competition's territory, offering more organic and good-for-you products at big chain prices.

Currently making up only a fraction of grocery sales but adding to this fragmentation of food retailing generally, and looming especially ominously on the horizon for traditional grocers, is the whole world of internet ordering and home delivery. "You know what keeps me up at night?" Jeff Heinen, grandson of the founder of his chain, asked me. He paused: "Amazon."

The delivery system of food appears to be on the cusp of great change, with not just Amazon but companies such as FreshDirect offering convenient home delivery of pretty much everything imaginable. This of course concerns the grocer, who depends on customers to get in their cars, drive to the store, then pick out and pay for their own food.

Every decade since the 1980s has seen substantial changes in food retailing—changes we ourselves have wittingly and unwittingly demanded to our benefit and detriment. The way we now sell and buy food has also transformed the way we grow, process, distribute, and consume the food we need to stay alive.

And we scarcely give it a thought.

For my father, this fragmentation of the food retailing business was a fantastic boon. Not only were grocers allowed to stay open late in the 1980s and '90s, they were open on Sundays as well. My dad could now shop multiple times a week. And he had many more stores to choose from. On nonwork days, he would visit as many as five grocery stores, filling up cart after cart with items he could find only at specific stores or taking advantage of sales (he was a coupon-clipper and ever on the hunt for bargains). When he got in line with his proudly chosen food, he didn't simply stand there and wait; he used the time to scan other shoppers' carts to see what they had, watched the continuous belts of food conveyed to the checkout girl and the bag boy. What was he missing out on? What did other shoppers know that he didn't know? He never hesitated to ask a stranger what was in this or that intriguing package.

"When I retire," he once said, "I think I'm going to bag groceries."

As my father made his merry way through the ever-expanding central aisles of the supermarket from the 1960s through 2008, he had little inkling what was happening to the food that companies were either preparing for him or manipulating in some way to make it cheaper (typically by removing whatever was nutritious about it in the first place). Dad didn't care—if it was new and tasted good, he wanted it.

Just so long as they had the food, he didn't concern himself with how it was made or where it came from. He trusted the grocery store and the makers of his food. One Super Bowl Sunday in the mid-1990s he retrieved a half dozen boxes of appetizers from the freezer and showed them to me with great excitement. "We're going to try all these different offerings throughout the game—this is going to be fun," he said. And it would all be so easy—put them in the microwave and tap some buttons. Convenience had been the explicit command within food manufacturing companies since the 1950s, and they had continued to deliver. Seven to eight minutes in the microwave? Too long, let's try to reduce it to three or four. The convenience of breaded and fried jalapeño peppers could not be denied—no breading or frying required. I remember not a single food we ate that wintry night; I remember only how miserable I felt by the fourth quarter and how desperately I wanted a salad after all that processed, precooked, and microwaved food.

America has always been conscious of diet and its impact on our health, but after five decades of eating processed food and not feeling good, combined with a recognition of the diet-related illnesses that were appearing, America's health-consciousness went into high gear. We began to understand, as the century changed, that we had better start paying attention to our food. Because the country *was* getting sick on an epidemic scale. One of every three adults in this country is defined as obese. Children were developing adult diabetes. Such illnesses have become rampant.

Another problem emerged in the first decade of this century, giving rise to the term "food desert," an acknowledgment that a huge swath of the population doesn't have easy access to fresh food. The US Department of Agriculture estimates that 23.5 million people, about 7 percent of the population, live in food deserts, where they rely on convenience food and fast food for their calories. While the media tends to focus on urban food deserts, food deserts in rural America, where people may not have a grocery store within ten miles of where they live, are equally prevalent and harmful.

It's a sad irony in a country as wealthy as America that people who live in food deserts have a higher rate of obesity, diabetes, and other food-related diseases than those who have easy and ready access to abundant food. A study in the *International Journal of Epidemiology*[7] notes, "Higher rates of obesity are likely to be found in those areas with the lowest incomes and the least education, particularly among women and certain ethnic groups." Not surprisingly, those with the lowest incomes are more likely to live in a food desert. Interestingly, this international study found the correlation between food deserts and obesity unique to

7 "Food environments and obesity—neighborhood or nation?," *International Journal of Epidemiology*, Volume 35, Issue 1, February 2006.

America. The authors cite a study in the *Journal of Preventive Medicine* finding evidence that "the presence of supermarkets was associated with a lower prevalence of obesity."

Why? People tend to eat what's easiest and cheapest to find, and in food deserts that typically means fast food and food that can be purchased in a drugstore or convenience store. I'm not sure that we need long-term, randomized, double-blind studies on the effects of eating food from these places, because the trials have played out naturally throughout the country in food deserts. Certainly other factors, such as education and tobacco use, have an impact on these populations, but the single factor in improving this high-risk population's health is improving the quality of the food it eats, and this means making that food easier to get to and also affordable.

But turning food deserts into oases is not easy. Wendell Pierce, the actor famous for his roles in the TV shows *The Wire* and *Treme,* wanted to give back to his home city of New Orleans by opening a grocery store in the town of Marrero, Louisiana, a so-called food desert across the Mississippi River from New Orleans. It closed in a year, suggesting that simply making fresh food available will not change people's eating decisions and habits.

For those who do have options, the situation became ever more complex in the grocery store, as more and more products lined the shelves catering to ever-changing dietary fashions, typically revolving around convenience and low-fat claims. One positive result of Americans' desire to avoid fat was that they began to eat more vegetables and greens.

Even my father, though he still leaned heavily on frozen Lean Cuisine entrées, began to load up increasingly on salad. Meals for him typically included a popcorn bowl filled with greens and cut vegetables, tossed with a vinaigrette he put together himself—albeit with a store-bought dried seasoning packet.

Alas, all the salad and whole grains in Cleveland wouldn't have been enough to save him from the lung cancer that appeared in January 2008.

All those aforementioned Lucky Strikes, though abandoned when he was in his forties, had done their damage, and by August, the bell tolled for him.

He had returned from the hospital on hospice care and within a few days was no longer able to climb the stairs. Hearing of the situation, my mother flew to Cleveland to see her ex-husband with whom she remained best friends. The night of her arrival I made one of my father's favorite meals, hamburgers on the grill with lettuce and tomato and homemade French fries, all from the grocery store. He was able to sit at the table and take a few bites before returning to the hospital bed we'd set up in the dining room.

By morning his breathing had become erratic, but on it went as we sat near him or busied ourselves in the open kitchen off the dining room, taking comfort in food. It was a clear summer Saturday and Mom had gone to our excellent North Union Farmers Market—yet another aspect of food retail that has changed radically. In 1994, there were fewer than two thousand farmers' markets in the United States. But with calls for eating fresh and local growing increasingly loud, such markets blossomed. By that summer of 2008 there were more than four thousand, a number that would double again in the coming years, to the point that this country now has one farmers market for every four or five grocery stores.

I boiled the corn Mom had bought and we stood at the kitchen island, munching away, salty butter dripping down our chins. I like to think that Dad could hear that munching during his final minutes on earth because he was always happiest when people around him were eating. We finished a dozen ears of corn.

My father died right there in our dining room, before noon, a month shy of his seventieth birthday.

I've always loved grocery stores without asking myself why. Surely part of my love comes from the happiness they gave my dad. And I suspect this was partly the reason I decided to look more seriously into grocery stores the winter after his death, to understand what they really mean.

Little has been written about them in terms of how they work and what they signify.

I chose my father's favorite grocery store, Heinen's, as my entry into this world. It's considered the best in Cleveland in terms of the quality of its products. I wanted a family-run business that was a manageable size for me to write about; Heinen's has twenty-two stores, not too big and not too small. They are both a traditional supermarket and one that looks to the future in terms of what the grocery store might become.

I should say up front that I don't make a distinction between a "grocery store" and a "supermarket."[8] Technically we don't really have stores that sell only groceries, shelf-stable products, anymore. Most stores sell a variety of shelf-stable and perishable goods. So most stores should be considered, technically, supermarkets. But there is a warmth to the term *grocery store* that encourages one to embrace it and hold on to it. In large part this is because it still does connote—in this era of fragmentation and impersonal service and a food world that grows ever more confusing—a place that can be depended upon, day in and day out, where you can get everything you need to nourish your family. We like to think that our grocery store is run by a grocer (not a supermarketer). And we want to believe that there are capable people in charge of our food, people who care for it and ensure that the products are good.

I met the grocers Tom and Jeff Heinen in March 2009, at the store where my father shopped, and where I often shopped, in Shaker Heights. Tom and Jeff, then fifty-four, are fraternal twins. They both have white hair. Jeff is tall and lean, with a narrow face and large, brown eyes. He no longer limps, thanks to a new hip ("I'm good on replacement parts," he assured me). Tom, with blue eyes and a rounder face, clearly enjoys his steaks and single malts. They grew up in suburban Cleveland the sons and grandsons of grocers, and they both moved into the business not long after graduating college. Though twins, their temperaments are quite different. Jeff is seen as the conservative one, a man who holds his

8 The word "grocery," by the way, derives from the old French *grocerie*, denoting a shop that sold items such as sugar, tea, and spices. The term moved over into English in the fifteenth century as "grocery," and crossed the Atlantic from there.

cards close to his chest, a grocer's grocer. He's active in the grocery store, eager to speak with customers. Tom, while every bit a grocer, is more inclined to shoot from the hip and pursue exciting ideas.

One of their managers, who has been in the business for more than forty years, told me, "Jeff is the real grocer. Tom's not. Tom is the entrepreneur." Theirs is a kind of spiritual yin and yang that seems to have served the store well.

One of the first things I said to them when I met them was how much my father loved grocery stores, and that he would visit as many as five in a single day.

Tom narrowed his eyes at me, gritted his teeth, and said, "We hate guys like your father." Meaning, of course, that they would have preferred my dad to do *all* his shopping at their store, something that used to be the case for most people, but was no longer—perhaps the most salient fact of this story.

We strolled the store and I asked questions and tried to explain why I was so curious about grocery stores, that there seemed to be a good deal of confusion regarding food in our country and that the grocery store seemed like a good place to start to get a better understanding of it. We happened to be in the produce section, and Jeff stopped in front of some plum tomatoes.

"People don't *think* about food," he said. He and Tom were dressed, as all employees were, in blue Oxford cloth shirts with the company's logo above the left breast pocket. "It can be frustrating. We don't want to give our customers peaches that are bad. You can get peaches now from Ecuador, but they're terrible. People see nice-looking peaches in Giant Eagle[9] and say, 'Why don't you have them?' Because we don't think they're very good. And yes, we think it's our place to tell people what's good and what's not good.

"We do try to educate the consumer," he continued. "There's a reason that tomatoes in February look and taste like a box. I had a woman

....

9 A Pittsburgh-based chain with 229 stores in this part of the Midwest and a strong presence in Cleveland.

come up to me last week, mid-thirties, nicely dressed, and ask me why we didn't have wonderful local heirloom tomatoes! I said, 'Have you looked out the window?' She did, paused long enough to consider the snow drifts, and said, 'Hmm, I guess you're right.' She'd never really *thought* about it."

Exactly, I thought. Thinking. It should be the first step in shopping.

Tom and Jeff said they were open to the idea of my hanging around in their stores. But first, they said, "You should speak to Chris."

Chris Foltz is a tall, slender man with sandy hair, protuberant brown eyes, an easy smile, and a slight twang retained from Topeka, Kansas, where he spent his teenage years. Chris is third in command here, a former consultant for Tom and Jeff who found that he loved the grocery business, and this company in particular.

"Chris didn't know squat about groceries," Tom told me, laughing, "and we made him director of operations!" Indeed, many of the managers I spoke with openly called Chris "the visionary."

I met Chris at another Heinen's, farther out in the suburbs and nearer to their headquarters, to stroll the store and talk about the grocery business. He had the enthusiasm of a motivational speaker.

"The more I began to learn about groceries, the more fascinated I became," he told me as we walked the aisles. "I kept saying to myself, 'This is *amazing*.'

"First," he said, "a grocery store combines a mercantile business model with a manufacturing model. We get product in, put it on a shelf, merchandise it as is. But we also get product in, *change* that product, and sell it as something else, so you've got two different businesses going on under one roof. And the balance between them is changing all the time as our culture, and how we eat, changes.

"This store here, this one store, does $35 million in sales every year, $675,000 a *week*. We've got 150 employees who work here. This one store is its own small company. Heinen's stores overall will do sales of $600 million this year. That's more than half a *billion* dollars, and we're still considered a small family business!"

"How so?" I asked as we moved past dairy (where, Chris noted, fifteen hundred cartons of eggs and sixteen hundred gallons of milk find their way into shopping carts every week of every year).

"Because we don't make a lot of money, because the margins are so small," he explained. "We run this on about a 1 percent margin.[10] Look at it from an investor's standpoint. You do sales of half a *billion* dollars and you only have a profit of $5 million—what kind of business is that?

"It costs us $10 million to open a new store. We're investing $4 million in new technology this year. A 5 percent shift in sales can really fuck us up. Nobody in their right mind would actually *invest* in this business because the return is so small.

"Plus, it's become incredibly complex. We've got forty thousand products in this store. Every week, we have about twelve thousand customers coming into each store, twelve thousand transactions at an average of forty dollars apiece at each store. So much has to be done to make that happen week after week, stuff that shoppers have no idea about. We have to order and keep track of forty thousand products, we've got to check it in and get it on the shelves, make it look good so people will buy it, then check it out of the store. If it's an ingredient, it has to be prepared."

As Chris talked, I continued to become more eager to explore groceries. Clearly there was considerably more to this subject than a business story.

It would be six years before my schedule and the Heinens' would align and I could devote time to watching a grocery store operate throughout the year, work in the stores, join them on sourcing trips and at trade shows. When I called Chris to reintroduce my idea of hanging out at his grocery store, he was more than enthusiastic.

"So much has changed since we first talked," he told me. "Local produce dominates our produce department, and what isn't local we buy directly from the farm, not wholesalers. Throughout the summer 70

10 Chris was rounding to keep the numbers simple; Heinen's runs on what most grocery stores do, a margin of 1.25 to 1.5 percent.

percent of our produce is local—70 percent! Local has established itself as a critical criterion because people see it as authentic, high quality, environmentally sound, and a good value.

"We now have grass-fed beef, lamb, and acorn-fed pork, in addition to our source-verified beef. Five years ago, nobody wanted hormone-free beef. Now transparency is critical. Where food comes from is huge. Huge. And it's happened so quickly. We work very hard to be transparent and we work very hard to source locally.

"There have been significant changes in *what* we eat," he continued, "*when* we eat, *how* we eat, and *where* we eat, but the traditional grocer hasn't changed what they sell or how they sell it. This has allowed niche players to enter markets and succeed—Trader Joe's, Whole Foods, Fresh Market—while traditional grocers struggle.

"Snacking now represents *50 percent* of our eating occasions. The solutions are across all categories of food, and yet we still merchandise snacks as a category in the snack aisle rather than highlighting snacks across all categories."

More and more I began to believe that the American supermarket was not only an important linchpin of a community, not only a place to pick up food for the home, but also an inroad toward understanding many of the critical food and health issues of our time. And perhaps even a mechanism for changing the way we grow and distribute food.

And what made these issues urgent to me, somehow, was the loss of my father.

Not long after finishing a draft of this book I was enjoying some pints of Founders IPA with the writer Andre Dubus III. When I told him I was writing about grocery stores, his face lit up. He grinned; he beamed. "I *love* grocery stores. I *love* grocery shopping!" When I asked why, he said, "I was never happier than when I was grocery shopping with my kids."

Dubus's mom and dad divorced when he was young. His mom raised him and his brother and two sisters on her own; even with her ex-husband's child-support checks, she struggled. They lived in a series of inexpensive rented houses and apartments north of Boston. He didn't starve, but there was rarely a food surplus at home.

"When a friend came over with a case of beer," Dubus said, "he could just slide it right into the fridge. He didn't have to move anything, because there wasn't anything in it."

Today, Dubus is an accomplished writer and teacher, living an upper-middle-class life in a house he built with his brother. There's always food in this house, something he didn't know in his youth. As a father, when he went grocery shopping with his kids, he could give them anything, anything at all. Shopping for groceries was a literal providing-for-the-family, the family he loved, but it also carried a complex emotional charge: a recognition of his mom and how hard she'd worked, how difficult it was to raise three kids, her struggle to feed her family, and how her struggle had helped lead him to success, success that now allowed his kids to never have to know how it *sucks* to be hungry, and what a great feeling it is to be so capable in this life as to feed one's family well. Dubus rolled his cart through the produce section, with his daughter and two sons, a father who likes to cook, picking out all the vegetables they wanted, past the meat counter for a slab of ribs, past the deli counter and through the aisles. *What do you want? You can have anything. Anything.*

I grew up with a dad like that, who got on the train every working morning of his life but for a single bout of flu to earn the living that paid for our house and car and food. You couldn't have fit a case of beer in *our* fridge, had you arrived with one, though it would already have had a dozen cans of Miller Lite and Carling Black Label (a client of his). As well as a gallon of whole milk, and butter, and lettuce, and jars of condiments, including his beloved Tabasco, and Hellmann's mayonnaise for his fried-egg sandwich, and the eggs, and the deli meats for more sandwiches, and limes for his gin on the rocks at the end of the day, his carrots and apples, and in the freezer compartment below, even more bounty: ice cream, frozen burgers and steaks ready to thaw and grill, a true surplus of food. Life was good.

So, in no small degree, my interest in grocery stores was an attempt to understand the nature of the grocery store's power over our imagination, its emotional force, as well as its measurable meanings.

And still, I had to ask myself, why was the loss of my father so bound up in my interest in groceries? On the surface it doesn't make a lot of sense.

About all this, I think my dad, slicing into his grilled chicken thigh at the dinner table, would have had one thing to say: "So, what should we have for dinner tomorrow night?"

2.

HOW THE A&P CHANGED THE WESTERN WORLD

The modern American supermarket stocks forty to fifty thousand individual items, each with a unique bar code. They are driven to do so because they want to appeal to everyone and be considered a place where you can get everything you need for daily living. You can't be assured of this by visiting a Sam's Club, Costco, or BJ's. These stores carry only about four thousand items, so we visit them for specific, money-saving purchases. Even Whole Foods carries only half of the items a standard grocery store offers.

A grocer may or may not like Honey Nut Cheerios, and Jeff Heinen might urge you to choose a better alternative to a sugary, refined-wheat product (the kind of Whole Foods–type products they now go to great lengths to offer in addition to the cereals we've been eating for decades). But if a mom or dad enters the grocer's store and looks for Honey Nut Cheerios, Jeff wants them to be able to find it, and anything and everything else that shopper might need. He knows if they don't carry it (or any of the other twelve versions of Cheerios), the shopper will go to a store that does. Thus their need to carry so many items.

We are currently in the midst of a gluten-free craze. Whole sections of aisles are now devoted to products that don't contain this protein found in flour, beer, soy sauce—too many foods to count. I asked Chris Foltz if gluten-free was a fad, and if he thought there were any benefits to healthy individuals buying all these gluten-free foods. "I have no idea," he said, "but I am lovin' the hell out of it." Because the stuff sells.

In the end the consumer rules, even if that consumer doesn't think about or understand why they are making the decisions they do. The consumer ultimately drives what grocers put on their shelves.

There's no better example of grocery stores responding to the customer than when our government makes pronouncements about what is good and bad for us. Eggs and fat are the perfect example. In the 1970s, doctors and nutritionists told us that eggs were bad for us and that fat must be avoided. And the consumer listened to what made intuitive sense: Egg yolks are high in cholesterol and high cholesterol in our bodies supposedly resulted in heart attacks, so don't eat eggs. (This despite the fact that there was little evidence that the food cholesterol in eggs raises our blood serum cholesterol.[11]) Fat, conventional reasoning went, makes us fat. So we traded eggs for Egg Beaters and egg whites. We traded traditional bacon for turkey bacon and looked for 2 percent milk rather than whole milk (which is only between 3 and 4 percent, anyway). And we put this low-fat milk on our kids' chemical- and sugar-laden Lucky Charms cereal. The food companies responded to the consumer, and the grocer stocked his shelves with low-fat and convenience foods.

The food companies also played a part in what was on our grocery store shelves, of course, learning through market research that they could sell more of a product if they offered increasing varieties of it, giving us more and more of what we once needed only one or two of, not because it was better for us but because it improved their bottom line. Have you tried to pick out a salad dressing recently? There are so many to choose from it's hard to make a decision. Barbecue sauce? The same. The supermarket began filling up with more and more products, often referred to as "skews" (for SKUs, or "stock keeping units," denoting specific items for sale). Traditional Triscuits are one SKU, reduced-fat Triscuits are another, and Triscuits with balsamic vinegar and basil flavor are still another.

The country's first grocery stores, in the late nineteenth and early twentieth centuries, carried about two hundred products. During the final decades of the twentieth century, the number of individual items,

11 But there is now. Many studies have since been published. According to Marion Nestle, author and New York University professor, the results depend on who paid for the studies. Studies paid for by the egg industry find no correlation between egg consumption and blood serum cholesterol (imagine that!). Independent studies are mixed, she said, in large part because how eggs affect you depends on how high your cholesterol is to begin with. For people with high cholesterol, eggs don't affect their cholesterol; for people with low cholesterol, eggs tend to raise it.

or SKUs, exploded. According to a January 2014 *Consumer Reports* article,[12] citing figures from the Food Marketing Institute, the average supermarket had fewer than nine thousand items in 1975. By 2008, that number had quintupled.

"More troubling is that when faced with an array of complex options," the article says, "consumers tend to throw reason out the window and pick a product based on what's easiest to evaluate, not what's most important, says Sheena Iyengar, director of the Global Leadership Matrix Program at the Columbia (University) Business School. 'We stick to the familiar or go by price because we don't want to deal with so many choices and scrutinize label claims or nutrition information,' she says."

It's easy to see how this can happen. I don't buy a lot of processed food. But after my divorce I found myself eating most meals alone, and I would occasionally fall back on that old standby, the frozen dinner, of which I had an extraordinary selection to choose from. But I would read the label, and if there were a lot of ingredients I didn't recognize or couldn't pronounce, I'd put it back. When my kids were young, their mother and I decided that if we were going to buy anything from the center aisles of the grocery store, it couldn't contain any unrecognizable ingredients. For instance, if a bag of potato chips had any ingredient beyond potatoes, oil, and salt, it was off-limits. And yet I adore and still eat Pringles. They're delicately crisp and salty, and taste vaguely of potatoes—perfect along with a ham sandwich. But with maltodextrin and mono- and diglycerides (both of which I had to Google—they're processed starch and emulsifiers, respectively) as well as dextrose, a form of sugar, they were a no-no for the kids.[13]

But the proliferation of new "products" is not simply what happened in the grocery section of the supermarket—it happened in all

---

12 "What to Do When There Are Too Many Product Choices on the Store Shelves?," *Consumer Reports*, March 2014.

13 These crispy little hyperbolic paraboloids that stack so neatly in a can were invented in 1967 and sold under the name Pringle's Newfangled Potato Chips. By the time they had become an offering nationwide in the mid-1970s, other chip makers complained about calling them chips, and the company has since referred to them as crisps, the name for potato chips in Great Britain.

parts of the grocery store. And then in all stores, until America created a single gigantic store that sold just about everything: Amazon.

Older grocers wistfully recall the days when all they had to worry about were three types of eggs: small, medium, and large. Now there are usually fifteen different types of eggs to choose from: regular, organic, cage-free, certified humane, omega-3, and so on, all in various sizes. And, of course, if hard-cooked eggs are your thing, but boiling and peeling them is just too much work for you, you can buy cooked and shelled eggs in a plastic pouch from Eggland's Best.

Produce managers who have been in the business for decades recall a time when they offered five different types of apples. Now there are dozens of varieties. The produce section didn't used to carry fruit that wasn't in season—you simply couldn't buy a cantaloupe or a peach in the northern states in January. Now we demand them year-round, even if the January cantaloupe doesn't taste anything like the ones you can buy in July. Older grocers remember a time when the only lettuce available was head lettuce, and they sold a ton of it. Now there are a dozen varieties of greens and a whole range of prewashed mixes in nitrogen-filled bags all year long.

In addition to the big food company's products, we also have a supermarket chain's private-label versions of the same foods. So, you can choose, say, Land O'Lakes butter or Heinen's own all-natural butter. (I read the ingredients of both: the Heinen's brand contains only cream and salt, whereas Land O'Lakes includes another intriguing ingredient: "natural flavors.") And, of course, new products enter the market each year, approximately twenty thousand of them, each struggling to find its way onto the shelves of the thirty-eight thousand grocery stores throughout America.

How exactly did we reach this extraordinary abundance, and where does it end? No one can say, but I would argue that it all began with the A&P.

The history of the grocery store doesn't begin with the A&P—records of purveyors of dry goods go back at least to the fourteenth century—but the Great Atlantic & Pacific Tea Company would over the course of fifty years dominate the entire industry, becoming by the 1920s not simply the biggest food retailer in the world but the biggest retailer of any kind.[14] In its heyday, the A&P took ten cents of every dollar America spent on food, and this was at a time when Americans spent more than 30 percent of their income on food, more than they spent on housing.

The history of the grocery store in America probably does begin with what was called the country store. It would have been more like what we consider today to be a general store in a small town, selling a variety of foods and necessities for the house. The first ones were built of logs chinked with mud, according to Laurence A. Johnson, a long-time grocer in Syracuse, New York, who began in the business as a boy in 1906 and would later write a book called *Over the Counter and On the Shelf: Country Storekeeping in America, 1620–1920*.[15] They carried soaps and spices, salt, dishes, books, hardware, leather goods, axes, log chains, kettles, pots, pans, saddles, harnesses, and shoes piled loose in a large box. Flour, sugar, molasses, and crackers were sold out of barrels. "A cat in the cracker barrel was commonplace," Johnson writes.

These stores sold patent medicines and sedatives, such as laudanum and paregoric, along with turpentine and Epsom salt. Whiskey was out of view but available. You could also buy pins, pens, paper, buttons and collars, black silk gloves, and palm leaf fans.

"When, about the turn of the nineteenth century," Johnson writes, "frame buildings made log cabins obsolete, up-to-date store quarters were built with cellars cool enough to store cheeses, butter, and eggs, and roomy enough for hogsheads[16] of molasses, casks of whale oil and camphine."[17]

---

14 Information on the A&P's history is derived in large measure from the eminently readable book *The Great A&P and the Struggle for Small Business in America* by Marc Levinson.

15 I discovered this book excerpted in another excellent work with the compelling title *The Food Industry Executive's Pleasure Reader*. Edited by Julian H. Handler, it is a small compendium of writings about grocery stores and the food industry.

16 A large cask, typically holding sixty-three gallons.

17 A mixture of turpentine and alcohol used for burning in lamps. It was volatile and replaced with kerosene after a method of distilling this liquid from coal was discovered and patented in the 1850s.

Platform scales were patented in 1831 but weren't perfected for another seventy years. Still, the store clerk used them to weigh out rolled oats, sugar, beans, or nails, which were then wrapped up in paper for the customer. (It wasn't until 1852 that the first machine to cut paper, fold it, and connect the folds with flour paste to create a paper bag was invented. Cloth sacks were also used, until a cotton shortage during the Civil War made them scarce, and paper bags took over.)

Colorful coffee mills were standard store equipment, Johnson says, but tea was the product that would launch the A&P.

The founder of this revolutionary enterprise was one George Gilman, born in Maine in 1826, who left the business of tanning animal hides in Manhattan to deal in tea around 1860. Tea at the time was one of the most profitable items a merchant could sell. Gilman first called his company Gilman & Company and then, proving himself to have a knack for promotion, the Great American Tea Company. Why mince words? Gilman already recognized what food manufacturers of the twentieth century would learn: that the promotion of a product was more important than its quality. By the end of the Civil War, Gilman had expanded his business to five New York retail stores, offices, a thriving mail-order business, a warehouse, and a plant for grinding coffee (coffee being another profitable trade).

Taking advantage of an important milestone in the development of America, the completion of the First Transcontinental Railroad in 1869, Gilman launched a second company called the Great Atlantic & Pacific Tea Company, which promised to distribute tea to merchants throughout the country (while keeping his other tea company alive separately).

While there were numerous stores selling what Gilman's shops sold in the years after the Civil War, Gilman's fierce promotional genius sparked a few critical innovations in the food retail business. Among the first of Gilman's ingenious ideas was to offer an exclusive branded tea, a black tea with a green tea flavor called Thea-Nectar.

"A brand-name tea was an extraordinary product to bring to market in 1870," Marc Levinson writes in *The Great A&P and the Struggle for Small Business in America*. "At the time, consumers had access to few branded products of any sort, save patent medicines. Almost everything offered in grocery stores, from flour to pickles, was purchased by the shopkeeper in bulk and sold from barrels or canisters, with the store clerk scooping out and measuring the quantity the customer desired. The widespread sale of brand-name foods in sealed packages was still two decades in the future."

Innovation number two: gifts for purchases made. Documentation is unclear, but Gilman seems to have been the first to give away mass-produced chromolithographs (color photos of sports events, presidents, still lifes, or landscapes), which were popular decorating items in American homes at the time. These freebies, which were referred to as "premiums," go back to the late 1700s, though surely purchase incentives aimed at customers are as old as trading itself. According to one account, it was the Jones Brothers Tea Company that began handing out colorful pictures in 1872. (The company later changed its name to Grand Union and eventually grew into a major supermarket chain, ultimately to be sold off to multinationals in the twenty-first century.) But Levinson dates the practice to 1871, by Mr. Gilman. In any case, so many tea companies began giving away the colored photos that Gilman decided to up the game by offering coupons (later known as "trading stamps") that could be collected and traded in for plates, glasses, and even lamps.

George Hartford had joined the company as a twenty-eight-year-old clerk in 1861 and within a decade had become one of the company's key figures. One of his first major accomplishments was to use Gilman's entrepreneurial savvy to turn a calamitous tragedy to the company's extraordinary benefit. When the great Chicago fire decimated that growing city in 1871, Hartford opened an A&P there (the first outside New York City)—before the bricks had even cooled, according to Levinson. That nice turn of phrase, apparently literal, implies a certain ruthlessness in taking advantage of a tragedy. But the city was desperately in need of resources and cash to rebuild its infrastructure, as well as food and, of course, coffee and tea. A&P was there to put up a store, employ people, and send wagonloads of goods into the city. The Chicago store, heavily promoted with Gilman-esque grand-opening hoo-ha, was so successful that Hartford began a rapid expansion from Boston to Atlanta to Kansas City.

While it was not the first retail chain in the country, it was likely, Levinson writes, the first with a national presence, and one whose methods and innovations became more widely known because of this presence. By the time Hartford's sons, George Jr. and John, entered the business in the 1880s, the Great Atlantic & Pacific Tea Company had one-hundred fifty stores and was doing $1 million in sales annually.

One product instrumental in the rise of the A&P was baking powder. Levinson goes so far as to call it "a controversial product." It was a relatively new concoction—a combination of sodium bicarbonate (an alkaline substance around since ancient times in various forms and still an excellent remedy for a sour stomach) and acidic salts. Not requiring an acid, only a liquid, to release the gases, it allowed for easily and consistently leavened breads, quick breads, and other baked goods, which most American families made at home. (Levinson writes that Americans bought fifty to seventy-five million pounds of the powder yearly.) The Hartfords slapped a red A&P label on one-pound tins, and the first of A&P's private labels was born—perhaps the first private label sold in a grocery store and certainly the first sold nationally.

This was the beginning of the A&P brand, a product customers felt they could rely on for consistency and quality. Recall that in those early days of the grocery business, the late 1800s, shelf-stable goods such as molasses and flour were scooped out of the barrels they arrived in, and customers had no way of knowing if those goods were clean or contaminated with moth larvae or mice droppings. A brand name implied consistency; a closed container promised purity.

But the A&P still wasn't in the grocery business per se. By all accounts, groceries were dicier in the 1880s than they are today from a profit standpoint, and stores were not much different from a trading post that Laura Ingalls's family would have frequented when venturing from their little house in the big woods. Most Americans grew some of their own food and often raised livestock. Selling food that didn't require refrigeration—sugar and slabs of bacon and salt pork and pickles and root vegetables—was left to local families, and they worked long hours in tiny stores.

George Hartford, who had taken control of the Great Atlantic & Pacific Tea Company after Gilman's departure in 1878, didn't have any interest in managing a chain of such stores. Perhaps he recognized their fundamental roadblock to growth: Because grocery stores at the time sold pretty much everything in bulk, there was no way to distinguish one product—say, crackers or sugar—from the same product in another store. A store's success was therefore completely dependent on outpricing its competitors. Surely the A&P could have done that (and would eventually), but in the late nineteenth century, the scale didn't make it practical.

Until, argues Levinson, the invention of two items we take for granted today.

How many practical items we take for granted! I sometimes have to remind myself that there was a time not very long ago when I didn't have a smartphone, let alone a cell phone. I'd wager that most people reading these words can barely recall a time when they couldn't crush an empty beer can between their two hands and reduce it to a quarter of its original size—the previous tin cans were simply too heavy and thick. Or a time when a can of beer, before the advent of the pull-tab, required a sharp-pointed opener (I'd kind of like to see those come back, actually, if any of you hipster craft brewers in Brooklyn happen to be paying attention).

But it was indeed the tin can that drove the Great Atlantic & Pacific Tea Company into the grocery business—that and the cardboard box. Cans and boxes: the stuff of revolution, as it turns out.

Tin cans had been around for a hundred years, but new technology allowed them to be manufactured so cheaply that by the 1880s, canneries had sprung up all over the country (more than a thousand by 1900, according to Levinson). By this time food processing accounted for a fifth of all manufacturing done in the United States.

The cardboard box was created by mistake at the Metropolitan Paper-Bag Manufactory. One of its operators set up the apparatus wrong, leading the company's founder, Robert Gair, to recognize that by setting the cutting blades at varying heights, one could create very thick, stiff paper bags—that is, cardboard—that could then be cut, scored, and folded into a box. Moreover, images and graphics could be printed on this cardboard. Tin cans, likewise, could easily be fitted with a paper label.

These two innovations, which happened at roughly the same time, paved the way for the modern grocery store as we know it today, filled with brand names such as Campbell's soup and Kellogg's cereal. And they also allowed the Hartford sons to load the A&P's shelves with all manner of goods.

Such advances in packaging would eventually allow major food processing to take hold. "The 1920s had been vintage years for large food-processing corporations," writes Harvey Levenstein in *Paradox of Plenty*. "Even at the beginning of that decade, a few large enterprises had dominated the meat-packing, sugar, and flour-milling industries. Then the same thing came to pass in dairy, baking, tropical fruits, and breakfast cereals." Massive conglomerates quickly formed, General Foods and Standard Brands, to feed the country this standardized, homogenized food.

The 1920s were also the years when the Great Atlantic & Pacific Tea Company was at its zenith; it owned nearly sixteen thousand grocery stores, seventy factories, and more than a hundred warehouses. In 1900, company sales totaled $5 million (with a healthy 2.5 percent profit margin, double what it is for today's grocery stores). Sales in 1925 would exceed $350 million—$4.8 billion today—more than any retailer in the world at the time.

To achieve such rapid growth, the A&P opened an astonishing seven stores a day, and they would have opened more if they could have found people to manage them. And they did what other major businesses would do throughout the first half of the twentieth century: They battled unions, pressed suppliers to lower their prices, cut out middlemen, and created volume.

These A&Ps weren't any bigger than the countless independent grocery stores they were putting out of business, and their products weren't all that different either. "Their great advantage," writes Levenstein, "lay in their enormous purchasing power and centralized warehouse systems, which allowed them to get price concessions from manufacturers and save on distribution costs."

Yes, they were vilified by the public for destroying mom-and-pop stores, and yes, they went to court in the 1940s on antitrust violations (losing, but suffering only small fines in legal battles that would go on for years). But Levinson notes the undeniable upside of such a Walmart-size impact on communities: "Few economic changes have mattered more to the average family. Thanks to the management techniques the Great A&P brought into widespread use, food shopping, once a heavy burden, became a minor concern for all but the poorest households."

"Once a heavy burden"—another of those small details of life that I believe we lose sight of at our peril: how convenient it is for us to acquire food.

While the Great A&P may have been the game-changer in how America got its food, it was not, of course, the only chain in the country, nor the only innovator. Barney Kroger had started his own tea company in Cincinnati in 1883, expanding it to a grocery and baking store in 1902. Today Kroger is our country's second-largest grocer (after Walmart) and operates more than twenty-six hundred stores with sales of more than $100 billion in 2015. (Also in 2015, A&P filed for bankruptcy and closed the doors of its last remaining stores. Bye-bye, Atlantic & Pacific![18])

In 1916, in Memphis, Tennessee, Clarence Saunders opened a store he called Piggly Wiggly.[19] His innovation was substantial: self-service. Before Piggly Wiggly, patrons of grocery stores were serviced by clerks; the customer read off a list of items and amounts and the grocer weighed

....

18 After World War II, when supermarkets began to expand, A&P was low on capital and had high labor costs. Following the death of George Hartford in 1951, the company made a series of strategic blunders. Its failure to respond to the changing nature of the industry would emanate through the company like rings in a pond. Levinson outlines the many reasons for A&P's long, slow collapse in a chapter of his book called "The Fall."

19 He refused to explain precisely why he called it that beyond the fact that it made people ask, "Why on earth?" Saunders's next grocery venture would be called Keedoozle.

them out and set them on the counter, or used a contraption called a long arm to retrieve cans off high shelves. At Piggly Wiggly, one entered and exited through turnstiles (surely a decision based on the fear that customers could pilfer at will in this new kind of food market), basket slung over the arm, and chose by hand from a variety of branded, packaged items. In 1929, *Time* magazine marveled at the "almost automatic process" of shopping there in an article called "The Piggly Wiggly Man."[20]

It would take years for the idea of picking out one's own food to catch on, and Saunders, in what appears to have been a blundering effort to corner Piggly Wiggly's stock, lost control of the company in the 1920s.[21] But by the 1930s, there were twenty-six hundred Piggly Wigglys throughout the South and Midwest, and most other grocery chains had, over time, followed suit with self-service stores.[22] Saunders's model spawned other innovations, too: the now-familiar checkout counters and lanes, as well as price stickers on every single item in the store. (These caused a serious headache for clerks until the advent of the barcode; when a price changed, they'd have to razor blade off all the old ones and put on new ones.[23])

The time was ripe for the next innovation: the shopping cart. In 1937, an Oklahoma grocer named Sylvan Goldman invented a rolling cart that folded up like a wooden chair (the source of his idea).[24] This allowed shoppers to *really* load up on groceries—but of course the only

....

20 *Time* magazine, February 25, 1929.

21 "On Wall Street, Saunders is remembered as the man who engineered the last real corner in a nationally traded stock—a memorable milestone indeed, since such a corner is the most drastic and spectacular of all developments that can occur in the stock market, with the possible exception of a general panic," wrote John Brooks in the June 6, 1959, issue of the *New Yorker*.

22 Piggly Wiggly is down to about six hundred stores now, most of them under the affiliation of a large private company, C&S Wholesale Grocers.

23 Scanning technology became available in 1974, Jeff Heinen told me, but Heinen's didn't begin scanning barcodes until 1980.

24 Here's a good article on the evolution of the grocery cart: "Who Made That Shopping Cart?," *New York Times Magazine*, December 18, 2011.

way they could get all these groceries back home was by taking advantage of the growing ubiquity of another innovation, one pioneered by a man named Ransom Olds and accelerated by the innovation of the moving assembly line (thank you, Mr. Ford).

But of all the technological innovations to shape the evolution of the grocery business, I would wager that the greatest by far was electric refrigeration, which didn't become commercially viable until the 1920s. In fact, refrigeration struck every corner of our food world. Commercial refrigeration units allowed for the creation of the supermarket, a single store that sold not just groceries, but also meat, seafood, dairy, and produce.

The first true supermarket was the brainchild of Michael Cullen, who opened King Kullen in Queens, New York, in a three-thousand-square-foot building—a size that was unheard of at the time. While grocery stores across the country had throughout the 1920s slowly begun to add food categories and called themselves "combination stores," it took Cullen's ingenious use of space to create what could be genuinely called, and used as, a one-stop supermarket.

Cullen's first winning idea was to take his grocery store off the main commercial thoroughfares, where rent was steep. Only by minimizing rent for such a large space could he afford to keep prices low. Cullen leased an abandoned garage on a street near, but not in, a busy shopping area. This location guaranteed plenty of space for parking, something that would become of considerable value throughout the United States as more and more families bought cars. By driving only slightly out of their way, they could shop at King Kullen, where the prices were low thanks to a combination of high sales volume and a cash-only requirement (most grocery stores at the time offered credit).

Cullen had been an employee of the Kroger chain and had suggested his revolutionary idea to top management, arguing that such a store could do ten times the volume of a typical Kroger. When he failed to get a response, he quit the company to do it himself. He surely had to have done this well in advance of the August 4, 1930, opening, and one can only imagine that Black Tuesday the previous October added additional concerns to the opening of this new kind of store. By 1930, the term Hooverville (a sarcastic nod to then president Hoover) had been coined to describe shantytowns popping up in cities throughout the country, including one in Central Park, just across the river from the shiny King Kullen. But hard economic times were a boon to Cullen, as he guaranteed the lowest prices anywhere in New York.

The American supermarket was on its way.

The power of this historical trajectory in terms of not only food retailing but *all* retailing cannot be underestimated. As Tracey Deutsch writes in *Building a Housewife's Paradise: Gender, Politics, and American Grocery Stores in the Twentieth Century*, a book that looks at the grocery store through the lens of politics and gender, "Grocery stores were by far the largest retail sector, in terms of both sales and numbers of stores, for most of the twentieth century. . . . [They] foreshadowed changes that would come to virtually all retail sectors. It was in food stores that mass retailing took hold most suddenly, first with the rise of chain stores in the 1920s and then with the sudden increase in popularity of supermarkets in the later 1930s and 1940s."

I am generally skeptical of the changed-the-world hyperbole found on so many book jackets these days, as I hope I would have been in the nineteenth century of a shop calling itself the Great American Tea Company. But I feel comfortable saying that it was, indeed, the A&P—the biggest retailer in the world of its time, with its high-volume-sold-at-low-cost philosophy, its management and expansion views—that shaped the way we make, distribute, buy, and use not just food, but all that we create. A grocery store.

But then, the grocery store is the keeper of our food, without which we don't survive. So perhaps it's not so surprising after all.

3.

GROWING UP

Grocery stores came of age in my hometown of Cleveland much as they did in other mid-tier cities throughout the country. My house is in Cleveland Heights, one of the first so-called streetcar suburbs that grew up around a new transportation system, eventually called the Rapid Transit. Cleveland Heights sits on a plateau about four miles east of downtown Cleveland. To reach it in 1890, a horse-drawn carriage would have to hike up a half-mile-long hill called Cedar Glen to the top, 275 feet above Lake Erie a few miles north. This was not a problem in dry weather. But during rain or certainly throughout the harsh Cleveland winters, reaching the plateau would be arduous. However, once electric railways became viable (starting in 1877, in Virginia, with power provided by overhead cables), Clevelanders could easily climb Cedar Glen in the new electric transit, so the real estate on the plateau could be developed. Cleveland was quickly industrializing (on its way to becoming in a few decades one of the country's largest cities), and middle-class families were eager to move out of the sooty, industrial city proper. Thus the suburb of Cleveland Heights developed around this streetcar line in the first decade of the twentieth century; Shaker Heights, the neighborhood where I spent my boyhood, likewise emerged, via a separate branch of the city's new Rapid Transit system. The Cleveland Heights streetcar would travel along Euclid Heights Boulevard, pass what would eventually be my street, and stop, a few moments later, at what was by the 1920s the busy shopping district along Coventry Road, which developed as a way to serve the community of this growing suburb.

Coventry remains an engaging commercial street, though short—a five-minute walk from end to end. It has an urban, not a suburban feel; were it to be set down in the middle of Bleecker Street it wouldn't seem out of place (in the 1960s it became, like that New York City street,

Cleveland's hippie mecca). But all around it were and still are streets lined with houses, front lawns, tall oaks and maples and sycamores. Residents of the 1930s and '40s could walk to Coventry, where all manner of shops and stores did business. A dairy store sold butter and milk. Four greengrocers offered various vegetables and fruit. Three butchers and a fishmonger plied their trade here (Lake Erie had a bountiful supply of perch and pike and walleye, and the rivers that fed this lake were filled with trout). One store sold live chickens. Three bakeries baked bread and fulfilled our love of pie, and three delicatessens sold corned beef and pastrami, pickles and sauerkraut. And, of course, there were grocery stores selling dry and canned goods—three of them on these two short blocks of Coventry, including *two* A&Ps just a block apart, with a Fisher Foods in between. A third A&P did business a few minutes farther up Euclid Heights Boulevard at Lee Road.

Among the families who did their shopping along Coventry at that time were Fred and Hildegarde Stashower. Fred helped found an advertising agency, Lang, Fisher & Stashower, which my father would eventually join as a copywriter in the mid-1960s. Fred and Hildegarde's son, David, born in 1929, would join his father's agency in 1954 and go on to become its president (and give me my first shot at copywriting as a nineteen-year-old intern). When David joined the agency, grocers were among their clients, so he knew the grocery business from that vantage point.

David still lives two blocks from Coventry. I asked to meet with him to talk food and culture and the way Americans in the burgeoning suburbs ate during the Depression and the war years as it was reflected by the Coventry shopping district. David's curly dark hair has turned gray, and he moves more slowly than when he and my father played racquetball in the 1970s, but he still has vivid memories of the Coventry of his boyhood and what food shopping was like then.

"I remember three butchers," he told me, seated on his living room couch, dressed in a sweater and khaki slacks, "countless produce stores, three bakeries, and at least one dairy store, a chain called Bruder's—

that's all they did was sell milk and cheese. If you wanted canned goods you had to go to a larger grocer, A&P or Fisher Foods.

"This was the Depression. Some people didn't have a car at all. Very few people had two cars. So, if the man of the house needed the car to go to work, the homemaker had to be able to walk and carry back what she bought, or she had to deal with a store that delivered.

"Also, dairy products were customarily home delivered. And there were home delivery bakeries. The Spang Bakery, the Star Bakery, Loeb's Bakery, Hough Home Bakery. And that's how people bought their food."

Small quantities from a variety of small merchants.

"People shopped much more frequently," he continued. "They shopped in smaller quantities because they were limited by what they could carry. And on top of that, refrigeration space was extremely limited. Most people had the GE Monitor Top refrigerator, which was a formidable piece of equipment.[25] But because of the insulation there was little space inside. So you didn't keep anything in there except some milk, butter, and leftovers.

"The idea of buying things in one store came about from the A&P, which dominated the market. A&P was, in its day, the object of more hatred than Walmart. The usual complaints: They were forcing independent businesses out of business. It was very impersonal. This was long before you selected your own stuff. A clerk waited on you. That lasted through the Second World War. There was a group of retail merchants like the Fishers, who were either butchers or grocers, and they decided there was no reason why they couldn't sell the other stuff."

Another Midwesterner of David's generation was born to the grocery business and would go on to renown as a writer about, among other things, food. Calvin Trillin's father (as well as his maternal grandfather) had a grocery store, then went on to open five more in Kansas City, Missouri. Trillin told me that his father, in an early abuse of so-called slotting fees, put Wonder Bread on special display in exchange for a one-

....

25 Do a Google image search—if the appliance had arms, it would look like a robot.

cent rebate from the company. His father used this money exclusively to put his son through Yale. "Some people have trust funds," Trillin said, "and some people have bread rebates."

Trillin remembers that his father got up at four a.m. to go to the produce market (as Joe Heinen, Tom and Jeff's grandfather, surely would have done), and the family never knew what a weekend was because Saturday was the busiest day in the store. Born in 1935, he remembers war rations, as does David Stashower, but when your dad owned a grocery store you weren't going to starve. "You could starve if the bank came and took the store away, of course," he added, over lunch near his West Village apartment.

His parents took inventory at the kitchen table with a hand-cranked adding machine. Most of their meals came out of cans. When labels fell off cans, his father had no choice but to bring them home. "Sometimes my dad would ask what brand these beans were," he said. "My mother didn't know—she didn't even know they were beans until she opened the can! They could have been onions for all she knew."

Trillin's father hated the grocery business and couldn't get out of it fast enough. And of course, he hated the A&P. His father hated them so much his writer son for years wouldn't go into one. "I was long out of college before I could walk into a big grocery store without feeling guilt."

To compete against the A&P, smaller, family-owned supermarkets often pooled their resources in order to buy in enough volume to lower their prices. It happened in Cleveland as it happened in Kansas City. But they couldn't muscle out every independent grocer or force him to merge. Some created grocery stores that didn't rely on price differentiation alone, but rather on something less measurable, something more alluring.

As David Stashower noted, "I had hell's own sweet time getting Sally to set foot in a Fisher Foods"—that is, his wife would shop at neither the A&P down the street nor his own agency's client. "She only went to Heinen's."

4.

THE VISIONARY CLEVELAND GROCER
AND THE ONE-STOP SHOP

In 1916, a thirteen-year-old boy named Joseph Heinen, the son of German immigrants who'd arrived at Ellis Island when he was ten months old, found after-school work in a butcher shop. The work suited him, he kept at it, and upon graduating from John Hay High School, he found full-time work in a variety of meat cutters' shops. By the time he'd developed some mastery of the trade, he sensed there was more opportunity to be had in the food business, and he suggested to one of his bosses that they could make more money if they sold more products than just meat. The boss, as company history records it, replied, "The way we make more money is by selling more meat." And left it at that.

Heinen, now a solidly built man with substantial nose and crew cut (he wouldn't have looked out of place in shoulder pads and jersey on a 1950s football team), was entrepreneurial by nature. He opened his own butcher shop, focusing on providing a higher quality of meat than his competitors. As his clientele grew, Heinen felt the demand from these customers to offer more products, so he put peanut butter, pickles, and doughnuts on his shelves.

"My grandfather always had the vision," Tom Heinen says, "recognizing that meat was the center of the plate and people always planned their meals around the meat. He realized, they *have* to come to us. We're their first stop. Why do we make them go somewhere else? Why not offer some produce? His thinking precipitated all the thinking we do about meal solutions today. Let's provide them a meal. And that meant offering produce. It was minuscule. It wasn't like he tried to be a full-scale produce store. He just wanted to offer enough so that people didn't have to go somewhere else. That's the way he started.

"One of my grandfather's big innovations was self-service meat. It was a full-service butcher shop, but he was the first one to sell meat self-service." That is, Joe Heinen also sold cut and packaged meat so that customers didn't have to wait for the butcher, something that would not become standard practice in the industry until the 1950s. In the early days, Tom says, "There was a poultry guy, a beef guy, a pork guy. My grandfather thought this was ridiculous. Why do we shuffle the customer around? You had to wait in the poultry section, then you'd have to go wait in the beef section. He said, 'No, once I get a customer, I'm going to take care of all their needs.'"

This notion of stores going beyond selling a single category of food had been alive for many years with what were called combination stores. And King Kullen, the country's first supermarket, would likely have been well known to most in the food business. In 1933, Joe Heinen opened what the company says was Cleveland's first supermarket near the intersection of Chagrin Boulevard and Lee Road, one block from the streetcar bisecting Shaker Heights. Here he had enough space to sell meat and fish, groceries (canned and boxed goods), dairy (milk, eggs, butter, cheese), and produce that he would buy daily at Cleveland's food terminal downtown, where all the other greengrocers bought their fruits and vegetables.

Heinen's claim to being the city's first, while difficult to prove, is not unlikely given that the food stores existing at the time had been created well before then and would therefore have had difficulty stocking many items outside their purview. The next recorded supermarket, Pick-N-Pay, emphasizing self-service with its name, wouldn't open for another five years. (And the A&P company wouldn't begin building supermarkets until 1937—as ever, slow to move on a new trend, but once it moved, it moved big.) So Heinen's claim to being Cleveland's first supermarket seems likely.

The store was a success and, as the strains of the Great Depression began to ease, Heinen opened a second supermarket in Cleveland Heights in 1940, always stressing the quality of the product and customer service. One of the bigger efforts in customer service included his

innovation of bag boys loading sacks of groceries, or parcels, into shoppers' cars, a practice that remains in effect today. This happened in 1953,
after automobiles became ubiquitous and people stocked up for the
week. As far as I know, and as far as the Heinen brothers know, Heinen's
today may be the only suburban supermarket in the country that won't
let you take your cart to the parking lot—at least in travels throughout
the country, I've never seen it elsewhere, so certainly it's an uncommon
practice. (I've never liked this rule because I'm always in a rush, and the
idea of driving to the front of the store to pick up my groceries seems an
unnecessary step, but a lot of people wouldn't do without it.)

Not surprisingly, the 1930s grocery store was primarily filled with
food that could sit on a shelf for a long time. Kraft mayonnaise, Franco-
American spaghetti, Clorox bleach, a product sometimes called catsup
(eleven cents for a fourteen-ounce bottle), canned vegetables (two cans
of green beans sold for about thirty-five cents), Campbell's pork and
beans, canned tuna, boxes of cornflakes and cream of wheat, matches,
table salt,[26] and Wesson oil. There was also a selection of fresh vegetables
and fruit, abundant in the summer but limited mainly to root vegetables,
potatoes, onions, head lettuce, and cabbage in the winter.

There was some Great Lakes fish available at the Cleveland supermarket. The meat cases were loaded mostly with cuts of pork and beef,
but also some lamb and chicken. In the 1930s, Americans, particularly
inland Americans, ate about fifty pounds of pork and beef per person
per year. There was considerably less chicken than we see now in our
supermarkets. We ate only about ten pounds of chicken per person
per year through the first third of the twentieth century.[27] This was no
doubt due to the fact that chickens were considerably less convenient

....

26 Iodized salt was created in the 1920s, according to Harold McGee in *On Food and
Cooking: The Science and Lore of the Kitchen*. Many Americans, especially people who
lived inland, weren't getting enough iodine in their diet at the time, and goiter was a serious health problem. Sea vegetables and fish such as cod and salmon are good sources of
iodine, but our food distribution system didn't allow for such fresh products to make it very
far inland.

27 "A Nation Of Meat Eaters: See How It All Adds Up," NPR, *The Salt*, June 27, 2012.

to prepare than they are today; they were typically sold plucked but not eviscerated, which was referred to as "New York dressed." My neighbor, Lois Baron, who lived in the Jewish neighborhood in Cleveland near 105th Street, still remembers her terror as a young girl of walking into Leizer's chicken shop, where her mom would head to the coops out back and point to a clucking chicken. The butcher would cut off its head and drain it of blood according to Jewish law.

It wasn't until 1942 that the country had its first government-approved chicken evisceration plant.[28] Chickens raised for their meat, known as "broilers," could then be processed and packaged rapidly and shipped in ice-filled wooden crates.

"We bought ice-packed chicken all the way into the nineties," Tom Heinen says, noting how long they did some things the old-fashioned way. "Other places went out of that long before we did, just like they were out of carcass beef [beef that arrived as whole hanging quarters] long before we were."

"Supermarket" though it was, the original Heinen's still stocked only the same number of products as the A&P on Coventry, a couple hundred, including meat, dairy, and produce. Photographs of the first store show a rectangular space of perhaps two thousand square feet, with deli-like cases running the length of the left wall, behind which various cutters sold beef, pork, lamb, chicken, and prepared meats such as tongue and corned beef. A dairy cooler ran along the back wall, and the right wall was split between dry and canned goods and produce. A single U-shaped case with cheeses and jarred items such as pickles and peanut butter created a large island in the center of the store, behind which was a smaller island of more boxes and canned goods on display.

Two things strike me about this early store. The first is how much wide-open floor space there is. There are no aisles to speak of, simply one broad track circling the central island, with the rest of the goods displayed around the perimeter. The second remarkable feature is how few groceries there actually are. One could fit all the dry and canned

----

28 "U.S. Chicken Industry History," The National Chicken Council, from their website nationalchickencouncil.org.

goods of this store into the smallest New York City bodega and still have room for more. Or imagine a single aisle of a contemporary supermarket, divide that in half, and you would have about the same square footage of product as would have been available in the 1930s. Today, we need the same area simply to display all the salad dressings and condiments we have to choose from. One wonders how on earth families got by with so few options.

After World War II, America entered its economic boom years. Its gross domestic product would quintuple from a prewar $100 billion to $515 billion by the end of the 1950s. White flight had begun, and middle-class families were moving out of cities in large numbers, something that was possible because of the ubiquity of the automobile and the great swaths of undeveloped land surrounding most cities. The Grandview Avenue Shopping Center, built in 1928 outside Columbus, Ohio, was apparently the first "shopping center" in the United States to include parking in its design. But now, with booming populations on plentiful land, real estate developers could create large complexes of stores with oceans of parking space.

In these new spaces, grocery stores could expand to ten and twenty times the size they were when they occupied stores built in shopping areas that had been created to accommodate foot traffic and streetcar lines. One of the under-recognized facts of American real estate development is how our modes of transportation are the fundamental determiners of the way we create our residential and commercial spaces. The advent of the streetcar, as previously noted, brought about the creation of America's first suburbs—with sidewalks and shopping districts within walking distance—in the first and second decades of the nineteenth century. Spaces that were developed after the automobile became a predominant feature of American life are far from city centers and spread out. It was the automobile, and highways, that led to suburban sprawl. And as the highway system grew, America created even more sprawling exurbs and office complexes centered around interchange cloverleafs.[29]

---

29 See Alex Marshall's excellent *How Cities Work: Suburbs, Sprawl, and the Roads Not Taken.*

"From 1948 to 1963 large chains increased their share of the nation's grocery business from 35 percent to almost half," writes Harvey Levenstein in *Paradox of Plenty*. "As early as 1956, the independent corner grocery store, while still visible, was a relic of the past. Full-fledged supermarkets accounted for 62 percent of the nation's grocery sales, while smaller, self-service 'superettes' took in another 28 percent of the food dollar, leaving the 212,000 small food stores to share 10 percent of the market."

At precisely the same time that the American economy swelled and middle-class families moved to the suburbs in large numbers, the major food manufacturers came into their own and began to dominate the American food scene. "Markets for [processed] foods exploded after World War II," according to the *Oxford Handbook of Food History*, "as food manufacturing became a powerful industrial sector in its own right. Food processing and manufacturing industries devised many new standardized food products, including packaged and frozen foods, turning commodity crops such as soy, maize, and wheat into inputs for industrial production."

And the surplus of nitrogen we had amassed for making bombs could be turned into fertilizer and sold to the farmers growing the commodity crops, most notably corn and wheat, that were required to create inexpensive processed foods.

Kellogg's Sugar Frosted Flakes were introduced in 1951 with a powerful marketing icon, Tony the Tiger, and exemplified what was happening to our foods. A simple product, Kellogg's Corn Flakes, was altered to a degree to create a new product—here, simply by coating those flakes with sugar. The introduction of Frosted Flakes signaled two changes that would dominate the grocery aisles: the development of multiple product lines and, perhaps more critically, the addition of increasing quantities of sugar to our foods. Advertising was also gearing up for its *Mad Men* heyday in booming America, and Kellogg's had gone to one of the most powerful advertising agencies, Leo Burnett, to help sell their new cereal. Cocoa Puffs, Rice Krispies, Shredded Wheat, Apple Jacks, and all the salty snacks from Kraft and Frito-Lay began to fill the supermarket aisles. And these food companies heavily marketed their packages of processed corn, wheat, sugar, and salt products, in seemingly infinite permutations, all with the promise of making life easier for the house-wife. As more women began to work outside the home, convenience became the main marketing lever food companies and advertisers used to sell their new products. "Cooking is a chore; let us do the work for you" was the overriding message of Jell-O instant pudding and Betty Crocker cake mix.

The three-thousand-square-foot store became thirty thousand square feet on its march through the 1960s and 1970s, toward the huge supermarkets of today, which can measure up to ninety thousand square feet. Don't get to the checkout line in one of these and realize you forgot the milk, because it's a hike to the dairy section at the back of the store.

Heinen's did what most family supermarkets did throughout the fifties and sixties—expand slowly, opening a store every decade. A news-paper account of the second store, which opened in 1940, noted that it was four times the size of the first store. By the time Joe Heinen opened his fourth store in 1959, he needed thirty thousand square feet to display all the goods customers now requested. (The current ideal size for Hein-en's stores is forty thousand square feet—plenty big for all they sell, but not so huge that you feel the need for a golf cart to navigate it.)

As the 1960s began, with little sign of the economy slowing, Heinen envisioned even more stores. Ever forward thinking, he recognized that they could save money and work more efficiently through such expan-sion by building a central warehouse and production facility. So by 1962, the year before I was born, a central warehouse fed the chain that was growing throughout the greater Cleveland suburbs, allowing national brands to make single deliveries to the warehouse rather than multiple direct store deliveries (a term important enough to be abbreviated by grocers today as DSD). The warehouse would prove to be the company's saving grace in the 1980s, when many of the city's (and the country's) family-owned supermarkets, unable to efficiently distribute goods to their far-flung stores, could no longer compete on price and were bought up by multinational food retailing companies. Indeed, it may be the single most important investment decision Joe Heinen made to ensure the long-term success of his stores. To this day, Heinen's is the only chain of its size that does its own distribution of all categories of food from a central warehouse.

By the 1970s, something of a groundswell was felt in the American home. After years of Julia Child's cooking shows and Craig Claiborne's food reporting for the *New York Times,* the increasing convenience of international travel brought more people into the kitchen for food beyond pot roast and potatoes. Even having more women in the workforce arguably brought increasing numbers of men into the kitchen. The cultural shift was distinct enough for *Time* magazine to devote its December 19, 1977, cover story, "The Cooking Craze," to it. In an article headlined "Love in the Kitchen," the magazine writes, "The sexual revolution is passe. We have gone from Pan to pots. The Great American Love Affair is taking place in the kitchen."

And to fulfill our new desires, food specialty stores began to cater to our new desires. A co-owner of Manhattan's specialty food mecca, Zabar's, told *Time,* "I have never seen such an explosion of food buying." Soon grocery stores were getting in on the business. "Supermarkets from coast to coast, the authors write, "now stock such one-time exotica as game pâtés, Beluga caviar, imported mustards, goat and sheep cheese, leeks, shallots, scallions, bean curd, pea pods, bok choy, capers, curries, coriander, and cornichons."

Scallions and pea pods, one-time exotica? Apparently: "Crisp, fresh vegetables, which used to be as rare as lapwings' eggs, have become a mainstay of any well-planned menu: at their best, the vitaminiferous vegetables are lightly steamed, or stir-fried, Chinese-style, or tossed raw in oil and vinegar." Moreover, the article announces that we had "rediscovered the glorious raw ingredients and inimitable provincial dishes of [our] own country," citing Maine lobster, Maryland crab, Gulf shrimp, Columbia River salmon, Kentucky burgoo, and Louisiana gumbo as evidence.

Yet for all its growth within the rapidly changing consumer culture, the grocery game itself remained relatively unchanged through the

1970s and 1980s, for both large and small supermarkets. Grocers did business pretty much as they'd been doing since the 1950s because they were the only game in town, as far as food you brought home to prepare was concerned. Then two different stores made 1988 a watershed year in the world of the traditional grocer.

It was in 1988 that the country's biggest nonfood retailer, Walmart, got into the food business, in its Walmart-size way. It became the biggest grocer in the world the day it sold its first apple, and it remains the biggest in the world, as the A&P once was. The opening of the first Walmart Supercenter signaled the beginning of the fragmentation of the food retail world—and caught the attention of other merchandisers who wanted to try to make a buck retailing food. At the same time, Costco and Sam's Club also exploded, offering a tenth of what a grocery store did but delivering great savings, especially on nonperishables and household goods bought in bulk. It wouldn't be long before Target, the discount department store founded in 1902, got into the business of selling groceries. As the 1980s became the 1990s, food stories, food concerns, and food issues, which had always been important but were more or less peripheral in our culture, began to take center stage.

Walmart's success in the grocery business relied on its genius for distribution. The next sea change in food retailing may come from another master of distribution, Amazon. It's too early to say, but Amazon does sell groceries and is experimenting with innovative methods of delivery. At the same time, independent grocery delivery services like FreshDirect are growing, while companies that offer "meal solutions" (in grocer parlance) take hold, such as Blue Apron and HelloFresh, which promise a delicious dinner you cook yourself, with no trip to the grocery store required. All these new options will of course accelerate the fragmentation of the food retail business.

The second big piece of news in 1988 was that Whole Foods Market, at the time a small but successful all-natural grocery chain in Austin, Dallas, and Houston, expanded out of Texas to become a thriving national chain. It first bought a New Orleans grocery store, coincidentally called Whole Food Company, then began a strategy of purchasing stores nationwide rather than building new ones. First in Palo Alto, California. Then in Illinois, North Carolina, and Massachusetts, all under the Steve Jobs–like leadership and charisma of its co-founder, John Mackey.

"If I reflect, in my lifetime, who has changed the world," Tom Heinen told me, "John Mackey is one of those people. He brought attention to the way food is grown. He really changed our industry."

Mackey opened a "health food" store in 1978 in Austin, Texas, partnered with another store, and opened the first Whole Foods Market in 1980. It was so beloved in its community that when a flood ruined the store, which was uninsured, its customers—and many of its vendors—chipped in to help put it back together. Whole Foods expanded beyond Austin in 1984 and would eventually grow to more than four hundred stores, including branches in Canada and the United Kingdom.

Not simply a successful entrepreneur, Mackey can truly be considered a visionary. It doesn't take a Sam Walton to recognize that whoever provides what the customer wants for the least amount of money wins. Walton's genius was in distribution. But that's not vision. What Mackey did was sense that people were starting to want to know where their food came from, and that the food's source mattered to increasing numbers of people who would be willing to pay a premium for that knowledge and that product.

Whole Foods didn't start out mainstream; its customers initially were on the fringe. But because increasing numbers of people began to want organic and/or all-natural foods, as Mackey had foreseen, he was able to open more stores. And as more stores opened, Whole Foods had to find more suppliers; where they didn't exist, it created them.

Whole Foods' buying power was strong enough to assure farmers that they could farm organically and make a living. "For a number of years," Tom Heinen said, "it wasn't that we didn't *want* to sell organic, it was that we couldn't get enough of it. And Mackey really converted agriculture—the farmers—to starting to grow things organically. It was a big deal."

Recognizing that its customers wanted beef that had been raised without hormones or antibiotics, Whole Foods worked with major beef suppliers to raise cows this way. Heinen's couldn't have done that, but today they are able to sell hormone-free beef because of the path Whole Foods blazed.

The chain did the same with groceries—sourcing natural and minimally processed versions of shelf-stable products. Of course, once traditional grocers saw that shoppers wanted organic and so-called all-natural products, they too sourced them and put them on their shelves beside the conventional versions. It was thanks to Whole Foods that they could expand their organic produce section, because the products were now available.

All of which has resulted in a significant problem for Whole Foods today, which Tom Heinen put concisely: "What makes them different now? The answer is, not that much." If traditional grocers can now offer what Whole Foods does at traditional-grocer prices, Whole Foods can no longer easily differentiate themselves, except insofar as they're more expensive. Not exactly a selling point.

Grocery stores today carry more than forty thousand different items; in virtually every food category, they now offer an all-natural or organic version. A typical Whole Foods carries around twenty thousand products. A grocery store has more options, and they can sell the products for less.

To adjust to the forces working against them, Whole Foods seems to be attempting to compete by offering itself as a community's social hub, touting their happy hour and craft beers on tap. And in 2016 it began launching smaller "365 by Whole Foods Market" stores (365 is the name of its private-label products), with Trader Joe's–like prices. They also seem to be investing heavily in their prepared foods offerings, which take up a major chunk of real estate in their stores relative to the size of the prepared foods section in traditional grocery stores.

Regardless of whether Whole Foods limps or bounds into the future, the overarching and encouraging lesson of John Mackey and his business, to me, is that this single store has had a measurable impact on the way America raises its food—and for the good.

As these massive changes rumbled through the grocery landscape in the 1990s—the fragmentation of the retail food world, the growth of organics and natural foods, the evolution of a new type of consumer—Tom and Jeff Heinen reached for the shelves to steady themselves and engage a new plan for moving forward. They recognized that they'd have to change if they wanted to keep the business for the long haul.

5.

"NEA, I THINK I WANT TO MOVE TO CLEVELAND—I THINK I WANT TO WORK FOR THESE GROCERS"

Chris Foltz, an Orlando-based business consultant, didn't know much about groceries, as Tom Heinen noted, and he didn't really *want* to know. His interests lay in technology. He ran a successful consulting business, specializing increasingly in developing leadership and building effective teams, and had a lovely home in a beautiful part of the country. He worked from there and traveled to help businesses develop successful teams. When home in sunny Florida, he cooked and relaxed with his wife, Nea, and their two boys. Chris takes good care of himself—he always carves out some morning hours even while traveling for a workout or a run. He is thoughtful about what he eats—raw almonds are his preferred lunch during a busy day. He loves to cook and is good at it. He appreciates great wines and cheeses and salumi. But pretty much the only thing he knew about the grocery business was that it seemed dull. His description of how he originally felt about my beloved grocery store was this: "Boring business, boring product—frozen dinners and milk."

Boring, that is, until D&W Fresh Market, a family-owned chain of two dozen supermarkets throughout the state of Michigan, contacted him in 1994 to ask for his consultation.

"I went up there," Chris remembers, "and the CEO—it was a third-generation family business—the CEO said, 'Can you help us?'"

"What kind of information do you want?" Chris asked.

The CEO said, "I'm not sure."

Chris paused, narrowed his eyes, and said more carefully, "What do you want to know about your company?"

The owner, somewhat desperately, responded, "I have no idea—can you help us figure it out?"

Chris realized then that he stood before a man who was running a business doing $350 million in annual sales but had no idea what to do with his business or even how to evaluate it.

"*That* was when I started to get interested in groceries," Chris told me.

Chris began to take on more grocers as clients. The business of retailing food had become so complex that the people who ran supermarkets didn't know what to do. D&W belonged to a "share group," a collection of a dozen family grocers of approximately the same size from across the country, who meet twice a year to share ideas and tactics—people such as David Ball of Ball's Food Stores in Kansas; Kevin Davis of Bristol Farms in Southern California and San Francisco; Russell Lund of Lunds & Byerlys in the Minneapolis–Saint Paul area; Mark Skogen of Festival Foods in Wisconsin; Edward Roche of Roche Bros. Supermarkets in the Boston area; Norman Mayne of Dorothy Lane Market in Dayton, Ohio. And Tom and Jeff Heinen.

It's likely that Tom, rather than Jeff, reached out to Chris on D&W's recommendation, because when Chris showed up at Heinen's headquarters, the first words out of Jeff's mouth were, "I just want to warn you, I'm allergic to consultants."

Chris thought, *Wow, I've never started a meeting like that before!* But he said, "How can I help?"

The brothers outlined the extraordinary challenges in food retailing, which Chris was by now familiar with. They knew they had to change, and they needed help defining and implementing a long-term strategy. The one thing Tom and Jeff did feel certain about was this: "For us to be successful in the future," they told Chris, "it's going to be because of our people, and they're going to have to have different skill sets. And we don't know how to teach that."

"The goal of Heinen's is the sustainability of Heinen's," Tom said. "It's not exit strategy or wealth management. We feel that it is not ours to sell, it's ours to perpetuate." And they believed that they could perpetuate it only if the satisfaction of their employees, not their customers, became their fundamental priority. But they had no idea how to train and develop their management team and associates.

"I'd never talked to senior leaders who admitted they didn't know how to do something," Foltz told me, recalling those years of consulting in the 1990s. "But they wanted to know. I'd never gone into a company where the senior leadership said, 'We want to do whatever it takes for our *associates* to be successful.' A company that is putting employees ahead of profit?" Chris shook his head. "I just hadn't seen that before."

On one of his frequent visits to Heinen's, in the winter of 2002—the company had been a client for five or six years by this time—it struck him. At the end of the day, he called Nea in Florida. "Nea?" he said. "I think I want to move to Cleveland. I think I want to work for these grocers." One can only imagine the silence on the other end of the line in balmy Florida.

But the reason was simple—something had become clear to Chris: "I felt part of something that was bigger and more important than me."

When Chris told Tom he wanted to join the company, Tom's first response was, "Why would you want to do that?"

Tom and Chris found Jeff, and Chris again explained what he'd just told Tom.

Jeff said, "Why would you want to do that?"

Chris laughed and Tom reminded him, "We *are* twins."

The twins were, ultimately, receptive. Chris remembers the negotiations as follows: "I came here and made them my offer," he told me, "what I needed to make in order for this to work for me. It was significantly less than I was currently earning, and Jeff said, 'We can't pay you that much—we don't pay *ourselves* that much.'" After Chris recovered from that news, he said, "Well, you two need to give yourselves a raise!"

Chris recognized that he was entering the grocery business at a time of rapid change. He began to rethink what a grocery store might and could be, given the speed with which America made its food choices and the changing nature of the people who buy what amounts to billions of pounds of food every day, not to mention Americans' health woes and the growing number of people looking for clear information on altering their diets. And it was not only a time of a continuous proliferation of foods, it was also a time when grocery stores had to compete with all kinds of food retailers that hadn't existed twenty years earlier. People now shopped at traditional grocery stores and super centers and discount clubs and niche markets. Once, shoppers had one or two primary places where they bought their food; today only one in ten shoppers can name a primary store where they shop.

And it wasn't just the types of food stores that had changed—the country itself had changed dramatically since the 1980s, and the shopper had changed as well. There had been just as much fragmentation among the people who buy the food as there had been in the people who sell the food.

Women used to be the primary shoppers in America—and that goes back to the earliest days of the grocery business. Now it's split nearly evenly (45 percent men), according to the Food Marketing Institute (FMI), a Washington, DC–based trade organization that works on behalf of food retailers nationwide and monitors such changes. FMI has also found that we shop differently depending on how old we are. People over fifty plan ahead, build their pantry, and shop for essentials as needed or as whim decrees. They have pasta and beans and salad fixings on hand and can make a range of meals based on their mood at the time without necessarily having to go to the store. Millennials, on the other hand, "shop backward." They more or less wait till they're hungry and crave something, then go out, bring it home, and cook it. (I witnessed this firsthand with my twenty-year-old daughter and her boyfriend.) More generally, there's been a shift in who decides what to buy, meaning more family members have a say in the matter.

There is also a growing focus on "wellness." And, in a food world so many people find confusing, there is an increasing tendency to see one's grocer as one's ally. An encouraging finding is that 25 percent of shoppers make decisions about what to buy based on the ingredients in the food and are increasingly trying to steer clear of overly processed packaged goods, something that never would have occurred to my father to do. Indeed, before the 1990 Nutrition Labeling and Education Act, we often had no way of knowing what ingredients a package contained.

So, not only did Chris Foltz have to help Heinen's respond to the customer, he had to figure out how to do so when that customer was rapidly changing in response to a media culture that confused as much as it edified. And looming in the background were changes in the broader American population, which was being made sick by much of the food this country offered for sale.

6.

HOW TO SAVE A LOCOMOTIVE THAT HAS JUMPED THE RAILS

Tom and Jeff Heinen grew up in the 1950s and '60s in comfort in Shaker Heights, then Pepper Pike, Ohio. Some of their earliest recollections are of joining their father on Sundays when he visited the stores. Tom and Jeff would race carts up and down the broad empty aisles (a practice that many a third-generation grocer mentioned to me with nostalgic fondness). They attended a private boys' school (the one I graduated from less than a decade later), played the same sports, shared the same friends. They would occasionally work at one of the stores—stocking shelves and bagging groceries—but were free to find work wherever they wanted. Some summers were spent painting houses. After graduating from high school in 1973, Jeff, the more reserved of the two brothers, headed west to Stanford while Tom went east to Bucknell in central Pennsylvania. They traveled abroad separately after college, reconnecting in London before returning home together. Once home, in 1978, into the family business they both went. As clerks under their father's direction, the brothers branched out to learn the grocery business over the course of the next sixteen years.

Jeff was put in the dairy department as a clerk associate. He likes to say, "I was the only Stanford graduate stocking milk eight hours a day."

The more garrulous Tom fried chicken at one of the stores that offered this prepared food. His father next sent him to baking school to learn how to work with frozen doughs; grocery stores were now creating full-scale bakeries, as local independent bakeries began to falter in the new food marketplace. Tom spent much of his time at "Central"—the central warehouse—where workers prepared salads and other foods, and he helped open proper deli departments, ultimately taking charge of the meat department, under which all these other departments fell.

While we were in discussions about this book, Tom and I met at a restaurant in downtown Cleveland, along with Chris Foltz. We began with local IPAs and small talk. When the beers were gone, Tom looked at the menu and asked to try the Laphroaig "triple wood." Having dispatched this woody one, he ordered rounds of the eighteen-year-old Laphroaig to compare (it was much better, the "triple wood" seeming to me a marketing device). I glanced at my watch. I was supposed to make dinner at home and it was getting late. We continued talking about the proposed book. When that whiskey was done, I felt for my wallet, anxious to depart. But the waitress appeared and asked, "Another?"

Tom looked at me and said, "Sure."

I looked at my watch again. Tom looked at me again. I told him I was expected home. He smiled at me as if to say, "Really, you're going to turn down an eighteen-year-old Laphroaig?"

I acquiesced. So dinner would be a little late.

Tom took a sip of his whiskey and said, "If you're going to do this book, you're going to have to get used to this."

I told him I didn't think this would be a problem.

And that, at a glance, is Tom Heinen. A lover of food and wine and spirits and also fiercely committed to his company and its employees. When asked recently by an associate what he would do if a multinational offered them an enormous sum for their stores, he reportedly turned red in the face and said, "The only person who can sell Heinen's is Joe Heinen!" The patriarch who had died in 1981.

I asked Tom what it was like to have a twin brother as his partner.

"The blessing of working together is that we've always had the same vision for the company. And that vision is to perpetuate the legacy of the company. It was never about getting rich. And the longer we were in the business, the more committed we were to that vision."

He reflected more. "And another thing is, when your partner is your brother, you know your partner is never going to screw you."

"When I was in high school, in 1973," Tom asked me, "how many items do you think we sold that you could buy somewhere else? The answer is zero. You could go to a gas station and buy a twenty-ounce bottle of pop,[30] but that was about it. Now, today, how many items do we sell that you can buy somewhere else? Everything. *Everything we sell is available somewhere else.* And nine times out of ten it's across the street."

Since the beginning of the grocery business, price was the primary way a grocer could differentiate his products, because every grocer sold the same things, and no other store offered what the grocer did. But beginning in the eighties, Sam's Club and Costco and Walmart came in to offer goods at prices traditional grocers couldn't beat. In addition, niche stores like Whole Foods and Trader Joe's and Wild Oats became national presences, offering specialty items not available in a traditional grocery store. Yet grocery stores continued to sell what they always sold, including mops and shoe polish, in the way they'd always sold it. It soon became clear that there were fewer and fewer ways they could differentiate themselves since cheaper goods were available elsewhere.

The major change for Tom and Jeff came in 1994, when their father was hospitalized suddenly with a stroke at age sixty-five. Tom still remembers watching O. J. Simpson's Bronco chase from his dad's hospital room. Jack wouldn't recover.

Tom and Jeff had been running the chain of eleven grocery stores, but until the loss of their father, they were not the ultimate decision makers. Once they did have that power, and they acknowledged the rapidity with which the food retail world was changing, they recognized that they weren't at the steering wheel of a sleek machine. They were on a locomotive that would jump the tracks if they didn't keep up with a changing society.

"We fell asleep as a company in the seventies and eighties," Jeff says, "and then we desperately tried to play catch-up to bring our stores into the twenty-first century."

Jeff returned to his roots in the dairy department to describe the trajectory of the changes. "Eggs were considered horrible," he said, when

30 It has always been customary in the Midwest to call soda "pop"; I had to consciously work myself out of this habit when I moved to New York so as not to reveal myself as a hayseed.

he first began as a clerk. "Eggs were in a death spiral. Yogurt was a small category. All the alternative milks didn't exist in a supermarket. Organic didn't exist. We had cheese, but started to move away from processed cheese. We still sold a lot of chunk cheese, but sales were declining. The *dairy* department was declining.

"So, when you have a department that's declining, you have to figure out how to allocate space when you redesign or build a store. It costs money to run dairy cases, so you wouldn't want to overspace it. We built our dairy cases according to what we understood the business to be at the time. Now go forward fifteen, twenty years, and dairy is this *massive* business. Milk sales are down a little, but alternative milk sales are through the roof. Organic milk is through the roof.[31] Yogurt is off the chart. We've got all these additional SKUs. Eggs are popular again, but it's not just small, medium, or large. There are fifteen different kinds—cage-free, organic—all these fancy butters, and on and on. All these cases that we built no longer made sense, so we're cramped now.

"That's why we don't think out twenty years, because nobody's smart enough to think out that far ahead," he said. "Ice cream is the same deal. Ice cream—you had the traditional half-gallon business, and you had a few novelties. For so long, the only upscale ice cream was Häagen-Dazs."

Ice cream is a great illustration of how products have diversified. Back before refrigeration, ice cream companies were small and local, and their business seasonal. But with the advancement of refrigeration, and the growing size of supermarkets, which could put large freezer cases in their stores, ice cream could be produced on a larger scale to be distributed nationally, and big ice cream companies came to dominate the market. And they did so by putting out the cheapest ice cream they could—as all products then differentiated themselves on price—by

---

31 Jeff didn't mention this at the time, but in addition to skim, lower-fat, and whole cow's milk, they also sell protein-specific milk. These milks contain only the A2 beta-casein protein, as some studies show that A1 may increase the risk of diabetes and heart disease and is the troublemaker for the lactose intolerant. ("Some studies show" is a catchphrase that you should read as "nobody knows for sure.") "Milk used to be milk," Jeff said, shaking his head.

using as little of the expensive ingredients as they could get away with and whipping it in a way that incorporated as much as 50 percent air in each half-gallon container.

Reuben Mattus, brought as a baby from Poland to Brooklyn shortly after World War I by his widowed mother, transformed what began as a family business selling Italian ices into a successful local ice cream company in a competitive market. But as the 1950s wore on and the bigger companies were able to pay for space and placement in supermarkets, Mattus knew he wasn't going to last by trying to compete with them. So he moved in the opposite direction, creating a product that was the highest quality he could make, which he would sell in smaller containers. His ice cream had a high butterfat content and contained only natural ingredients—long before anyone even thought of touting "natural" ingredients as a marketing device—whereas the big ice cream companies used artificial flavorings.[32]

Naming his ice cream was critical. Mattus had to differentiate it from those of the American companies. He knew that in Brooklyn there were people who were prejudiced against the Irish, against Italians, Poles, Jews. One country, though, Denmark, was well known for a high-quality ice cream called Premier. When he was casting about for a fancy-sounding European name, he looked there. No one is prejudiced against the Danes, he reasoned. So after much thought he came up with the made-up words Häagen-Dazs and put a map of Scandinavia on the packaging, though the ice cream would be made in New Jersey. The weird name would also, he argued, force people to stop and look at it to try to figure out what in the ham sandwich it was.

Mattus thus introduced what he would dub "superpremium ice cream" in 1960, and through sheer doggedness managed to begin placing his product in supermarkets. The ice cream was a hit. Two former competitors in the small New York ice cream business, one of them a relative, wanted in on the racket and immediately created their own knock-

---

32 This story is hilariously laid out by Calvin Trillin in a July 8, 1985, *New Yorker* article. Trillin focused on the feud between Häagen-Dazs, by then owned by Pillsbury, and the upstarts Ben Cohen and Jerry Greenfield, creators of Ben & Jerry's.

offs, Frusen Glädjé ("frozen joy") and Alpen Zauber. Mattus tried to take them to court, arguing that they were, in Trillin's account, stealing his scam, but to no avail. Nevertheless, these brands weren't nearly as successful, and for two decades, as Jeff Heinen notes, Häagen-Dazs enjoyed 70 percent of the superpremium ice cream market.

Ben & Jerry's, celebrating their ice cream as made by a couple of Vermont hippies, entered the scene in 1978; by 1981 the company started to take off, despite Pillsbury's efforts to shut it out of the market. (The hippie upstarts sued Pillsbury—they had bumper stickers printed with the line "What's the Doughboy afraid of?" and benefited from the extraordinary publicity.)

"And then Ben & Jerry's came along," Jeff told me, "and now the half gallons have shrunk to twenty-five ounces or whatever. And there's still a market for those, but it's now mainly pints. You have a thousand varieties and you can never have enough."[33]

This proliferation of products is more or less what has happened in every department of the supermarket. A retail store once comprised four departments: meat, dairy/frozen, produce, and grocery. Today there are ten to fourteen departments, depending on how you combine or don't combine them. Here, in order of gross revenue, are Heinen's:

Grocery, that broad center of the supermarket, accounts for about 27 percent of sales. It includes one of the fastest-growing categories in the store, the "wellness" category, which encompasses vitamins, supplements, antioxidants, probiotics . . . nothing, that is, you'd consume for pleasure (except perhaps the matcha green tea), and nothing that has any noticeable effect when you do consume it.

Produce is typically the first department you encounter when you enter a grocery store; it accounts for 17 percent of sales, but it's also one

---

33 There is, for instance, an excellent homegrown company just two hours south of Cleveland, in Columbus. In 2002 Jeni Britton Bauer created Jeni's Splendid Ice Creams, using whole ingredients and dairy from pasture-raised cows. Jeni's is so beloved in these parts that Heinen's all but has to carry it. But when I saw it in a freezer case at Living Foods, on a trip to Kauai, one of the most remote islands on the planet, I had to shake my head at the global nature of our food supply (and tip my hat to Jeni for making it all the way to Hawaii).

of the most profitable areas of the store. Today you'll find fruits and vegetables from all over the world.

Frozen/Dairy brings in 15 percent of sales; note that these three departments bring in nearly two-thirds of all grocery store sales.

Meat now includes specialty meats and organic, grass-fed, pasture-raised, antibiotic/hormone-free offerings, along with traditional ("commodity") meats.

Deli/Prepared Food is, according to Tom and Jeff, the eternal money loser for all grocery stores, and yet this department continues to grow in size thanks to customer demand.

Beer/Wine is a category that has seen extraordinary growth since the turn of this century, especially with the range of craft breweries appearing all over the country.

Seafood departments offer fish farmed both well and badly, wild fish, line-caught fish, fish on the Monterey Bay Aquarium Seafood Watch list, and fish overnighted from around the globe.

Bakery offerings include cakes and cookies and muffins baked from scratch or parbaked, and specialty cakes.

Floral departments account for only 1.4 percent of sales, but they remain an important product to make available to customers. (Did you know you can order your teenager's boutonnière or corsage for prom night from the grocery store? I didn't till I saw one set on a grocery store conveyor belt. When I got a corsage to give to Elizabeth Eels before our eighth grade prom, I had to be driven to Gali's, a local florist.)

In 1994, grieving the loss of their father, Tom and Jeff tried to come to grips with the fact that they were now responsible for not just eleven stores but also twelve hundred employees. It was clear that while once overseeing four departments seemed perfectly manageable, they couldn't possibly handle the ten to fourteen departments that a supermarket now comprised, and they were worried. "We would either fail, or we'd die," Tom recalls thinking.

"That's when we got into this whole Treacy Triangle thing," he said, "and [thinking about] how do we differentiate ourselves. We realized there's no way the two of us can do all this work. We need leaders who can make good business decisions. And that's when we stumbled on Chris."

The Treacy Triangle was created by Michael Treacy and Fred Wiersema and written about in their book *The Discipline of Market Leaders*. It is a visual display of the three primary ways a company can differentiate itself from its competitors. Tom, Jeff, and Chris were going to use it to help move Heinen's into the future.

Chris Foltz was born in Brooklyn the same year as Tom and Jeff, 1955. He graduated from the University of Kansas in 1977. He earned his MBA from Oklahoma State University, then worked his way up the business ranks in the technology sectors of *Fortune* 500 companies such as Phillips Petroleum and Farmland Industries. But it was while he was at Sprint Communications that he began to notice how weary his colleagues were and how unpleasant the atmosphere was. The political nature of advancement in these companies turned him off, with colleagues working against each other to advance rather than helping one another. His coworkers, moreover, seemed to have little interest in the work itself and seemed to live only for weekends. Relentlessly upbeat and energetic, Chris realized that this was not how he wanted to work.

He left that world and, with Nea, bought a camper van and traveled the country. This decision describes all the facets of Chris Foltz that make his walking the aisles of a Heinen's grocery store as its director of operations so unusual. First, he'd made enough money that he and his wife could take a year or two off. Also, he was clearly so good at whatever it was he set his mind to, and so confident in his abilities, he had every assurance he'd be able to make more money after returning from being off the grid for a year or two. He was essentially a businessman, but he wanted to travel the country with his love. When the two happy voyagers settled in Florida, Chris began working for himself as a business consultant.

When he came on board with Tom and Jeff, he recognized that they, like the previous grocers he'd consulted with, had no long-term strategy, and this was what he began to implement. He helped them identify what their goals were.

Chris, Tom, and Jeff frequently speak with new employees. And when they open a new store, they must indoctrinate the employees with Heinen's business culture and ethic. At these meetings, a fundamental part of Chris's presentation is the Treacy Triangle, and the authors' observation that there are three basic "value disciplines" that companies can excel at to become successful. The first discipline they identify is "operational excellence"—offering goods at the lowest price with the least amount of inconvenience to the customer. They point to Walmart as the paragon of this value. The second discipline they call "product leadership"—offering the best-quality products available and remaining innovative by coming up with new products of the same or better quality. The authors cite Nike; had they been writing in 2007 rather than 1997, they might have focused on Apple. And the final discipline they call "customer intimacy"—cultivating meaningful relationships with customers to ensure them of the best possible solution for their needs and the optimal way of achieving that solution, whether it's help purchasing goods or providing a service. The authors use Airborne Express as an exemplar of customer intimacy.[34]

An oversimplification of the Treacy Triangle is that a company can focus on one of three things: price, product, or customer service. I like that they don't fall back on those dull terms, especially the latter. Customer service—what does that even mean? Customer intimacy has a kind of thrilling, well, intimacy to it. And it is here, as Chris explains to new hires, that they hope to distinguish themselves. (Treacy and Wiersema note that no company should simply ignore the two disciplines that they don't focus on, but rather recognize where their focus is and do an above-average job at the others.)

Heinen's believes it has a high-quality product insofar as it's possible in a grocery store—that is, grocery is often grocery; Cheerios at Heinen's are going to be identical to Cheerios at every Giant Eagle in

---

34 Airborne was acquired by DHL in 2003.

town. But they also work hard to source the best produce and the most interesting new products entering the market.

So, in addition to identifying some tactical strategies that they could implement, such as inculcating employees with a company ideology, Chris, Tom, and Jeff also did things such as introduce a new dress code. They checked with Nordstrom to find out what color most people look best in. They ended up choosing the *second* most flattering color, blue. (Chris, Tom, and Jeff didn't have to think long before nixing the idea of using the number one color that most people look good in; they would have a very hard time, they knew, requiring their bag boys to wear periwinkle. I doubt they fancied wearing it themselves.)

So the standard was set for all employees—light blue shirt and trousers that aren't jeans. The department managers, who once wore ties that distinguished them in the pecking order, were initially upset. How will customers know who's in charge, who has seniority? Chris explained that it shouldn't matter—every associate should provide the same level of service. If a manager was needed, the associate would find one for the customer. But foremost in this decision was the message that all associates are of equal value. "We don't want everyone to be compensated equally," he explains to new employees, "that would be communism. But everyone from the manager of the store to the sixteen-year-old part-time bagger is equally important." Tom and Jeff wear the same uniform as the checkout clerks.

The biggest change in the industry, the reason Tom and Jeff had to bring in Chris, has been the diversification of stores. People now have a dozen different types of stores where they can shop for food. For 85 percent of all American adults, grocery stores remain the primary place to shop for food, according to the Food Marketing Institute. The next biggest choice, used by 46 percent of American adults, is the super center, which combines groceries with clothes, toys, electronics, and jewelry. An unfortunate 15 percent of our adults shop for their food at a drugstore. And online grocery shopping, while small, continues to grow.

And yet the Heinen's business model had to remain fundamentally the same, despite the sea changes in food retailing. Jeff tried to simplify it for me.

"Think about it this way," he said. "For every dollar of sales, the average margin for Heinen's is 32 percent, or thirty-two cents. We are at the high end; perhaps the 'average' supermarket is somewhere between 25 and 28 percent margin. So with that thirty-two cents of profit on each of our dollars, we have to pay our expenses. For Heinen's, twenty-four cents of it—three-quarters of our earnings—goes to labor (wages, benefits, and payroll tax), leaving eight cents to cover all our other expenses. Those other expenses are utilities, rent, insurance, repairs and maintenance, marketing, supplies, and bank fees, plus a host of other small expense categories. One factoid that points up the difficulty for supermarkets is that of that dollar of sales, we pay 1.4 cents to the banks for credit card fees. That fee barely existed twenty years ago and now, after labor, it is our second-highest expense line item."

To recap generally the grocer's P&L: sixty-eight cents for cost of goods, twenty-four cents for labor, 6.75 cents for operating costs, leaving a little more than a penny in profit.

Labor is their biggest cost after goods. But again, one of their two main goals is taking care of their associates. "If you pay your people a decent wage and try to provide benefits," Jeff said, "there is very little margin of error. Heinen's is definitely at the very upper end of the wage expense, which is one reason our margins need to be higher."

Chris put it more simply. Noting that Heinen's pays their managers and long-term associates about 10 percent more than union rules require, he said, "If we paid our staff the minimum requirement, we would *double* our profits." An extra $7.5 million, roughly speaking, which would certainly be enough for Tom and Jeff to give themselves the raise Chris had suggested.

And yet not only were they able to remain viable in a changing food retail market and pay their committed associates a better than average wage, they were able to grow. When Tom and Jeff took over, they operated eleven stores. In a little more than a decade, they added seven more and began construction on a major food-processing facility for prepared foods. And they had a clear strategy for moving forward. In 2012, after the Chicago chain Dominick's went out of business, the brothers decided to make the move into a new market, opening four stores there in the course of two years, an astonishing rate for a relatively small chain.

PART II

HOW TO THINK ABOUT FOOD

7.

SHE BOUGHT THE FAT-FREE HALF-AND-HALF

I was standing in line at an independent grocery store in my neighborhood with my La Croix orange sparkling water, some hamburger buns, a bag of chips, a couple of bottles of wine—last-minute purchases for dinner. In front of me was a middle-aged woman dressed in business clothes, loading up the conveyor belt. She set a carton of Land O'Lakes Fat-Free Half-and-Half on the conveyor belt. I paused and thought, *No, keep your mouth shut.* But I couldn't help myself. Half-and-half is *defined* by its fat content, about 10 percent—more than milk, less than cream. I had to ask.

"Excuse me, can I ask you why you're buying *fat-free* half-and-half?"

A bit startled to be put on the spot by a stranger, she recovered enough to say, "Because it's fat-free?"

"What do you think they replace the fat with?" I asked.

"Hmm," she said, lifting the carton and reading the second ingredient on the label after skim milk: "Corn syrup." She frowned at me. Then she set the carton back on the conveyor belt to be scanned along with the rest of her groceries.

The woman apparently hadn't even thought to ask herself this question; rather, she accepted the common belief that fat, an essential part of our diet, should be avoided whenever possible. Then again, why *should* she question it given that we allow the food companies, advertisers, and food researchers to do our thinking for us?

The encounter crystallized many issues for me about the nature of our food and the nature of the people buying that food, and how food companies, nutritionists, doctors, and governmental recommendations influence what we buy. And, frankly, it drives me a little crazy.

Chief on my list is this fat business, and also salt. I address these two items first because, with regard to how we're encouraged to think about food, they are the biggest of the boils on my ass and I won't be able to think straight until I lance them.

We have a serious fat problem in America. It has nothing to do with our obesity problem. We also have a salt problem, and it's not about hypertension. While signs of change are in the air, fat and salt remain the leading bugaboos in consumers' ongoing national diet strategies, the wrench in the spokes of our quest for nutrition, the evil forces that, in our fearful, helpless craving for them, prevent Americans from achieving their whole-grain, high-fiber, all-natural health. And what can we do about it?

We should eat fat as we wish. We should cook our own food and season it with salt to taste.

There's little disagreement that Americans have a hopelessly neurotic relationship with what they consume. It's a neurosis that's built into our culture from the broadest levels of agriculture and government, which demand that we subsidize farmers to grow crops you can't eat without industrial processing, all the way down to our grocery store shelves, which are packed with confusing, marketing-spun messages about what's good for us and what's not.

There's no better example than Snackwell's, the low-calorie cake-like cookie. Who's the clever executive who came up with that name? Want a healthy snack? Try buying *Snackwell's*! This is a way to snack well—it says so on the package, and it's low-fat, so it must be good for me. Are Americans stupid enough to buy this? You bet. By the mid-1990s these cake-like cookies had sales of $500 million.

Nabisco, which makes Snackwell's, was acquired by Kraft in the early 2000s, so Kraft became responsible for Snackwell's as well as one of America's all-time favorite snacks, the Oreo cookie.

A *Chicago Tribune* article[35] uses these cookies to exemplify big food manufacturers' hustle to cater to America's rapidly changing desires, and describes the pertinent issues well.

---

35 "For Every Fad, Another Cookie: The Oreo, Obesity and Us," *Chicago Tribune*, August 23, 2005.

"Food fads and conflicting research force Northfield-based Kraft and other foodmakers to shift gears from one new product to another," the paper reported, "in an endless quest to develop the next big thing out of the same old things: sugar, flour, and fat.

"In an era of fleeting health fads and niche marketing," the article continues, "there has been an Oreo product for just about every new trend, whether low-fat, low-carb, low-sugar, or low-calorie.

"The Oreo now comes in forty different flavors, colors, and package sizes—from Mini Oreo Go-Paks that fit in a car cup holder to the Double Stuf Oreo Peanut Butter Creme. The cookie's many variations are emblematic of a food industry that has sought to placate an overweight nation bombarded with conflicting information of what makes a healthy diet."

Forty different kinds. Of one cookie.

Just about every box and bag on grocery store shelves has some kind of "low-fat" version of its "original" self, sometimes even if the real version doesn't require fat in the first place. On a recent flight, I was handed a Quaker granola bar touting "low-fat" on its label—granola is good for you, and it's low-fat, right? What the company doesn't say is that granola doesn't need much (if any) fat in the first place, but it *does* need sugar—worse for you, it's now suspected, than fat—and you can bet abundant sugar is the reason my Quaker low-fat granola bar was every bit as sweet and chewy as a Milky Way bar. And a check of its "Nutrition Facts" (yet another form of misleading labeling) confirms that it contains 7 grams of sugar. But will moms who shop and read labels know what those 7 grams actually mean? Here's what the 7 grams mean: The bar itself weighs 24 grams, so it's nearly one-third sugar and two-thirds carbohydrates (17 grams according to the label).

On yet another flight, I was given a blueberry muffin in cellophane. The first ingredient in this item was not even flour—it was sugar.

What drives me crazy, though, is my fat-free half-and-half friend, the American consumer, who truly does care about food and cooking but is continually misled, largely by an uninformed media and unchecked marketing by food companies, notably regarding two of the most fundamental components of cooking—fat and salt.

I say unto you: Fat is good! Fat is necessary. Ask any chef. Fat does not make you fat—eating too much makes you fat. We aren't filling our bodies with sodium because of the box of kosher salt we use to season our food, we're doing it with all the processed food that's loaded with hidden salt (case in point: those same granola bars). American cooks and American diners need to understand the differences between food we cook ourselves and food that's manufactured for the grocery store shelf.

I hope it's obvious that a diet composed of vast quantities of saturated animal fat is not good for anyone. This kind of fat has been linked to elevated blood cholesterol and heart disease—people who are at risk of these medical problems need to be cautious. And some people have serious issues with high blood pressure—salt will exacerbate this.

But most people don't have these problems, and for them, fat is not bad, not evil, not dangerous. It's a pleasure in the right quantities and we shouldn't be made to fear it. If all you ate was lettuce, you would eventually become very ill, so I would like to caution you about the hidden hazards of lettuce. Consider yourself warned. But if you eat a variety of natural foods, including plenty of vegetables, and avoid foods that come in a box or bag or are in some way processed, you should be able to salt your food to pleasing levels.

Yet listen to what the media tells us. ABC News led a 2014 story announcing a "new" health crisis: "The danger is salt," Diane Sawyer intoned ominously. At about the same time the *New York Times* published an anti-salt op-ed, in which Thomas Farley, a former New York City health commissioner, warned, "A lifetime of consuming too much sodium (mostly in the form of sodium chloride, or table salt) raises blood pressure, and high blood pressure kills and disables people by triggering strokes and heart attacks."[36] Two days later, reporter Nicholas Bakalar called the studies Farley relied on flawed: "A report commissioned by the Institute of Medicine just last year found that there was no scientific

---

36 "The Public Health Crisis Hiding in Our Food," *New York Times*, April 20, 2014.

reason for anyone to aim for sodium levels below 2,300 milligrams a day. A study published in 2011 found that low-salt diets may increase the risk of death from heart attacks and strokes and do not prevent high blood pressure."[37] *Increase* the risk—that's something you don't hear much.

Who to believe?

Regrettably, I'd say no one at this stage. The only thing about salt's effect on our bodies that we do know for sure is that if you consume *no* salt, you will die. That's how important salt is to your body. Just like fat, we need it to be healthy.

As ever, the French can teach us about a healthy relationship with food. Americans scratch their heads over the so-called French paradox—how can the French eat all that rich, fatty food and have lower levels of heart disease and associated problems? I'll bet their red wine helps, as has been suggested, but what is more likely the case, in my opinion, is that the French eat more natural foods than Americans, and they eat it in appropriate quantities. That, I would wager, is the root of their ability to eat a heavily salted duck confit dripping with duck fat, to luxuriate in Époisses and Reblochon, and have none of the health or weight problems we're led to believe are associated with these foods. The French can do this precisely because they don't eat "low-fat" granola bars and blueberry muffins that have more sugar than flour and eggs.

I've been an unabashed Francophile ever since I began writing about food. For most of that time I thought it was simply a love of that style of cooking—butter sauces, confits, pâtés, rillettes, the list goes on. But listening to an episode of *This American Life* that profiled a series of Americans in Paris to find out what living in that city was really like, I heard an illuminating comment on our country's relationship to its food. One of the people interviewed noted the joy with which the French eat, and contrasted this joy with the way Americans consume their food: "Americans treat their food like medicine," he said.

How true. We even have a governmental agency whose name underscores this message: the Food and Drug Administration.

37 "Study Linking Illness and Salt Leaves Researchers Doubtful," *New York Times*, April 22, 2014.

Americans need to be better educated about the food we eat, what's truly good and what's harmful, quantities that are necessary, and super-sizes we don't need. Until we find out for ourselves from reliable sources the answers to these questions, we will instead rely on knee-jerk media alarmism and marketing hooey, and we're not going to eat the food that satisfies both our souls and our bodies. Our fat and salt dysfunction will carry on unabated.

We shouldn't take any information at face value. Too often, it doesn't make sense, and much of it has been warped to some degree by lobbyists in Washington (there are approximately five hundred lawmakers in Washington and more than ten thousand lobbyists,[38] or twenty lobbyists for every lawmaker).

Moreover, there is little evidence that doctors and nutritionists are making decisions based on reliable data, but rather based only on inferences—just as in the seventies, when we made a country-wide appeal to cut fat and eggs from our diet. Ultimately, there is little hard evidence as to what is good for us and what is bad for us.

In a *New York Times* opinion piece in 2014 headlined "Why Nutrition Is So Confusing," the journalist Gary Taubes addresses this very issue.

"We're going to have to stop believing we know the answer," Taubes writes, regarding what is good and what is bad for us to eat, "and challenge ourselves to come up with trials that do a better job of testing our beliefs."

Taubes is a founder of the Nutrition Science Initiative, whose website dares to say, "Americans are unhealthy, diabetic, and obese—not because they are making conscious decisions to eat unhealthy foods—but because the information and guidance they receive about what to eat has been poorly tested and is quite likely incorrect."

The current state of affairs, he continues, "is an unacceptable situation. Obesity and diabetes are epidemic, and yet the only relevant fact on which relatively unambiguous data exist to support a consensus is that

---

38 From the Center for Responsive Politics, a nonpartisan, nonprofit organization that tracks money in US politics and its effects on public policy.

most of us are surely eating too much of something. (My vote is sugars and refined grains; we all have our biases.)"

That last parenthetical sentence is critical, because increasing information does indeed point toward the veracity of his biases. Reducing sugar, which has little nutritional value on its own and of which we consume inordinate amounts in everything from fat-free dairy products to bread to jarred tomato sauce to, of course, soda, is the primary new directive from the government (surely someone in the sugar lobby lost their job when the report was issued in January 2015).

But reducing the consumption of refined wheat products was not among the mandates. This is significant because refined grains are but one dietary step away from sugar, as these carbohydrates are converted quickly to sugars once they enter our system. Moreover, we do know *why* these refined grains are scarcely different from eating pure sugar in terms of how our metabolism handles them.

But before I get into that, let me conclude this little rant by returning to the Woman Who Bought the Fat-Free Half-and-Half. What actually happened? Our middle-aged businesswoman had followed one of our government's nutrition guidelines, but only by consuming more of those guidelines' main concern: sugar. In other words, she replaced natural dairy fat, good for you (about which more anon), with corn syrup, bad for you. How on earth are we to make good decisions when the processing of our food has made those decisions so complicated? Life is busy, stressful, and complicated enough; we consumers don't want to have to agonize over what to put in our shopping carts at the grocery store. We expect our food not to be harmful to us, but who is making that call?

No one you can rely on, that's who. Ergo: It is our job to think for ourselves, not the lobby-influenced government, not the nutritionists, and certainly not the food companies trying to sell you their convenience food. It's our job to make commonsense choices as best we can.

But how does most of America actually shop? How do we make decisions? To find out, I contacted Harry Balzer, a food industry analyst and a vice president of the NPD Group, which consults for restaurant chains and food manufacturers. He's been studying what food people buy for thirty years. I first read about him in a *New York Times Magazine* cover story by Michael Pollan.[39] The accompanying photo showed a modern kitchen filled with cobwebs and addressed the strange fact that though America seems to have become more interested than ever in cooking, food, and chefs, and is watching more cooking on television than ever before, American families are cooking less and less.

Pollan has been one of the most important voices in the food world, with such books as *The Omnivore's Dilemma*, and has been a fierce advocate for the notion that cooking our own food is an important part of our culture that has been disintegrating for decades.

He spoke with Balzer for an hour and could only say how depressing it was.

Why? Because Balzer, having studied Americans' food buying and cooking habits for three decades, says that Americans are moving steadily away from cooking, and that it's going to keep going that way. While 58 percent of our evening meals require some assembly, that number is dropping. Even the definition of cooking had to be refined for our new food system, Balzer said. Microwaving a pizza was not considered cooking by Balzer, but pouring bottled dressing over lettuce or making a ham sandwich was. "Some assembly required" was about all Balzer needed to consider a process "cooking."

"A hundred years ago," Balzer told Pollan, "chicken for dinner meant going out and catching, killing, plucking, and gutting a chicken. Do you know anybody who still does that? It would be considered crazy! Well, that's exactly how cooking will seem to your grandchildren: something people used to do when they had no other choice. Get over it."

When I talked to Pollan about his interview with Balzer, he said he was so depressed by what he heard that he had to struggle for even a glimmer of optimism from the gleeful cynic. Balzer explained precisely why cooking more nutritious meals would never be in our future: "Because

---

39 "Out of the Kitchen, Onto the Couch," *New York Times Magazine*, July 29, 2009.

we're basically cheap and lazy. And besides, the skills are already lost. Who is going to teach the next generation to cook? I don't see it.

"We're all looking for someone else to cook for us," Balzer told me, separately. "The next American cook is going to be the supermarket. Takeout from the supermarket, that's the future. All we need now is the drive-through supermarket."

Pollan persevered in his effort to pull something, anything, hopeful out of Balzer. How would Balzer suggest people eat food that enhanced their well-being and might reduce the damage already done by a diet of industrially processed foods? Balzer's words conclude the article:

"Easy. You want Americans to eat less? I have the diet for you. It's short, and it's simple. Here's my diet plan: Cook it yourself. That's it. Eat anything you want—just as long as you're willing to cook it yourself."

Of course, I thought when I read that. Simply buying food that requires you to cook it ensures that not too many manipulations have been done to the food. You don't *cook* a bowl of cornflakes. Yes, you can crush them and coat chicken pieces with them (one of my dad's favorite ways to prepare chicken, which I denied him most of his life because I couldn't stand the flavor of cooked cornflakes), but the majority of that dish is chicken meat, nourishing protein. And I bet that if we bought only whole foods and cooked them ourselves, just about every one of our food-related diseases would fall away like butter off a hot knife.

The idea that we could radically alter the health of our country simply by cooking is a powerful one. Pollan even made it the foundation of his next books, *Food Rules: An Eater's Manual* and *Cooked: A Natural History of Transformation.*

"He's a really interesting guy," Pollan told me, of Balzer. "You should try to have dinner with him if you're ever in Chicago." I could be pretty sure Balzer wouldn't offer to cook it himself.

Having no plans to be in that city (although it's my favorite restaurant city after New York), I reached Balzer by phone to see if anything had changed in the seven years since that article had been published. Short answer: nope. Had Balzer become any more hopeful about the American diet, with our enhanced interest in food and its impact on our health? Nope.

"We're in a state of flux right now," he said during our conversation about the food we buy and how we prepare it. "Nobody knows how this is going to shake out. They're trying to get out of processed food. And yet most of the food we eat is processed.

"I remember in the last recession people said more people were gardening, growing their own food. What a *load*. Maybe some people were putting seeds in the ground, but I watched. There was no movement toward growing your own food. What [people] discovered was the farmers' market."

In other words, we wanted freshly grown food, so we found the people who would do the work for us. In Balzer's world, farmers' markets are not a fad. Because they do one main thing: save us time in getting something we desire. "We will always move to the two great values of our life, our time and our money." Therefore, all food companies try to create products that save us one or the other. But he doesn't even think saving money will result in lasting change. It's all about time, he said, "because I can always make more money. I can't make more time."

But so much of the marketing these days, I noted, was not about time, it was about health. I didn't get into my beef about eating "healthy," a term that shouldn't apply to our food, because it's too ingrained.

"If we didn't have healthy to market to, I don't know what we'd market to," he said, noting that the push toward "healthy" food began in the 1970s—again, about the same time our food-related illnesses began to appear.

How about this move away from processed foods, how even Kraft Mac & Cheese was trying to offer a less chemical-laden product?

"I think this is a backlash from the eighties," he said. "When we tried to make our food better by altering it. By getting rid of the fat, getting rid of the cholesterol. Then what did we create? Low-fat foods. But that's not *food*. . . . And what happened to all that fat we took out of the dairy products? Where *is* all that fat? Is it up in Wisconsin? Are there great mounds or tourist traps somewhere?

"So, people start eating low-fat foods. What changes? Am I healthier? I don't know. There are no immediate benefits, like buying something cheaper or something that saves you time. You and I only eat fries cooked with no trans fats anymore. What have you noticed in your life now that you eat trans fat–free fries? What is the key benefit in your life?"

And this goes back to something I alluded to earlier. This is part of America's food problem, the issue of eating more nutritious food. If you have a really nutritious meal, you feel good afterward. But you go to sleep and you still have to get up in the morning and go to work, and the work is stressful. You bolt a quick lunch, and the work keeps you late and you don't have time to go to the store, figure out what to buy, take it home, prepare and serve it, and clean the kitchen afterward. And this is not likely to change. The only way for this to change is for society to recognize the long-term benefits of carving out the time to cook. That's all it really is: being organized and making time. You never hear people say, "You know I would really love to shower more, but I just don't have the *time*."

I asked Balzer what some of the trends were that he was seeing. And even here he was cynical.

"By 2000 we were hearing 'eat more whole grains, eat more dietary fiber.' And I'd say we've run the course on *that*. Whole grains are going down, antioxidants are going down. And there was the gluten-free—which is really just a digestion issue. Probably all of us have digestion issues. But gluten-free has already jumped the shark. As all health issues will eventually jump the shark.

"We will never have a healthy food supply. This country will never have a healthy food supply. Never. Because the moment something becomes very popular someone will find a reason why it's not."

He did acknowledge that meat remains a big problem in our diet, that we do eat too much of it, and that meat consumption is indeed going down.

"The snacks that are growing are healthy snacks. Yogurt, nuts, meat snacks, and granola bars and fruit bars and nut bars. The sweet snacks are not growing. We're snacking on savory things now. But those snacks are not growing at snack time, they're growing at mealtime—they're *replacing* mealtime."

"So when we do prepare or at least assemble dinner, what is it?" I asked.

"The main dishes for dinner in America, it's either going to be a piece of chicken or a sandwich," he said. "Those are tied for the main dinner dishes. At lunchtime it's clearly a sandwich. Even at breakfast, sandwiches are growing. Why? Because they're easy to make and they're almost an entire meal in themselves. And the accompaniment to a sandwich—it's not soup, soup and sandwich, that's just something that Campbell's said. It's chips, sandwich and chips. The easiest side dish in America." And by far the most popular, as it had been when Pollan interviewed him in 2009.

"And the number one side dish is vegetables, number two is potatoes, mashed potatoes or something like that, number three is salad, and number four is bread. But of those, what's the easiest side dish to make? Because all those other four are going down. Chips. Chips are going up. A man can serve chips. 'I'll take care of the side dish, hon.'"

Among the changes to cooking in America over the last few decades, the most prominent of them by far has been the microwave. Microwave ovens were invented in the 1940s but were only feasible for residential use by the 1970s. In 1986, 25 percent of all households had them. By 1990, Balzer said, 90 percent of American households had microwaves.

"The stovetop is still the number one appliance used to prepare foods, that fire we create in our house, even after all these years," he said. "The microwave is number two."

Some 20 percent of all meals assembled in the home use the microwave. Which is substantial, but that's not the most significant influence of the microwave. That would be the fact that it changed food manufacturing. Suddenly, frozen food could truly evolve, offering all kinds of meals that would have been difficult to heat in an oven, such as spaghetti and meatballs. With the microwave oven in most households, food companies could devise any number of exotic dishes to feed our desire for new and different options. And, of course, there's microwave popcorn. By the mid-2000s, microwave popcorn had become so ubiquitous, many people born after that time didn't even know you could make popcorn on the stovetop.[40]

But Balzer has noticed another major change in his lifetime. "We discovered that men can cook," he said. And who was promoting this? "Every wife in America was telling her neighbors that nobody can barbecue like her husband. And for only one reason. Then and today, the number one person preparing the food is a woman. And she wants to do one thing, which the ages of humanity were trying to solve, and that is *get out of it*. So supermarkets come along and say, you know what? We're going to start preparing food, because we are a food-service operation.

"The history of mankind always follows one path when it comes to eating," Balzer concluded, "and it never deviates from that path. And that's who's going to do the cooking. The answer to that now is the same as it was since we began cooking: *not me*."

Or to repeat his words to Pollan: not going to happen, because we're cheap and lazy.

---

40 I like the convenience of microwaved popcorn, but I'm wary of all the chemicals in it. Popcorn cooked on the stove is, of course, a different product altogether, far superior to microwaved popcorn, especially with melted butter and salt. It's so good that my son came to me and said, "Dad, could you make pot popcorn?" I knew he couldn't mean *that*, but what *did* he mean? "Popcorn that you cook in a pot," he explained. I found this so funny I wrote a blog post about my technique for stovetop popcorn, and many parents wrote to tell me their kids had no idea you could make popcorn in a pot on the stove.

8.

BREAKFAST: THE MOST DANGEROUS MEAL OF THE DAY

In the middle of a long book tour promoting a cookbook, *Egg*, my love song to that miraculous ingredient, I returned briefly to Cleveland, where I made an emergency appointment at my internist's office at the Cleveland Clinic to evaluate a painful knee ailment. My regular internist was out of town, so the doctor who knocked before entering the examination room was a stranger. When I introduced myself, Roxanne Sukol said, "Oh, I know who *you* are." Sukol happens to be a self-taught expert on nutrition ("They didn't teach us anything about nutrition in medical school," she told me). She is a preventative medicine specialist, medical director of the hospital's Wellness Enterprise, and the author of a popular blog called *Your Health Is on Your Plate.* And she was familiar with my books and the rants I occasionally post on my site.

Knowing that I often address the topic of thinking clearly about what we eat, she immediately broached her main nutritional concern with me: stripped carbs. That is, carbohydrates stripped of all their nutrition—the germ and the bran, which contain essential oils that would go rancid on a grocery store shelf. This, she believed, was at the root of much of our country's diet-related health problems. To explain this, she backed up to the topic of sugar. Too much sugar is bad for you in a specific, known way. When you ingest sugar, it goes straight to the blood, triggering an insulin release; the hormone insulin is the mechanism for guiding sugar to the right places in our bodies, where it can be burned as fuel. When we take in too much sugar, though, the insulin becomes overwhelmed and can't get all the sugar to the right places, so the sugar is stored as fat.

Sukol compared what happens in our blood to a valet service at a large gathering. If guests arrive at intervals, the valets can get the cars parked in the right place in a timely fashion. If all five hundred guests show up at once, the valets (insulin) can get only some of the cars to the lot, while the backed-up cars (excess sugar) sit there waiting (stored as fat).[41] Sukol maintains that this happens not only when we drink a Big Gulp, but also when we eat a bowl of cereal or a pile of pasta.

Items composed of simple carbohydrates, such as refined wheat and cornstarch, are converted quickly to sugar, which enters our bloodstream and results in the same rush of insulin that sugar generates. Over time, the insulin simply can't handle the load, and the result is type 2 diabetes.[42] And this is significant because since the 1970s, when the call to reduce fat spread throughout the land, we altered our diet so that we consumed considerably more of these low-fat, refined-wheat products. Which happened to be the same time all these food-related illnesses began.

"All carbs aren't bad—people need to understand there are nutritious carbohydrates," Dr. Sukol said. "Now, I'm afraid I'm going to have to ask you to lower your shorts."

The kind of statement that kills a decent conversation.

But I was so fascinated by what she had to say, I asked to meet with her to pick up where we'd left off and to ask her some more questions about her nutrition convictions and the stripped-carb situation.

Fruits and vegetables are examples of "good" carbs—even sweet corn and peas and grapes—but especially good are beans and legumes. These are all "good" because they have what she calls a "fiber matrix" that slows their conversion to blood sugar, and this has all kinds of metabolic benefits, especially in reducing the stress on our insulin system. Stripped carbs, on the other hand, are scarcely different from a spoonful of sugar as they are converted so quickly into sugar, triggering a flood of insulin to carry this sugar to our cells.

How did this explosion of bad carbs happen? Sukol believes it began when "some very savvy marketers in Battle Creek, Michigan, began to

41 Dr. Sukol has a very good TEDx talk describing these issues called "Our health is on your plate."

42 This type of diabetes was once referred to as adult-onset diabetes, but so many children developed the disease over the past couple of decades that this became a misnomer.

teach us to behave in some certain ways." Battle Creek is the birthplace of Kellogg's and Post cereals. Corn Flakes were invented in 1894 by Dr. John Harvey Kellogg, who ran a health sanatorium there, and he touted this unique product as a cure for the diabolical practice of masturbation. One of the people who stayed at the sanatorium was a man named C. W. Post, who, evidently impressed with this "health" food, went on to found his own cereal empire.

Kellogg's first cereal was basically an unsweetened wheat mush run through rollers and roasted. But it was Dr. Kellogg's brother, Will, the entrepreneur of the two, who began experimenting with flaked corn and also, importantly, the one who first added sugar to the mixture. This new version was considerably more popular than the unsweetened version. Kellogg's competitor, Post, followed suit.

The cereals proved so popular that others moved into Battle Creek to make their own, so many that it was considered a "cereal boomtown" by 1911, where 108 brands of cereal were being made.

But it wasn't until 1949 that Post created a cereal coated in sugar, called Sugar Crisp, which, according to reporter Michael Moss, was an immediate sensation.[43] The other two major cereal makers, Kellogg's and General Mills, followed suit with Sugar Pops and Sugar Jets. Two years later, Kellogg's introduced Sugar Frosted Flakes, "unleashing a marketing force of nature known as Tony the Tiger," writes Moss. That pretty much cemented the cereal makers' MO: Add more sugar. By the 1950s, Moss says, "cereal makers were not only adding sugar, they had made it their single biggest ingredient, pushing levels past 50 percent."

To reiterate what these breakfast cereals were and are: a combination of refined wheat, which turns to sugar almost as soon as we eat it, and sugar. In other words, ingredients: sugar, sugar.

Breakfast cereals, often marketed as a health food, got a major boost owing to an important cultural shift in America: the working woman. As soon as women entered the workforce, there was suddenly

....

43 Michael Moss's well-reported book, *Salt Sugar Fat: How the Food Giants Hooked Us*, recounts the entire cereal story, along with the genesis of many of the processed foods that now fill the grocery aisles.

a need for a quick way to feed the family before everyone left the house in the morning. Breakfast was, after all, widely regarded as "the most important meal of the day." (The first reference to this spurious wisdom appeared in a 1917 issue of *Good Health* magazine, edited by Dr. John Harvey Kellogg.)

And breakfast cereals were at the ready for a quick early cure. Back before women began to work, says Harry Balzer, cereal was something typically eaten on Sundays, when we were a churchgoing nation. Once women were working, the true cereal boom began.

By the 1960s and '70s, breakfast cereals had penetrated between 70 and 90 percent (depending on the source) of American households—and that's pretty much exactly the time our health started to go south. No more eggs and bacon (bad for you, back then). Instead, pour a bowlful of cornflakes, cover with milk, sprinkle with sugar, and off you go.

I used to eat Special K because I thought it at least wasn't bad for me; certainly it tasted like something that should be good for me. Did I look at the ingredients in Special K? Not back then, but I did recently. It turns out that 98 percent of a Special K flake consists of rice (a stripped carbohydrate), wheat gluten, sugar, and defatted wheat germ. (Please take note of that "defatted wheat germ." Defatted is good, no? No. Wheat germ is nutritious *because* of the essential oils it contains; when you remove the oils—defat it—what you're left with is more stripped carbohydrates.)

Not only are these stripped carbs bad for us, but Sukol has a hunch that they are particularly bad for us when we eat them first thing in the morning (as most people do), when our stomachs are empty. She's read studies that suggest our insulin may be especially quick to jump in the morning. Or, she says, "Maybe the problem is the huge quantity of nutritionally bankrupt foods that are supposed to stand in for breakfast." Even though we don't yet have the answer, the first thing Sukol advises her patients to do is stay away from the bad carbs before noon, or until they have some form of fiber and nutrition in their system to mediate the incoming sugar bombs.

And don't think that buying your cereal at Whole Foods changes anything. They offer their own 365 brand versions of all the cereals children beg for, like a Froot Loops replacement called Rainbow Morning O's. I'm going to write that again just for the fun of it. Rainbow Morning O's. Ingredients: grains processed to prolong shelf life, and sugar. Yes, that's organic whole grains (wheat, corn, and oats) and organic cane sugar. But please be aware that cane is where we get most of our sugar. It's still sugar, but it sounds better if you say organic cane sugar, doesn't it? We also get sugar from beets, which would sound even better even though it still does the same thing once it's in your blood. The least harmful-seeming cereal I could find at Whole Foods was Arrowhead Mills Organic Sprouted Multigrain Flakes: a variety of whole grains sweetened with organic pear juice (aka pear sugar).

One could certainly argue that if there is actual danger in the American grocery store, it is that Transformer-size aisle smack in the middle filled with boxes and boxes and boxes of breakfast foods—a dozen varieties of Cheerios, some with a little sugar, some with lots, not to mention those sugar-in-your-face cereals such as Cocoa Puffs and Froot Loops—that hulking behemoth in the middle of the grocery store so vast and diverse it astonishes people from poorer countries. Here is stripped-carb ground zero, and if Sukol is correct, a kind of unrecognized terrorism wrought on parents by our own food makers in every city, town, and suburb of America, given that most American households have a box of cereal in the cupboard and that we spend $10 billion annually on them[44]—at a 40 percent profit margin for those companies making them.

Groceries, no matter their importance to our lives and our health, and notwithstanding their contribution to our national illnesses, can seem to be a bland, uniform landscape. I returned to one of my favorite nonfiction books, *Great Plains* by Ian Frazier, as the American supermarket seemed a kind of consumer version of that great swath of flatland in the center of our country. Frazier takes that seemingly endless expanse of nothingness, dotted with small cities and tiny towns, and animates

44 "A Brief History of How Breakfast Got Its 'Healthy' Rep," *The Huffington Post*, October 6, 2014.

it with story—Sitting Bull, Crazy Horse, Custer, and Lawrence Welk; hitchhikers he picks up; gas station attendants and park rangers he talks to. He visits a Founder's Day parade in Nicodemus, Kansas (population "about fifty"), and experiences transcendent joy.[45] He describes how wheat became the dominant crop during World War I, when the Turkish Navy blockaded the Dardanelles in 1914 and shut down the flow of wheat from Russia. American farmers intensified their efforts and land use, as wheat prices doubled. "Farmers became rich," Frazier writes, "bought better equipment and more land, acquired more debt." But when the war ended, wheat prices dropped. Instead of planting less, farmers planted as much as possible to stay out of debt. "Then, in 1932, the rain stopped." The Dust Bowl catastrophe began. And it wouldn't really end until rains returned in 1941, the economic good fortune of World War II, and, after the war, the ability to tap the Ogallala Aquifer, which eventually "turned a number of Dust Bowl counties greener than they ever were before."

But it isn't American wheat production that led me to think of Frazier's work at this moment. It's what's under that soil of the Great Plains. Namely: nuclear missiles. Frazier was writing at a time when nuclear warheads sat on 1,850 Minutemen and MX missiles below the Great Plains ready to be launched through silos toward Russia. Many of the missiles have been dismantled, but about 450 remain active in Montana, Wyoming, and South Dakota, all of them coming at a cost of countless billions of dollars.[46] And in the end, Frazier, after much humor, characters, story, and history, gives a sad, brief summary of the Great Plains, a verbal time-lapse film, about how the new settlers of this

---

45 This is surely part of Frazier's Midwestern temperament and good-naturedness. He hails from Hudson, Ohio, thirty minutes south of Cleveland. He found joy on the Great Plains and I find joy among groceries, a kind of food Great Plains. When and if he returns to Hudson, he can buy groceries at a Heinen's grocery store that opened in 2005. "Joy seems to be a product of the geography, just as deserts can produce mystical ecstasy and English moors produce gloom."—from *Great Plains*.

46 When Frazier contacted the Office of Air Force History to get an actual figure on how much was being spent on these things he was rebuffed; determining the amount would be too expensive, he was told.

country destroyed the Native Americans and the buffalo and elk and prairie dogs, tore up the soil till it blew away to the Atlantic, shipped off the wheat and the cattle, killed off the small farmers, piped away the natural gas, and sucked up all the water.

"And in return," he writes, "we condense unimaginable amounts of treasure into weapons buried beneath the land which so much treasure came from—weapons for which our best hope might be that we will someday take them apart and throw them away, and for which our next-best hope certainly is that they remain humming away under the prairie, absorbing fear and maintenance, unused, forever."

That kind of sums up my feelings about the cereal aisle from all that I've read, from all the questions I've asked of people who seem to know what they're talking about. Breakfast cereal is a kind of unseen, underground threat, humming endlessly away, like those missiles. Only the cereal aisle is not inactive; it's one of the most active parts of the store. So bright. So cheerful. And of course plentiful, endlessly so. Convenient, nourishing-seeming, innocuous at worst. And we consume it without a thought.

Just last week, staying with one of my best friends on a visit to my hometown, I was up at the breakfast hour. J.D.'s wife had departed early for work and J.D. was in charge of getting eight-year-old Danny to baseball camp. J.D. went to the cupboard, retrieved a box of Special K, and set two white bowls on the kitchen island. He filled the bowls with cereal, poured organic nonfat milk over it, and slid one bowl to Danny. He took the other himself and ate it standing up. "Come on, Danny, we've got to leave in fifteen minutes."

I didn't say a thing. What good would it do? What could I even say without being an annoying crank, not to mention a bad houseguest?

9.

NO FOOD IS HEALTHY

A few aisles up from cereals, you'll find the equally huge "snack" aisle, also loaded with stripped carbs, corn syrup, and other non-nutritious ingredients.

Is it any wonder, Dr. Sukol asked me, that all the popular diets that seem to be successful in reducing people's weight (South Beach, Atkins, Weight Watchers, paleo) have one attribute in common? All of them limit or eliminate altogether stripped carbs.

The availability of more nourishing food is growing. For example, you can't buy Cap'n Crunch at Whole Foods. The chain is committed to offering food that supports health, or at least food that isn't harmful in the long term (though, as noted earlier, you can find plenty of stripped carbs there as well). It offers humanely raised meats that haven't been pumped with hormones and antibiotics, fish that has been caught in a sustainable manner. And traditional grocery stores have responded to increased demand for that same kind of food—food that is lower in sugar and refined grains, better for us, and sustainably grown or caught. Look for the kale chips across the aisle from the potato chips, for instance, kale being the current trendy "healthy" choice.

But even though many of our food choices are changing, at least among more educated, affluent Americans, we still have a long way to go in terms of how we think and talk about food. That businesswoman I accosted at the checkout counter regarding her purchase of fat-free half-and-half remains a great example of the need first and foremost to *think*. The compulsion to reach for the package with a "low-fat" label on it is hard to break. We don't know what "low-fat" really means.

An article on the National Public Radio website's food section (called, happily, "The Salt") describes long-term studies of thousands of people comparing their dairy fat consumption. It explains that there is now evidence that dairy fat can reduce our risk for diabetes and help us control our weight.[47] "'It appears that children who have a higher intake of whole milk or 2 percent milk gain less weight over time' compared with kids who consume skim or nonfat dairy products, explains [Mark] DeBoer. . . . With all the new evidence that challenges the low-fat-is-best orthodoxy, [Dariush] Mozaffarian[48] says it may be time to reconsider the National School Lunch Program rules, which allow only skim and low-fat milk."

Of course I'd have loved to pull up that article on my smartphone to show to the fat-free half-and-half lady, but I feel pretty certain that she would have bought it anyway, and that she continues to buy the fat-free version. Why? Because words are powerful.

How many of us use the word "healthy," for instance, to describe food or our meals? Do we stop to consider what this means? Eat healthy food, we are continually told.

I submit to you that our beloved kale salads are not "healthy," and that we are confusing ourselves by believing that they are. Because kale salads are not in and of themselves healthy. They are certainly *nutritious*. They may be delicious when prepared well, and the kale itself, while in the ground, may have been a healthy crop. But the kale on your plate is not *healthy*, and to describe it as such obscures what is most important about that kale salad: that it's packed with nutrients your body needs. This is not strictly about semantics. If all you ate was kale you would become sick. Semantics, rather, shows us where to begin.

"*Healthy* is a bankrupt word," Dr. Sukol said. "Our *food* isn't healthy. *We* are healthy. Our *food* is *nutritious*. I'm all about the words. Words are the key to giving people the tools they need to figure out what to eat. Everyone's so confused."

In March 2015, the US Food and Drug Administration (FDA) sent

---

47 "The Full-Fat Paradox: Dairy Fat Linked To Lower Diabetes Risk," NPR's *The Salt*, April 18, 2016.

48 Mark DeBoer is a Virginia pediatrician who has studied the effects of dairy fat on the weight of children. Dariush Mozaffarian, dean of the Friedman School of Nutrition Science and Policy at Tufts University, is an author of the study cited here.

the fruit-and-nut-bar maker, Kind, a letter warning that their use of the word "healthy" on their packaging was a violation—there was too much fat in the almonds to be considered healthy by their definition of the word, which specifies "healthy" to the gram. Kind responded with a citizens' petition asking the FDA to reevaluate their definition of the word. Most nutritionists would agree that the type of fat in almonds is good for you, and yet our FDA wants you to believe that it is not.

If I may reiterate the doctor's words: Our food is not healthy; *we* will be healthy if we eat *nutritious* food. Words matter. And those we apply to food matter more than ever given our confusion over what to eat.

There are some guidelines as to what we can and cannot call a processed food. For instance, Kraft American Singles cannot be called cheese, but must be labeled "pasteurized prepared cheese product." It was only about twenty-five years ago that the government mandated "nutritional" labeling on all food. The Nutrition Labeling and Education Act of 1990 gives the FDA "the authority to require nutrition labeling of most foods regulated by the Agency; and to require that all nutrient content claims (i.e., 'high fiber,' 'low-fat,' etc.) and health claims be consistent with agency regulations," according to the FDA's site. But I put quotation marks around the word "nutritional" because, when it comes to labels, they don't do a lot of good. As the market researcher Harry Balzer noted, "The nutritional facts label is mostly about stuff that's bad for you."

Here is a word we think we understand: protein. Protein is good, right? Builds strong muscles, has positive health connotations. That's why "protein shakes" are a multibillion-dollar business. Pork cracklings do not have positive health connotations because we think of them as having a high fat content. But pork cracklings are little more than strips of fried pigskin. Skin is one of the many forms of connective tissue in all animal bodies and is composed almost entirely of protein, typically undergirded by a layer of fat. When these strips of pig skin are fried, the fat is rendered out and the connective tissue puffs, resulting in a delectable, crunchy, salty crackling. I therefore recommend them to you as a go-to "protein snack" during your busy day.

Perhaps you opt for turkey "bacon" and turkey sausage because turkey is a lean meat, leaving aside the fact that even if the sausage is made of turkey, it can have just as much fat in it as a traditional pork sausage (fat is why all sausages, for those who eat meat, are so satisfying). Read the label on these turkey products and you will most likely see an ingredient called "mechanically separated meat."

This refers to meat still on the butchered poultry carcass, which is removed by machine. When you look at how it's actually done—augers take the carcass through grinders, and various sieves filter the meat from the crushed bone, cartilage, and nerves—it's not exactly mouthwatering. But the benign term "mechanically separated meat" attracts little attention on the ingredients list. The idea of processed meat engages our imagination only when someone attaches new words to it, such as "pink slime"—basically beef bits that have been removed from the carcass by centrifugal force, frozen, and then extruded through tubes. And even pink slime may have unfairly sinister connotations—Tom himself, Heinen's Mr. Beef, considers pink slime essentially "a natural product without additives that got banned due to some activists' misgivings." It's banned in Canada, that is, though when the pink slime brouhaha broke in 2012, many American companies either stopped using it or disavowed its use.

All of which is to say that neither mechanically separated meat nor pink slime will likely kill us, but the verdict is still out on whether they're good or bad, and why. My point is only that words are powerful: "I'll have one order of the mechanically separated meat, but I'm afraid I'll have to pass on the pink slime, thanks."

Given the infinitely malleable language of food, it's no wonder that shoppers are confused. "Refined" is another critical food word. Refined means elegant and cultured in appearance, manner, or taste, or with impurities removed. Yet refined is also what food companies call wheat from which the germ and bran have been removed, leaving the endosperm, which is in effect pure starch, devoid of the fiber, oils, iron, and vitamins that make wheat nutritious. This is why Dr. Sukol uses the word "stripped" rather than "refined"—flour stripped of the nutrition that makes it valuable to our bodies but reduces shelf life.

And then, because it has been stripped, we must "enrich" it. "Enriched." "Fortified." Good, yes? To make rich, to make strong. Food companies add the iron they take out during the refining process, but not enough of what we need. "Refined flour—this resulted in B vitamin and iron deficiencies," Sukol said, "so they added vitamins and iron. And what do they call that? Enriched and fortified. But they forgot to add folate, vitamin B$_9$, until the 1990s." What we don't know, Sukol said, is how these additions, not to mention the diglycerides and sulfates, combined with the lack of fiber, will affect our metabolism in the long run. So far, she said, "it has resulted in diabetes and metabolic syndrome." The latter condition is a term for a variety of risk factors that result in diet-related diseases, Dr. Sukol explained. Then she threw up her hands and said, "I don't even know."

We will be healthy if we eat *nutritious* food.

This is not a judgment on what you choose to eat. If you hunger for a cheese product grilled between bread that's been stripped of its nutrition, along with a bowl of Campbell's tomato soup (made with tomato paste, corn syrup, and potassium chloride), fine. It was one of my favorite childhood meals. Just be aware. Buy fat-free half-and-half if that's what you like, but know what it is you're putting into your body (and your children's bodies) and why. Because, and this *is* the judgment call, fat isn't bad, stupid is bad. And until we have better information and a clearer, shared language defining our food, smart choices will be ever harder to make.

We would also do well, in our thinking about food and abundance and food deserts and groceries, to consider these long, packed aisles of cereals and sugary breakfast foods, and aisles of snacks and shelf-stable breads in the very center of the grocery store. This too might well be considered a food desert, so lacking in nutrition is the food on these shelves. Nearly everything here contains some form of sugar and some form of refined cereal grain (either wheat or corn).

We might pause and reflect on the irony that even at the heart of abundance, in the very center of the American supermarket, we find a food desert.

10.

SHOPPING WITH MY DOCTOR

My final request for the good doctor Sukol was to see how she, as a physician with a passion for nutrition, shops at a grocery store. Would she meet me where she shops? She said sure and asked me to meet her at the Heinen's near her house in Pepper Pike, a tony eastern suburb of the city.

Sukol is on the shorter side, with black hair finely streaked with gray, black glasses, black attire, and a disposition I can only describe as one that combines scientific professionalism with an almost childlike voice ever on the verge of a giggle—until she mentions her overarching goal: "I'm intent on reversing the epidemic of obesity and diabetes and associated chronic diseases in this country," noting that two-thirds of Americans are either overweight or obese and that half us are either prediabetic or diabetic. Thus her willingness to tour her local grocery store with me.

She arrived after a long day at the Cleveland Clinic, so we got straight to it, entering produce, the first stop at this Heinen's, as at most grocery stores. "This is where people should spend most of their time," she says straightaway. Immediately she points to a cart being pushed by an after-work shopper, calling attention to the child-seat section of the cart filled with produce. "I'd like to see the carts redesigned"—that is, in a way that encourages shoppers to fill their basket first and primarily with vegetables and fruits, rather than using the small, child-seat portion for this, which is what most people seem to do.

Not here to shop, she looks around and evaluates: "They do a nice job of displaying it—this is where the local and seasonal stuff is. This is where I do most of my shopping, when I'm in this section." She walks to the left, to a section of misting produce shelves signed ORGANIC.

"This is way too small," she says, staring at about five feet of shelves of organic vegetables. "This looks kind of ratty. But organic is less homogeneous. It's not part of the food machine. . . . This is what I choose.

I'd rather buy these dry-looking carrots than the nice-looking carrots there," pointing to the bagged carrots in a central case, "because I know these were grown without pesticides. I don't want to eat pesticides. Just like I don't want to eat antibiotics and steroids that weren't prescribed for me.

"I also work to eat more colors." Pointing to some purple carrots, she says, "I would buy these because of the colors. Each color is a phyto-nutrient. But long before we understood that, we said things like 'Eat the rainbow.' My mother always said, 'Put as many colors on your plate as possible.' I try to go shopping once a week for just vegetables. To replen-ish." She cooks for her husband, a twenty-nine-year-old daughter who lives at home, and a middle son who lives next door.

We stroll to the opposite corner and she points to Heinen's freshly ground peanut butter. "I buy a lot of this," she says. When I ask why, she says only, "Look at the ingredients." Peanuts, period. "Have you ever had a roasted sweet potato with peanut butter?" she asks. "It's delicious."

We pass a display of avocados, another fruit she loves. "What would happen if the government subsidized these vegetables and made them easier to buy for more people? We'd spend less money on Medicare. We're all in this together. But it's stupid when an avocado costs three dol-lars and a loaf of Wonder Bread costs ninety-nine cents. That's wrong."

Dr. Sukol had said something that I didn't understand amid all that pro-duce and on our way to the wellness department, conveniently located next to produce. She talked about the "shikimate pathway" and a chemi-cal called glyphosate. There was so much ground to cover in the grocery store I didn't want to ask her to explain, beyond the fact that it had an impact on gut bacteria, sometimes referred to as our microbiome. But when I began to look into genetically modified organisms (GMOs), this shikimate pathway was apparently a not insignificant player.

Normally I don't have a lot of patience for this kind of thing—trying to avoid genetically modified foods—and considered it to be another fad akin to our sudden embrace of gluten-free products. As Nathan Perc, director of packaged goods at Heinen's, had told me, he had no idea if all these non-GMO-verified products were any better or worse for you than the food we've been eating for decades, he just knew that they sold. I thought it was mainly hooey.

Because this is true: We have no idea if products that use GMO ingredients are better or worse than those that don't, as Sukol says herself. Also, we've been modifying plants since the beginnings of agriculture.

But the GMO ingredients may not be the point.

The key is to ask why companies are modifying crops, and by companies we're mainly referring to Monsanto and its weed-killing product Roundup (great name—conjures up open plains and harvest time). The answer is to make plants increasingly tolerant of the powerful weed killer.

"That, in my mind," Dr. Sukol told me later, "is the problem. If we're talking about glyphosate, the active ingredient in Roundup, the genetic modification confers on the crop an ability to remain alive despite ever higher levels of weed killer, which are required more and more as the plants themselves develop their own tolerance.

"Here's the deal with glyphosate," she continued. "It targets, and poisons, the shikimate pathway, a metabolic pathway that is not present in humans. Monsanto sold Roundup on the basis of an assumption—faulty, in retrospect—that it would kill plants but not affect animals. But here's the rub: Our intestines contain trillions of bacteria that *do* have a shikimate pathway. So it poisons our intestinal microbiome even as it leaves us standing."

So the problem may not be the GMO crops themselves, but rather the chemicals required for their growth. Not to mention all the non-GMO crops that are also sprayed with glyphosate. We certainly are beginning to understand the importance of our gut bacteria. We've even devised something called fecal microbiota transplant, ingesting the feces of someone with healthy gut bacteria as a treatment for *Clostridium difficile* and chronic gastrointestinal disorders. The chemical glyphosate is not directly harmful to us, Sukol said, but it may be killing our gut flora. And she suspects this may be the cause of a host of medical issues: non-celiac gluten sensitivity, irritable bowel syndrome, rheumatoid arthritis, the exponential rise in Crohn's disease, even the increased frequency of children born with autism.

"The last thing we need is more glyphosate in our food," Sukol said.[49]

Curious about GMOs even before I started hanging out in grocery stores, I contacted the chef-author Dan Barber to try to get the lowdown: good, bad, or we just don't know. Barber, who was writing about agriculture for his book *The Third Plate*, responded from an agricultural standpoint.

"What we know is that diversified agriculture," he said, "a mix of grains in the proper rotations, like wheat, barley, a leguminous crop, a cover crop, and then a brassica, will dramatically improve the fertility of the soil. If the health of the soil improves, pest resistance is bolstered, and nutrition generally improves, dramatically. Which is why, as you know better than me, we need a *cuisine*—a whole pattern of eating to encourage a diversity of crops—because that's what the soil is demanding it needs for optimum fertility and health.

"Planting GM crops allows you—it begs you, really—to plant a monoculture and repeat that monoculture year after year. Because the GM crop is modified in a way that, for example, the most obvious pest will be eliminated. That works, and it works well, for a few years. But, for *sure*, it doesn't work well into perpetuity because nature doesn't work that way—it develops ways to circumvent the resistance. That's the problem with GM, and it's a big one. It's the 'one gene can solve our problems,' and we know that doesn't work, not in the long term. It's not possible. What *is* possible is that Monsanto can profit from a technological 'breakthrough' by patenting a seed. That's for sure."

....

49 Many scientific sources cite the herbicide glyphosate, introduced by Monsanto in 1974, as a chemical that disrupts the endocrine system, damages DNA, and drives mutations that lead to cancer. As tolerance to the herbicide inevitably rises, more is required to control pests, thus more of it ends up in our food. A quick online search will turn up more information than you probably want; see, for example, Nancy L. Swanson et al., "Genetically Engineered Crops, Glyphosate, and the Deterioration of Health in the United States of America, *Journal of Organic Systems* 9(2), 2014; and Carey Gillam, "FDA to Start Testing for Glyphosate in Food," *Civil Eats*, February 17, 2016.

So, is it bad to eat genetically modified foods? No one knows for sure. Something is responsible for this marked rise in gastrointestinal diseases, but we don't know exactly what and why. Sukol thinks that GMO versus non-GMO is a nonissue. She says, "We've been genetically modifying plants for all of history. . . . Even before GMO corn, we humans had turned it into a very different crop from the one that existed ten thousand years ago." If it is the case that GMOs do not directly harm our bodies, the next question to ask is whether they adversely affect the way we grow food and our impact on the environment. And the answer is likely yes. So when you choose a non-GMO-verified product, it's not necessarily any better for you than a GMO product, but it is a vote for better agricultural practices. As for organic, it seems certain that the pesticides on both non-GMO and GMO crops alike are harmful and may be the cause of numerous current diseases and allergies that largely didn't exist fifty years ago. So, if you can afford it, buy organic.

Organic produce is near the wellness department—all the vitamins and supplements now available—and I mention to Dr. Sukol on our stroll through the grocery store what Chris Foltz had said to me: "We think that grocery stores can be the health care clinics of the future."

"I like that," Sukol says, and would back it up at the end of our tour. "Because what we're doing right now isn't working." I sense her lack of interest in the variety of bottles of pills, and she replies, "There's a place for this. So many people don't eat the way you and I do." She adds, "This is a billion-dollar industry. The bottom line is that people feel like crap and they don't know what to do about it.

"The food industry," she continues, "has been so extraordinary at getting us to internalize the messages that they've promulgated: that when we respond as predicted to what we're fed, which is not what they promised—but it's certainly going to happen if you eat Special K—then we don't think there's a problem with the *message*, we think there's a problem with *me*. That's tragic. That's why there's all this." Row after row of vitamins and supplements. "People feel inadequate. There *are* good things here. A lot of people *need* more vitamin D. We don't live at the equator." (The sun releases this important vitamin.)

Moving toward dairy, where all kinds of fruit juices are on refrigerated display, she cites the John McPhee book *Oranges* and says, "Before the current era, 75 percent of the oranges that came off the tree were sold as oranges. Now it's the reverse. And you're not really drinking orange juice. You're drinking juice with all the fiber removed. You're drinking other ingredients added to it that sit in great big tankers on the ocean for months. If you want orange juice, buy a little thing and juice it yourself. It's food, and it's so much better for you."

She barely pauses as we pass the many feet of granola bars. "Granola bars are just candy. They've got so much sugar in them."

Across from the granola bars are a range of alternative snacks, either organic, natural, or gluten-free. A single packaged lemon tart catches her eye and she picks it up, reads the ingredients. "It's expensive, but it's food. You can buy all the ingredients in a grocery store."

This is a good rule of thumb when evaluating food that's in a box or a bag: Read the list of ingredients, and if you can buy each one of them in the grocery store, it's probably real food.

We arrive at the dairy case and she stops at the packages of cheese, many of which promise low-fat. "Anytime anything says reduced fat, that's a sign it's not food. They used to call this processed American cheese, now they're called American cheese products. One of the things I tell my patients is that if it has to tell you its food, it's not."

In the cereal aisle, she stops at some whole-grain Cheerios. "The first ingredient is whole-grain oats—so far, so good," she says. "But the second ingredient is food starch and the third ingredient is modified food starch—that's nonsense. That's just like corn syrup. It's stripped carbs. So really three out of the first five ingredients are sugar and I don't know what this is—tripotassium phosphate?—but I'm pretty sure it's not food. It's disingenuous to call this a whole-grain product."

We stroll past the cooking oils. "Canola stands for Canadian oil association—that's not food. Crisco stands for crystallized cottonseed oil—that's not food in my mind, cotton's not food. I did a little research on Crisco last week and they're also running to catch up, so they're creating this," pointing, "Crisco with omega-3s." This brings her to two important fatty acids that we eat—omega-3 (which we hear a lot about) and omega-6 (which we don't). "We need both," she says. "Omega-6s potentiate the pro-inflammatory cascade, 3s achieve the anti-inflammatory cascade. We need 6s—if there's a foreign invader, you need search and destroy. But then you need to cool off. Nuts and seeds in nature are rich in omega-6s, because they're more chemically stable, so you need them. Omega-3s are more predominant in leafy greens. Which is why fish are so high in omega-3s—because they feed on phytoplankton, the biggest source of greens on the planet.

"Before the twentieth century people ate a one-to-one ratio of 3s to 6s. But now, because the processed food industry is based on seed oil, the standard diet is fifteen or twenty to one of 6s to 3s. And if you're a kid living off fast food, that ratio is as high as forty to one. So there's pretty good thinking that the omega-6-predominant diet is partly responsible for all these autoimmune and anti-inflammatory diseases. So that's why I don't eat any of these seed oils. I'm getting what I need in the edamame and in the nuts. You don't have to go out of your way to measure this— you just have to eat *food* and it takes care of itself."

When we arrive at the seafood case, a large spread of ice in which lie butchered fillets, whole fish, raw and cooked shrimp, and a range of shellfish, Sukol simply shakes her head in wonderment. "This is remarkable to me," she said. "Last time I was here there wasn't any of this. This is the first time I've seen it where almost all of this fish is wild. They're responding to what people want and people are buying it."

I, too, was amazed by the seafood case. It wasn't unusual to find whole parrot fish and live scallops in their shell here. Marty Gaul has been Heinen's seafood buyer for the past sixteen years and is a forty-year grocery store veteran. When I first started looking into groceries in 2009, I talked to her about her work, and she sounded harried by the complicated position she found herself in as a fish buyer trying to please a range of customers. "Chilean sea bass, I can't win," she said. "Half my customers get mad if I don't have it, the other half gets mad at me if I do. But it's getting close to being off the endangered list." That generous and delicious fish, which also goes by the eminently more colorful name Patagonian toothfish, had become so popular it was in danger of being fished out of existence. She doesn't want it fished out of existence, but she also wants to please her customers, knowing they'll go elsewhere if she doesn't have what they want.

As a fish buyer, she's all too aware of sustainability issues: "About half the fish I sell is farm-raised," she said, "and a good thing, too—otherwise our oceans would be empty." And yet she has an uneasy relationship with the main watchdog of the industry, the Monterey Bay Aquarium Seafood Watch, which monitors the ocean's fish supply, recommends the best choices for consumers in terms of sustainability (as of this writing, arctic char, bluefish, rockfish, and swordfish, if it's from United States or Canada caught using buoy, handline, or harpoon), and notes fish to avoid (as of this writing, Atlantic cod, pollock, orange roughy, and swordfish, if it's caught by long line or imported). "If I listened to them," she said, "all I'd be able to sell would be herring and sardines." (But that was seven years ago, and sardines are now on the Seafood Watch's "avoid" list, if they're caught in the Atlantic.)

When I returned to speak with her recently, Marty had all but done an about-face on sustainability issues. "The government regulations," she said, "they finally woke up." The availability of fish had increased as more quotas were adhered to. In fact, the most pressing issues for fishing in the future will likely be how to continue to regulate the industry as the warming ocean forces fish toward cooler waters.

I asked about her uneasy relationship with the Monterey Bay Aquarium Seafood Watch. She said they had a problem with Heinen's selling Chilean sea bass. "They said in order for you to partner with us, we have to have an end date as to when you'll stop carrying [it]. And I said, 'Well, you guys may not recognize these fisheries as sustainable. However, other organizations do, and I have documentation. And I am not going to stop selling it because my customers want it and I believe we're purchasing it from a sustainable fishery, and if they don't see it here, they're going to go find it somewhere else.'"

Later in the year, she met with representatives of the Seafood Watch, which agreed to add Heinen's to their list of businesses that source environmentally responsible seafood purchases.

Marty sources fish from all over the world. Shrimp come from a variety of countries. Peal-and-eat shrimp are from Vietnam, wild and farmed shrimp from Mexico. "Raw pink shrimp from Argentina," she told me, pointing to them in the fish case. "They have the flavor and texture of lobster and they're cheap."

"Our walleye fillets are coming out of our own lake,[50] from the Canadian side," she said. Fishermen can't fish commercially for walleye in US waters, but they can fish for perch (both are fabulous, and perch makes an especially good fish-fry). She buys these from Classic Seafood Market in the Flats, the area on either side of our crooked river, where the city's first white inhabitants lived. Classic's boats cruise off the lake, into the mouth of the river, and off-load directly, the fish still flopping and dancing as they land on the dock. They're weighed so that the Department of National Resources can verify that the weight isn't over their quota.

"We have our catfish, all-natural catfish, from the Carolinas," she said, continuing her tour of the case. Here all-natural means the fish are fed no hormones or antibiotics. "Then we have our beautiful tuna and sea bass. Bluefin is controversial, but yellowfin is not, and sea bass is not either. It's MSC certified." This was a happy change from seven years earlier—the Marine Stewardship Council certifies those fisheries that are fishing the Patagonian toothfish sustainably.

While I was asking her to describe her fish case, Marty had to excuse herself to tend to customers who'd arrived to pick up the goods for their

---

50 This would be Lake Erie. One of the things this city is famous for is that its main river, the Cuyahoga, which feeds into the lake, was so polluted in the 1960s it caught fire. I prefer to call attention to singer-songwriter Alex Bevan, who notes in one of his songs that Cleveland is the only city in America that has a tower that is Terminal overlooking a lake that is Erie. The river is slowly cleaning itself up, but I'd still prefer the kinder, gentler fish caught on the Canadian side of the lake.

clambake. In the fall, Heinen's does a thriving business in these—Marty told me that Cleveland buys more clams between September and October than the rest of the United States combined. Marty believed our penchant for the clambake was a custom started by the city's most famous robber baron, John D. Rockefeller, who founded Standard Oil here in the late nineteenth century (creating, in addition to the clambake, enough wealth for the founding of many of this city's most important cultural institutions, including its excellent art museum and Severance Hall, home of the renowned Cleveland Orchestra).

After Marty had helped load five huge boxes of clams and corn and sweet potatoes into the customers' van and explained to the couple how to cook everything, we returned to the store. I noted she seemed less fraught about what she was able to sell and what she wasn't. I asked her if we need to worry in the same way we did seven years ago.

"I don't think so," said Marty, who oversees fish sales of $19 million annually. "They're doing so much with aquaculture. They keep making great strides. And the government has regulated the wild. We've done a great job in taking care of it."

She led me to the Verlasso salmon—"my baby," she called it. Verlasso salmon is grown in the Pacific Ocean off the coast of Chile, a joint venture between AquaChile, which grows the fish, and DuPont, which creates the feed, genetically modified so that it is high in the omega-3 oils salmon need. Most salmon farms use feed made from feeder fish. Salmon need lots of this to grow, about four pounds of it for every pound of salmon grown. Verlasso claims that it uses a little more than one pound of fish per pound of salmon. That, combined with its farming practices, which reduce the common problems of aquaculture (overcrowding, disease, and parasites), make this salmon the first ocean-farmed fish to meet the approval of the Monterey Bay Aquarium Seafood Watch.

"I love that stuff," Marty said. "I love the flavor of it. I love the support the company gives Heinen's. And I love what they're doing for the oceans. I like to think of farm-raised fish as we're not killing fish to make fish. What are you going to do when the sardines are gone, the mackerel are gone, all those different feeder fish? Think what you're going to do to the environment. All those fish that rely on feeder fish for their diet. They're going to go."

Another program that interested me was that Heinen's overnighted seafood, one more way the grocery store was behaving like a restaurant. It started when Marty received a call from an Alaska seafood purveyor, Karl Gustafson, who simply asked to ship her some samples. She said sure, why not.

The next morning she saw the Federal Express deliveryman bringing in a forty-pound box and didn't know what it was until, to her astonishment, she saw that it had been sent from Anchorage. She said, "It was like Christmas morning. It was Alaska gold. The fish was gorgeous: rockfish, king salmon, cod, and halibut." She was so excited she called Tom Heinen and said, "You need to stop by and see this stuff!" And that was the beginning of their overnight program: The boats off-loaded the fish in Alaska, and by the following morning, thanks to FedEx, the fish were in Heinen's stores in Cleveland.

Marty thought if they can do it in Alaska, they can surely do it in Hawaii and Boston. And so they now receive overnight, just-off-the-boat fish from five different regions.

When Sukol reaches the butcher's case, I ask her where she stands on animal fat.

"Here's what I tell patients. We all grew up in a time when we thought fat makes you fat. Nothing could be further from the truth. There's all kinds of arguments about this, but everyone agrees that certain fats are good for us. So I eat tons of them and I list them—deep ocean fish, and avocado, and olive oil. And then there are other fats that are inventions of the twentieth century—they're not food. They're causing inflammation—nondairy creamers, margarine and seed oil and corn oil. Don't eat any of that.

"Then there are fats that are in between—beef, lamb, etc. At the highest levels, among the real nutrition thought leaders in this country, there's a war going on. Some of them think that [animal fats] are good for us; some of them think they're rat poison. In the next ten to fifteen years we're going to know a lot more. In the meantime, don't eat them too often. We should be eating a plant-based diet to support our need for phytonutrients and antioxidants anyway. So eat more plants, moderate meat consumption, and stay away from the processed fats. And stay tuned."

Her final message about the grocery store was simple: "We can spend our money here or we can spend it at the drugstore. I sometimes have my patients put out all their medications and I say to them, if you start eating X, I think we can cut out this medicine in a few months. It's a real one-to-one trade-off."

This hews to the uniquely American think-of-your-food-as-medicine mindset that rubs me the wrong way, but I guess if your food can make you sick, it can make you well, too.

11.

THE NEFARIOUS PRACTICES OF
THE MODERN-DAY GROCER

My father was not alone in his love of grocery stores. There is at least one man still alive who shares my dad's enthusiasm, the esteemed journalist and author Jack Hitt, and it's a love he described in a 1996 article in the *New York Times Magazine*.

"I confess to a supermarket jones," he wrote. "I go to them. I stand in them. I wander around in that singular alpha state triggered by those automatic doors and sustained by a hallucinogenic sea of primary colors. I like to fondle fruits and examine vegetables. I admit to a savannas-of-Africa high upon seeing slabs of meat along the length of a wall. I like to stare down dead fish nested in ice. I contemplate new offerings of foodlike substances. Frozen spicy popcorn shrimp, for example, lofted me into a state of pure Zen abstraction."

Here is a man after my father's heart, but also one who understands his trumpeting of the grocery store. Indeed, he stretched even further than I'm wont to do when he made a great, and to my mind accurate, claim on behalf of the American supermarket: "It is, on some level, our greatest achievement." And make no mistake: By "our" he clearly means *Homo sapiens'* greatest achievement. "The painted cinder blocks of the average Food Lion," he continues, "are the true heirs to the walls of Jericho, built to protect the earliest stores of wheat and strike the first blow for post-nomadic culture."

I don't consider this an overstatement. Humans began to cultivate land and grow food about twelve thousand years ago, the same time a short, fat wall in the city of Jericho on the West Bank was constructed. The beginning of agriculture meant that we no longer roamed the earth in a daily search for food. Indeed, we *had* to stay put to watch over the crops. The crops gave us a food surplus, which allowed us to stay put.

Staying put resulted in communities. Communities resulted in rules of conduct and other tools of organization—government, class structures, religions, and, ultimately, everything we now consider to be human culture.

Such ideas about the critical nature of food are often best recognized by farmers. On a recent trip to Hawaii, I met Adam Asquith, a taro farmer on the island of Kauai. Taro, there called kalo, was the fundamental staple cuisine of these islands. Early inhabitants, dating to the fifth century, used it to create a dish called poi by cooking the tuber to death and mashing it with water until it was the consistency of furniture glue. Poi, left to sit out, would ferment, and the resulting acids prevented spoilage. It was thus an early example of preserved food—one rich in complex carbohydrates and vitamins and teeming with beneficial bacteria. "Poi is what created Hawaiian culture," Asquith told me. "Because they didn't have to worry about what they were going to eat, they could do other things." Thus, in this unique land, a food surplus in the form of mashed and fermented taro root resulted in, among other things, surfing, a dance style called hula, and, crossing the Pacific to the commercial mainland as it did in the 1950s, the hula hoop.[51] As with duck confit in southwestern France, lardo in the hills of Italy, and kimchi in Korea, to name just a few, poi helped further a particular culture.

Because food surpluses were so important to a society, they were vulnerable to plunder. Thus the food surplus can also be said to have created some of the more pernicious aspects of human society—warfare and slavery, and, eventually, traffic in Los Angeles and smog in China. The latter of course add to the greatest current threat to our species, the

....

51 At least nominally, as forms of the hula hoop have existed for centuries. According to various internet sources, swiveling hoops around the midriff was a form of exercise used by ancient Greeks; in Australia they were referred to as "exercise hoops"; the practice became a fad in fourteenth-century England; Native Americans employed the activity as a form of storytelling. It was British sailors in the eighteenth century who, on arriving in Hawaii and observing the native dance over bowls of poi, attached the word "hula" to "hoop." Two centuries later, the Wham-O company created a plastic version that, thanks to savvy marketing, became a national rage and a symbol of its era. From poi to the hula hoop in just fifteen hundred years.

heating of our atmosphere, which is caused in no small measure by the way we now grow and distribute food.

Yes, it's all connected. And I digress to this degree to underscore the fundamental importance of the grocery store, your local food surplus, to human culture. Do a quick thought experiment: Imagine if every food retailing outfit, from pharmacies to gas station convenience stores to grocery stores, vanished. Your first issue of the day would be to figure out where you're going to get food, and life wouldn't be so much fun.

Strangely, though, after his initial rhapsody on the great achievement of the supermarket, Hitt begins an extended criticism of the people who run these modern-day wonders. We hear this sort of thing with such uniform regularity from the media that the message has become accepted as fact: Grocers are out to trick us. Hitt says that "the supermarket has been subjected to an absurd level of scientific inquiry: complex experiments regarding display, observational studies of human movement, and intricate work on the effects of lighting, color and music."

Marion Nestle,[52] the esteemed professor of nutrition and food studies at New York University, would agree, and points to the influential 1957 book *The Hidden Persuaders* by Vance Packard. Writing in her own book *What to Eat*,[53] Nestle notes the "breathtaking amounts of research" that seem to have gone into designing supermarkets. "There are precise reasons why milk is at the back of the store and the center aisles are so long. You are forced to go past thousands of other products on your way to get what you need." As we walk past the dizzying array of food, twice—once to get the quart of milk, then again on the way to the checkout lanes—it is hoped we will be persuaded to pick up numerous impulse purchases.

....

52 I do, of course, love the irony that this prominent nutritionist and writer, who understands well the dangers of sugar in our food supply, shares the name of one of the most famous confectioners in America, but it is in spelling only. Marion's last name rhymes with the word "pestle."

53 This book, published in 2006 and every bit as pertinent today as it was then, looks at every department in the modern supermarket, evaluating what's in it, the good and the bad, and the way it's marketed to the consumer—I highly recommend it for an informed and informative take on what's available to us and how it affects our bodies.

Type "supermarket design research" into an internet search field and among the top hits are articles on the psychology behind supermarket design, one from a *National Geographic* blog titled "Surviving the Sneaky Psychology of Supermarkets" and two from Business Insider titled "15 Ways Supermarkets Trick You Into Spending More Money" and "A Few More Ways Supermarkets Mess With Your Minds."

"Grocery shopping, start to finish," writes Rebecca Rupp at *National Geographic*, "is a cunningly orchestrated process. Every feature of the store—from floor plan and shelf layout to lighting, music, and ladies in aprons offering free sausages on sticks—is designed to lure us in, keep us there, and seduce us into spending money."

And then she launches into the myriad ways in which grocers do this. They put produce in front, so the first thing you see is a virtual farm stand of fruits and vegetables; that "makes us feel upbeat and happy" and encourages us to buy lots of food. Citing Martin Lindstrom's 2011 book *Brandwashed*, Rupp says that the produce in the cases is periodically misted to give the vegetables a "deceptive dewy and fresh-picked look," when in fact the water makes the food spoil sooner.

She goes on to note that the most expensive products are placed at eye level, and the piped-in low-tempo music makes us move more slowly—the more time we spend in the store, the more likely we are to make impulse buys.[54]

This is the kind of media that drives grocers bananas. I spent several days in Philadelphia hanging out with that "share group" of family grocers who meet twice a year to discuss business, share successful strategies, and note unsuccessful ones in an effort to remain viable in the fragmenting food retail world. These are men (and one woman, Carole Friedman Bitter, who runs four Friedman's Freshmarkets in Pennsylvania) who have been lifelong grocers. One of these grocers is Mark Skogen.

---

54 "Surviving the Sneaky Psychology of Supermarkets," The Plate, *National Geographic*, June 15, 2015; "15 Ways Supermarkets Trick You Into Spending More Money," Business Insider, July 26, 2011.

Mark is the CEO of Festival Foods, a chain in Minnesota and Wisconsin. In 1946 Mark's grandfather opened his first grocery store in the family's three-thousand-square-foot home. "It was all in one—you lived in the business," Mark told me as we visited Pennsylvania and New Jersey stores in a small tour bus.

In the 1970s they "knocked down the house and built a twenty-thousand-square-foot store," Mark said. "I have positive memories of growing up in the business. My sister and I would ride our bikes through the aisles when the store was closed when we were young. We'd build forts in the back room, sort pop bottles, and fill the beer cooler. It was fun."

Mark, age forty-six, now oversees twenty-two stores that do sales of more than $783 million.

I had my recorder running, using bus time to interview as many of these grocers as possible, and thus was visibly in journalist mode, which likely elicited Mark's next comment: "You know what really bugs me?" he asked, apropos of nothing.

"What's that?"

"That silly knock that a grocery store gets over the years. Some knucklehead journalist[55] comes in and says, 'This is how you need to be careful in a grocery store. You know they put the milk in the back on purpose. You've got to go all the way back to get this popular item.' Who says milk is the most purchased? And 'Here's what grocery stores are trying to do to you.'

"There's no science or trickeration," he said, "other than just a nice easy flow through the store. Our stores are just logical.

"You want to know why dairy is in back?" he concluded. "Because that's the most efficient place to put these huge refrigerated cases."

As if the supermarket gods were personally underscoring the non-sneakiness of the grocer, the very next store our tour bus pulled up in front of was one of Joe Colalillo's ShopRites. In the vestibule where the shopping carts nest was a refrigerated glass case filled with milk and other dairy products, with a sign on the door that read GRAB AND GO!

---

55 The implication was clear.

Mark passed by it without notice, but I called out to him, pointing to the case.

"See?" he said, still annoyed.

"Doesn't every retail store want you to spend more money?" Jeff Heinen asked me when I inquired which "sneaky methods" Heinen's employed. He seemed as annoyed as Mark. "If you're successful at that, is that being sneaky, or being a good retailer? The idea that the grocery retail business is any different than other retail business seems ludicrous to me.

"Every retailer designs their store to reinforce their brand and their product," he went on. "Think about Aldi [the discount supermarket]: bare-bones decor, simple signage, no service, etc., to reinforce their image as being inexpensive—is that sneaky or good retail? Think about Trader Joe's: simple decor, Hawaiian shirts to reinforce their image as being cheap and fun. Think about Heinen's: clean, tasteful, and high service levels to reinforce our image for quality food and being a comfortable place to shop. Is that sneaky or good retail?"

I got down to brass tacks. "Admit it, Jeff, you put dairy in the back to force customers to walk past your cornucopia of food products, trying to trick people into buying stuff they don't need."

"*Produce* is most shopped," he responded, "so the theory about placing dairy in the back is already suspect.[56] Dairy has to be placed on a wall. It would not be on the front wall." (Heinen's front walls include large windows looking out into the parking lot, rows of nested carts, numerous displays of foods that are on special that day, and, in summer, a large display of vegetables from local farms.) "I have seen dairy on every other wall—both sides and the rear wall. I don't think there is a preponderance of evidence that it is placed mostly on the back wall. As you know, we place it on the side wall after produce."

I admitted that he had me there. But since he brought up produce, I wondered whether he would cop to the fact that, as the *National Geographic* writer Rupp claimed, they mist the vegetables to give them

---

56 Mark Skogen also said produce was the most shopped department at his stores.

that "deceptive dewy and fresh-picked look," when really all that water increases spoilage.

"Misting is about keeping the produce fresher and in better condition," Jeff responded. "Produce has a high content of water, so placing water on it is good for it, especially since the refrigerated air blowing over it dries it out. Yes, it is more visually appealing because the product is healthier and no, it does not trash the product unless you overwater it."

This made me want to write to Rupp to ask something that hadn't occurred to me when reading her article: Why would a grocer do something to speed the spoilage of a product they had to make money from? But I sensed Jeff was inches from tripping up so I could get to the bottom of his sneaky tactics.

Despite having spent countless hours in Heinen's, wandering the aisles and interviewing staff, not to mention years of shopping there, I couldn't remember whether they played music at all. I was sure that they must, and I had learned from my research that low-tempo music was used as a way to slow shoppers down. Hitt, in his *New York Times Magazine* article, referenced a "groundbreaking" study finding that sales could be substantially increased if slow music was played.[57]

"I've heard every kind of music in the store," Jeff said, "slow and fast tempos. I believe in most cases, the employees in the store select the music they want because they have to listen to it the most. Stores play music because there is a lot going on in grocery stores that is noisy, and music is more soothing than a lot of supermarket noises. But the idea is that the customer does not consciously even hear it.[58] Sometimes we have to tell stores to tone it down because it gets turned up for the associates. We let the store GM select the music because we get complaints from customers no matter what music we choose."

---

57 Quoting Hitt: "If background music is slowed from a lively allegro of 108 beats per minute to a simple adagio of, say, 60 beats, then the speed of the average buggy slows . . . and purchases soar. Sales have been measured to increase by 38.2 percent—a truth that, as any ambitious bag boy would know, is found in R. E. Milliman's groundbreaking study, 'Using Background Music to Affect the Behavior of Supermarket Shoppers.'"

58 The idea had obviously worked on me.

All right, then, my last question while I had him on the stand: "Isn't it true, Jeff, that you put the most expensive items at eye level because those items that get looked at most are most likely to be bought? And, furthermore, isn't it true that you put candy and sugary cereals at toddler levels, for tots who will then pester their parents into purchases the parent didn't intend?"

"First and foremost, placement is by category," he answered, "so using the example of candy, yes, there is candy at eye level and every other level as well.

"Once you place the category, then it is by size of package. I would guess most everybody places the bigger and heavier items in the category on the bottom shelves and the smaller, lighter ones on the top shelves. Not a perfect science, but it certainly makes the most sense for the customer.

"The only rule of thumb that most grocers abide by," he continued, "is placing their private-label items more or less at eye level versus the bottom shelf or the top shelf. There is research that shows the middle shelves get seen better by the customer. It certainly makes sense, but I would argue it gets a bit mitigated by today's proliferation of, and ever-changing, items and size of packaging."

I think he was having about enough of me by this point.

"All of this is a conspiracy theory," he concluded. "But the fact is that the customer's drive for ever-lower prices means the retailer does not even have *time* to overthink all these issues. Heinen's carries forty thousand items, and we barely have time to tie our shoes let alone try to psychologically outsmart our customers. Maybe fifty years ago in a slower time, smaller stores, and with less informed customers, people spent time trying to outsmart their customers but in today's age, those people would not remain in business because they'd be focused on the wrong things."

Like Jeff, I find this "conspiracy theory" annoying for a couple of reasons. After all, with forty thousand products, *something* has got to be in the back of the store. And produce is the most shopped section of

Heinen's, so if Tom and Jeff wanted to lure their customer past all those products in order to encourage impulse buys, they'd put produce where all their frozen foods are. Sure, at Thanksgiving they put out big displays of cranberry juice between you and the checkout aisle to encourage sales of this particular item, sales of which are tepid all year long and go through the roof during the winter holidays. But should they hide it in order to make well and sure that the customer truly desires this Ocean Spray product and is not giving in to baser impulses?

So why don't any of these journalists, especially one writing for such an influential venue as the *New York Times Magazine*, ask for comment from an actual grocer? I've been unable to find any story in which the reporter sought a response regarding merchandising tactics, let alone tricks of the trade.

I had lunch with Marion Nestle to talk about groceries and asked her about the validity of the grocery store being laid out to encourage impulse purchases, as she'd been critical of their methods. I explained what grocers had told me, but she wasn't backing down on this. She said she had spoken with supermarket executives at a conference and cites her sources in the book.[59]

My other criticism of the sneaky-grocer theory: Why do journalists appear to hold grocers to a different standard than other retailers? We are unlikely to see, for instance, an article titled "The Sneaky Methods Nordstrom Uses to Get You to Buy That $200 Sweater You Don't Really Need." Are jeans or laptops or frying pans somehow different from food? We expect retailers to merchandise their merchandise. We don't criticize online sites for sending out email blasts announcing sales on Tumi suit-

---

59 The book she references is *Grocery Revolution: The New Focus on the Consumer* by Barbara E. Kahn and Leigh McAlister. Those authors don't spend much time on layout, beyond mentioning a few grocery stores that moved product around in order to boost sales, and did so successfully. They cite a *Wall Street Journal* article titled "James Bond Hits the Supermarket: Stores Snoop on Shoppers' Habits to Boost Sales" (August 25, 1993)—there they go again, those sneaky grocers! I should also note here that, like Roxanne Sukol, Nestle thinks the GMO issue is a nonissue; the GMO lobbies' big mistake, she told me, was in arguing against mandatory labeling; if they'd said fine, happy to label it, there would be no GMO/non-GMO debate today.

cases or Ray-Bans. We aren't annoyed by Barnes & Noble's display tables or Amazon's helpful "frequently bought together" suggestions (indeed, I hope these booksellers will use such sneaky tactics to sell this book!). And yet we seem quick to assign blame to the grocer, none of it founded as far as I could tell, for using underhanded methods.

To be fair, the books *Brandwashed* and *The Hidden Persuaders* don't single out grocers, but rather all manner of companies and the tactics they use to merchandise all kinds of goods—as well as the advertisers who help them to do it. But in these books, the criticism focuses primarily on the product manufacturer and the advertising, rather than on the venues in which these products are sold. Except in the case of the grocer and his or her store, which seems to me to be uniquely singled out as a culprit.

We are well aware that food companies, in an effort to lower the cost of food (demanded by the consumer) while increasing their bottom line (demanded by their shareholders) employ dubious tactics. For instance, food manufacturers may reduce the amount of actual food in a package, while keeping the package size and price the same. *Washington Post* reporter Roberto A. Ferdman confirmed that Frito-Lay (a PepsiCo subsidiary) uses the same size bag—and charges the same price—for all its potato chips, but puts fewer flavored chips in the bags than plain chips. By presenting the two varieties as having the same value when they do not, Frito-Lay seems to be betting that consumers won't scrutinize the package labels and will be duped. One could argue that the "honest" thing to do would be to keep the quantities the same and sell the flavored bags for more to cover the added expense of flavoring the chips. One could simply file this under *Caveat emptor,* "Buyer beware"—or, better, *Emptor scire,* "Buyer aware."

While the half-ounce-per-bag reduction in flavored chips may seem small, Ferdman says that a reduction of 5 percent could add as much as $80 million to the company's bottom line, given the volume of chips sold ($1.6 billion annually).[60]

---

60 "No, you aren't crazy: Some Lay's potato chip bags actually do have fewer chips inside," *Washington Post,* July 26, 2014.

PepsiCo is not alone. All major food companies look for ways to keep prices low while raising profits, so it's up to consumers to make themselves aware. And this really is Marion Nestle's beef—the big food companies and their methods of continuously driving sales to increase their bottom line rather than the consumer's knowledge or health. I asked her why the onus isn't on the consumer to make educated decisions.

"I would say $17 billion on marketing," she told me, gobbling up a delicious salad as we talked. "It's not a level playing field. For consumers to make informed choices they need to be correctly informed, and they're not. Why aren't they? Nobody teaches it, and it's countered by this vast amount of marketing, which is designed to sell products and not health. And it's unrecognized."

I agree, and I find fault with companies that package their products with deceptive labels claiming that their cereal reduces our risk for heart disease and any number of dubious claims, countless examples of which Nestle cites in her book.

And yet the grocer still routinely comes under fire for putting their heavy, high-maintenance refrigerated cases along the back wall (where there is, typically, the most space available to push back without reducing square feet of retail space), misting produce to keep it fresh, and playing leisurely music to slow customers' progress through the aisles. My bias—that these charges are specious at best—should be clear by now.[61] And frankly, it's of little concern to me whether they're true or false, as I believe the onus is on me, not the grocer, to determine how best to spend my money. We now have a consumer base that is genuinely and rightly skeptical of claims. I am. I wouldn't complain indignantly, "You tricked me!" if I lost a twenty playing three-card monte in Times Square (if I could find a game, that is—where did they all go?).

....

61 The worst "tactic" that I've been able to find are all those "Buy 3 for $4.99" types of offers. This really does encourage me to buy three Honeybell oranges rather than the two I'd intended. The sign implies that you need to buy three in order to get the deal, when in fact at Heinen's and most other grocery stores, the oranges will ring up on the register as costing $1.66 each no matter how many you buy.

Indeed, if it were truly up to the grocer, he or she would probably have me buy the expensive organic and genuinely all-natural products because, first, they give the grocer a margin well above the processed commodity versions, and second, because they are better for me than if I went for the processed food filled with unnatural ingredients. That way I'll ultimately be healthy and fit enough to produce offspring (future customers!) and I'll live longer (more years to shop their stores!).

But it's we who make the choices, and while grocers would prefer their customers to be healthy rather than ill, their first obligation, they say without exception, is to make available everything that the customer wants. Most grocers find that the single biggest driver of customer satisfaction and repeat business is the availability of product. This is why checkout clerks are so often instructed to ask, "Did you find everything you wanted?"

So, since we do seem to hold the grocery store to a different standard than retailers of non-consumable products, my interest lies in figuring out *why*.

I suspect that part of the reason is that it is our food we're talking about here, and our food has the potential to make us healthy or sick, something that a pair of jeans or sunglasses cannot do. Also, not everyone shops at Nordstrom or is on the lookout for bargains on high-end luggage. But just about everyone shops at a grocery store. The exceptions lie at both ends of the spectrum: the ultra-elite (the Manhattan investment banker who eats out seven days a week or the Malibu movie star who employs a full-time chef) and those who rely on fast food and convenience-store processed food for all their meals. (The latter is particularly upsetting to imagine, since it's been made clear by books such as *Fast Food Nation* and documentaries such as *Super Size Me* that eating this way results in discomfort and, eventually, serious illness.)

So, the vast majority of American families share a reliance on a single type of retail store, the supermarket, which makes these places unique in the world of retail. Pretty much every family in the country visits a drugstore for one reason or another, too, but I could find no studies or articles describing the "sneaky" ways that drugstores mess with our heads. I would guess it's for the same reason: because we don't rely on them as our main food source. Clearly, without recognizing why we're doing it, we're placing grocery stores in their own category—it's a store that has a value to us like no other. And because they are so important, we put them under a stronger microscope than other kinds of retail stores, even ones that sell some kind of food or another.

I would argue further that we are *right* to place them in their own unique category, right to liken them to the wall of Jericho, even if it does result in suspect claims regarding their motives and methods. And Nestle concurred: "We're talking about *food*," she said, as if I were a tad dimwitted. "We're not talking about clothes. People have to eat to live. People don't have to go to Nordstrom to live. Food is essential. You have to have it. It's not optional. Clothing is not optional in our society, but Nordstrom clothing is."

Grocery stores are the primary keepers of our food. They are our food surplus, open seven days a week and filled with all the food we need. And we count on them for our survival.

INTERLUDE: CHECKOUT

I owed it to my father to spend a couple of days bagging groceries, something he'd always wanted to do but didn't get around to during the four and a half healthy years of his retirement. So I headed out to the Heinen's in Pepper Pike, also known as store #05. This is the location where I'd met Dr. Sukol, and the one that is my favorite of the eighteen Cleveland stores. I can't put my finger on why it is my favorite—perhaps because it's spacious without being too large, and it has an elegance the one closest to me lacks. That would be the Shaker Heights store, store #01, across the street from the building where Joe Heinen opened the first Heinen's supermarket in the 1930s. It's smaller than store #05 and has a more confining feel to it, which affects how I feel when I shop there. (This is not something I would have consciously recognized had I not been writing about the two stores—that's how subtle the impact of a grocery store can be.)

When I was writing *The Making of a Chef*, I shopped at store #01, because I still did my writing in my childhood bedroom, at the desk where I'd done my homework starting in sixth grade and all through high school. At the time, 1996, my wife, toddler daughter, and I lived in a small house in Cleveland Heights a few miles away. I had a home office, but because of the looming deadline for the book, I asked my dad if I could work at his house, where I would be undistracted by the aforementioned toddler. When I took my midday break, I would often shop at store #01 for my lunch, as well as anything I needed for that night's dinner.

I often found myself in the checkout line of Fatima Harrison, a brown-skinned woman with black hair and lovely dark eyes. One afternoon as she rang up my items, she asked me in her Moroccan accent, "Why are you always in a hurry?"

I had learned to cook professionally at the Culinary Institute of America in order to write the book, and I'd instilled in myself the importance of hustling. The chef in my final restaurant had described getting kicked off the line at the first restaurant he worked because he wasn't fast enough, an experience so humiliating that from the next day forward, he told me, "I *ran* everywhere I went." This made sense to me. And because I had just four months to write an entire book, I knew I had to apply the hustle I'd learned in culinary school to my daily life.

"What do you mean?" I asked her.

"When you leave, I always see you running through the parking lot."

"I can get more done that way," I told her. But what impressed me was the fact that she noticed, and was curious enough to ask me about it at the checkout. And it really impressed me to discover, twenty years later, that Fatima was still working the register at Heinen's, now out at store #05, when I arrived there in my blue Heinen's shirt and chinos to begin work. I would bag groceries for her. And I would learn to do so under the tutelage of Chris Kenski, a fifty-year-old woman with short blonde hair who'd been working for Heinen's for thirty-four years. It was beginning to strike me how long so many Heinen's employees had been with the company.

When I'd first gotten to know Fatima, what cell phones existed were called mobile phones and were the size of a brick. Now I could pull my iPhone out of my pocket, take a picture of Fatima, and post it to Instagram, which surprised and delighted her. I could also use the QR reader on my phone to scan just about anything in this grocery store to find out where it came from, yet another new facet of our retail world.

Changes in the grocery store were no less dramatic. "Every aspect of our business has changed," Chris told me. "When I started we had hanging beef. Now the butchers are more about production, making things like value-added meats, things like shish kebabs. They're not cutting down the carcass, cutting your steaks—those things are already cut when they come in.

"When I was young, I thought I hated fish, because all we had was Mrs. Paul's fish sticks, which are disgusting. Now people in Cleveland can get mahimahi and moonfish."

Tom Heinen had told me that at the time Chris started, Heinen's would get their one fish delivery early in the week, and that fish had to last into the weekend. By Friday, he acknowledged, the fish section would be taking on something of a low-tide odor. Now, thanks to overnight delivery, on any given Tuesday Clevelanders can have that moonfish—a rosy-colored deepwater fish as big around as a car tire—which was off-loaded at the Honolulu fish auction on Monday.

"Produce," Chris said, "we have things that we never—we have Buddha's hand and dragon fruit!"

Chris, dressed in Heinen's blue shirt and chinos like mine, was the store's front-end manager, in charge of the cashiers, baggers, registers, and customer complaints. She would teach me the nuances of proper bagging, a skill she was "OCD about." And obsessive-compulsive was just what I was after.

Staking out the last of the nine checkout aisles, nearest to the customer-care desk, she got to work, bagging and teaching.

"The first thing I'm going to do is look at what's going to be coming down the belt," Chris said as Fatima scanned the first items and placed them on the conveyor. "Paper or plastic?" Chris asked the shopper.

"Plastic is fine."

"We always try to separate cold and dry items," Chris explained to me. "So right now I'm starting a grocery bag. Kind of give it six items, make sure you separate all your glass. If you alternate your glass and your cans, it does not clink. That's when you know you've done a good job. So I've got my cold things in here, my dry things here. Laundry soap I always give it a little twist on top because I've seen those puppies leak. Miss, would you like your soap in a different bag?" To Fatima she said, "And can I have a freezer bag for the cut fruit [half a cantaloupe] and two freezer bags for the meat?" Then back to me, "We always want to make sure that anything that can leak on other items is put in a freezer bag. Never put different kinds of meat in the same freezer bag. Chicken goes with chicken, pork goes with pork, beef goes with beef.

"We ask the customer would they like their raw meat product in separate bags—the customers that do are adamant about it. Cut fruit should always be put in a freezer bag because once it's cut it starts letting out its juices, so if you don't put it in a freezer bag—and I've seen this happen—you have cut fruit start to slide out of its packaging, which can be very, very messy." Chris had not really begun yet to bag—she was separating the items, almost like a cook setting up a station. "So you can see, all my dry goods are together, all my refrigerated goods are together, my raw meats are separate, and I'm always aware of what I'm putting in the cart because, on a large order, you want to make sure you're not putting a bag of cans on top of your produce.

"When they have their own bags"—many customers arrive with their own reusable bags—"you want to look at what you have. Some are lined bags; some are insulated bags. You want to save those for the correct products, but the rest of the principles are the same. It's a great idea to work with your cashier because your cashier is the one who is having more interaction with the customer than you are yourself. Good morning, miss, how are you today? Now you want to pack light. If you have a lot of cold items and there's no way you can get them in this one bag, still continue that packing light idea. And everybody's idea of light is different. When somebody tells me to pack light, I'm thinking about five pounds. But your typical bag should be about six to eight pounds. You always want to make a good base first, so you should never start with things that if you set other items on them they're going to fall over, so start with items like your clamshells, your cans, and then build up. The clamshells will actually provide a nice base. You see how I'm always communicating with my customer? How else am I going to find out what her needs are unless I'm talking to them?

"Chemicals"—detergent, furniture polish, and so on—"always get packed by themselves. You don't pack them with any other food item. Always start with your heavy items on the bottom and build up. I'm a firm believer in putting a rubber band around the eggs because it's happened to me; I get home, I unpack the bags, and suddenly I've got scrambled eggs on the floor. People think that eggs are the most fragile item—they are not. Lettuces are. They are 95 percent water. Now that

Snapple, did you want that in a separate bag? Okay, starting with cold items, I've got the milk, I've got this"—a half gallon of orange juice—"and then I can put the other produce items with them. The idea with this is that when she gets home, the entire bag is going in the fridge. You wouldn't want to take a bag all around your kitchen to put it away. Another thing a great packer will do is they can go back and forth; a great packer can work two lines. I'm going to do one more paper"—she opens a paper bag inside a blue plastic Heinen's bag—"because I've got all this yogurt coming down. I've got this Claussen pickles. A lot of times packers think that all boxes are dried goods—they're not. There's Go-Gurt yogurt, there's butter—they come in boxes but they're refrigerated items. All jars are not dry goods. You've got ghee, clarified butter, just be aware—look at what's in your hand. Lunch meat should always go on top. People are paying ten dollars a pound for lunch meat—the last thing they want when they get home is to find out that their lunch meat has been damaged. I'm always aware of what I'm packing and how it fits in the bag. The idea is when you pack a plastic bag, believe it or not, it can stand up if it's packed well." Chris set the final bag into the shopper's cart, smiled, and said, "You're all set, ma'am."

The above transactions took place over the course of about ninety seconds, and the next began immediately as Chris departed, leaving me to it. And for the next several hours I bagged groceries, bag after bag after bag. I used mainly blue plastic Heinen's bags, but many customers, when I asked, responded with a request for a combination of paper inside plastic. This sets you back five or ten seconds a bag, as the conveyor belt sends boxes of crackers and cereals and pancake mixes and sugar and butter and eggs, and takeout soup (two rubber bands required) and other takeout containers from the prepared foods section—roasted carrots, roasted Brussels sprouts, roasted asparagus, twice-baked potatoes, sautéed shrimp with garlic and parsley, grilled peppers and zucchini, filet mignon, curried couscous with chickpeas and spinach, pulled pork, chicken parmesan, and on and on—and wine and paper towels and Heinen's brand tissues, and flour and sacks of russet potatoes and bananas and bananas and bananas, and grapes and broccoli. All of it stuffed—or, rather, carefully arranged—into bags per Chris's instructions.

An endless river of food it seemed to me—*it didn't stop.* If I got backed up and my end of the conveyor belt began to feel like an over-stuffed closet in which everything threatens to cascade down on you, I could turn the belt off with a little button on my end (Fatima had one, too). If things got *really* backed up, she would help bag to catch me up. And if the action in my lane slowed, I could hop over to the next aisle where another bagger might need a hand. And vice versa. You could find yourself in the weeds when the store had a big lunchtime or post-work push, and you really had to hustle.

For the most part the customers were appreciative of my bagging, and cordial, thanking me more often than not—except for a few moms, who were exhausted and distracted by their young kids in tow, and older women, who asked me not to make their bags too heavy. One mom had a toddler in the child seat[62] sucking a lollipop, which the toddler dropped on the floor, much to his evident dismay. The mom retrieved it from under a rack, looked at it, looked at her crying child, shrugged, gave the lollipop a solid suck to remove the debris, and stuck it back in her child's mouth. Some local chefs recognized me and wanted to talk, and of course several shoppers were people I knew socially. Those aware that I was in the midst of a divorce gave me a hug (I don't think there's a policy against hugging your bag boy), and a couple of acquaintances cast nervous glances at me, presuming I was bagging groceries due to a dramatic reversal of fortune and a need to make ends meet. (Had that been the case, I'd have been earning between ten and twelve dollars an hour; teenagers start at $8.50 and work up in monthly increments to ten dollars.)

Generally, bagging groceries was fun—though, like any manual labor, I knew it would get tired fast. But I liked organizing the foods by

62 Sylvan Goldman, inventor of the shopping cart, introduced the child seat in 1947, ten years after inventing the first cart. More than twenty-four thousand children were taken to the emergency room for treatment of shopping cart injuries in 2005 (according to an article by Gary A. Smith, "Shopping Cart–Related Injuries to Children," *Pediatrics*, August 2006), and some children have died from falls and cart tip-overs.

types, checking the cart and belt to see what would be coming in order to plan, putting a kind of puzzle together in my head. I enjoyed having conversations with the shoppers (and refrained from harassing any of them for buying fat-free food). And, like my dad, I was fascinated by this boggling variety of fresh and packaged food, half of which I'd never have even looked at had I been walking the aisles. But ultimately there was too much to keep track of and I was too busy bagging to pay much attention.

I bagged Earth Balance Vegan Buttery Sticks, Organic Valley ghee (*this* is what they do with the fat they remove from their milk—turn it into clarified butter! Applause to Organic Valley!), Southwestern-style Egg Beaters, Silk cashew milk, Chameleon cold-brewed black coffee, flax milk, and cold-pressed juices; bottles of probiotics that cost thirty dollars and up, some for oddly specific purposes (one just for vaginal care, for instance—probiotics for one's privates?); five different Temple Turmeric juices, Melissa's Hollandaise Sauce in a microwavable pouch, frosted animal cookies, Special K Fudge-Dipped Pretzels, Uncle Sam Toasted Whole Wheat Berry Flakes and Flaxseed, and organic amaranth flakes; Dora the Explorer fruit snacks, Kind bars, and a dozen different Greek-style yogurts, including Noosa, a hot new brand from Australia.

There were Bays English muffins (my favorite, so much better than Thomas'—they're in the dairy case, along with Farm Country fat-free crumpets; since when does crumpet dough require fat?), Heinen's American Cheese Product Singles (thirty cents cheaper than Kraft Singles), Duke's Jerky (along with turkey jerky, which sounds disgusting and doesn't taste much better), Jeni's pistachio ice cream, frozen peas, frozen berries, and, well, 39,950 other items. Almost every one of these items sells, or it wouldn't be in the store. (Those items that don't sell and must be discarded are called, in grocer speak, "shrink"—grocers are ever on the lookout for ways to reduce shrink.)

And of course there was all manner of minimally processed food or, rather, food that we don't think of as being processed, namely our animal protein: beef, pork, chicken, lamb, venison. Fish from Alaska, Hawaii, and Boston, as well as farmed salmon and tilapia, shrimp, whole parrot fish, branzino, oysters, clams, and mussels. And produce, of course, the least processed of foods and happily one of the most shopped departments in the store. Almost every basket I saw contained something from the produce department.

Every now and then there would be an idle cashier, but not for long. The food just kept coming. And coming. And coming. Eight a.m. till nine p.m. every day except Sundays, when their hours are eight a.m. till six p.m., and holidays, when they close to give all Heinen's employees time off to be with their families. A river of food flows down each of these conveyor belts—each week $675,000 worth of food comes down the conveyor belt of my checkout lane and each of the nine others here. Bagging it all made me think not just of these lanes, but of every lane in the eighteen Heinen's stores in Cleveland—$500 million worth of groceries are scanned and set on those conveyor belts in, on average, thirty-five to fifty-dollar increments. Not to mention down the conveyor belts of the fourteen Dave's Markets, and the forty-odd Giant Eagles in Cleveland alone, and the fifty-odd Marc's, a discount grocery store, and the twenty Aldi grocery stores, three Whole Foods, two Trader Joe's, and a handful of family-owned grocery stores with one, two, or three stores such as Constantino's and Zagara's (my go-to grocery store in Cleveland Heights). The volume astonishes even the grocers themselves.

The grocery store at the end of the day feels almost serene. While there are few people in my Heinen's thirty minutes before closing, produce clerks are still restocking pint containers of strawberries. In a few minutes those same clerks will put those strawberries on a cart, along with all other produce that requires refrigeration, and store them in refrigerated rooms. Fifteen minutes before closing, another produce clerk will begin to empty the misting racks of lettuces, so that the racks can be cleaned and dried before closing up. The central aisles are now filled with clerks "blocking" shelves—that is, filling any holes that remain so that come eight a.m. tomorrow, every single shelf is as fully stocked as it was on opening day. That's the goal of Rick Gonzalez, manager of store #05: "I want the store to open every day as if it were the grand opening."

The cashiers thoroughly wipe down their conveyor belts and the stainless steel around them so that it shines. They hand over their cash-filled tills to the front-end manager. These will be wheeled to the back of the store and placed in a safe, to be counted and balanced the following morning. One register stays open for the final two or three shoppers as a few lights in the center aisle begin to go out, a gradual, timed shutting down.

The rows and rows of nested shopping carts are rolled away from the front wall so that the floor can be swept and mopped.

A lone fish guy stacks all the unsold fish on ice to be stored. Next to him a young man behind the meat case is wrapping the butcher cuts in plastic, which can remain where they are in the refrigerated cases. One of the kitchen crew collects twenty-four sets of salad bar tongs and puts them in a cleaning bucket, breaking down that station. A woman behind the prepared foods case loads the unsold cooked food onto sheet trays and slides them onto speed racks, racks she will completely enclose with plastic wrap, turning it as a spider encases its prey, and roll them into one of the many refrigerated rooms in back. And whoever is acting as manager that night will see that the safe is locked, the last lights are out, and the alarms are set.

And the grocery store sleeps.

PART III

THE CENTER AISLES

12.

A FEW OF THE TWENTY THOUSAND NEW PRODUCTS FOR YOUR CONSIDERATION

"I got private-label coconut chips for eighty-six cents *a bag*," says Nathan Perc, "a *five-ounce* bag."

"Stop being so proud of yourself!" Chris Foltz tells him.

Chris and Nathan, and a half dozen other Heinen's people, are at the bar of the Kimpton Shorebreak Hotel in Huntington Beach, California, standing around a large table, cocktails and beers in hand. They flew here from Cleveland to attend Expo West, an annual trade show in which three thousand vendors of natural, organic, and "healthy" products present their goods to seventy thousand food retailers. The show is held each March at the Anaheim Convention Center, which is the size of a small city (nearby Newport Beach has the same population as those visiting this enormous complex of buildings).

Expo West, which Nathan told me is the biggest and best new-food show, is the premier venue for a company like Heinen's to find new products—beef jerky and all-natural heat-and-serve meals and kombucha (the fermented tea that's currently the rage in the booming beverage category); probiotic chutney and kale chips and dehydrated broccoli; specialty sausages and yogurt and pet food. It's also where larger, more familiar companies, such as Bob's Red Mill and Tom's of Maine, purchase booth space. I don't believe there's a single center-aisle category of food not represented here. And it's not limited to food. Companies are here to interest buyers in reusable sandwich bags and toxin-free laundry powder and, from a company called Bamboobies, "mom-invented" disposable nursing pads and Boob-Ease Organic Nipple Balm.

Heinen's will find a hundred or so new products to put on the shelves of their twenty-two stores, displacing a hundred others. For start-ups and small companies, landing a client the size of a Heinen's can make their name—that is, if they can figure out how to produce their products in the quantity the grocery chain needs and, critically, get them there. Sometimes distribution can kill a deal; transporting a product made in, say, Seattle all the way to Cleveland may be impossible without using a food distributor, a middleman, which can be prohibitively expensive. And if they can't produce in enough volume, a middleman may not even agree to take them on.

After the first of three days of Expo, Nathan Perc beams energy and confidence. He's six-foot-four, an athletic 260 pounds, with a shaved head and blue eyes so deep and intense they can seem to turn green when he's making a deal. You wouldn't want to mess with him outside a nightclub, where he could easily be mistaken for a bouncer. Few of the many tattoos covering his arms, shoulders, chest, and back—a crown, a diamond, a hundred-dollar bill, portraits of both his mother and father, a grenade, a sacred heart, an eagle—are visible. He's delighted to have negotiated a sweet deal with Calkins & Burke, a company that packages coconut chips, to do a version in a Heinen's private-label bag.

Nathan takes a sip of his gin and tonic, turns to me, and says, "The thrill of the deal. That's what it's all about for me."

At age thirty-four, Nathan has found his company and his calling. "I played three sports in school," he tells me, "till I found my favorite sport, which is making money."

Despite having graduated from Kent State University with degrees in finance and business management, he could find work only as a bartender, followed by a job at a T.G.I. Friday's, where he soon became manager. After a stint as a mortgage broker (felled during the 2008 crash), he returned to bartending.

His mother is a long-time grocery store worker—"I grew up in a grocery store," Nathan told me—and currently a director for the Tops chain based in Buffalo. She called on a former Tops colleague, Jim Whalen, who had become a Heinen's store director. Jim hired Nathan as a front-end manager, where Nathan was in charge of all the associates at the registers; he was also responsible for distributing cash to each register and balancing them at the end of the day, and he handled customer care and complaint issues. It's an important position, but Nathan would also find himself bagging groceries during crunch times, mopping the store entryway during winter weather, greeting customers and saying, "Thanks for shopping at Heinen's" as they departed. For these reasons he considered himself the low man on the manager totem pole.

A talker by nature, he was always eager to engage the customers. "As a front-end manager," he said, "you're the first person to touch the customer and the last one to touch them before they leave, and that's big. You can set the precedent and you can set the tone of what they feel when they leave"—a practice of customer engagement explicitly encouraged by Tom, Jeff, and Chris. But some people, Nathan sensed, didn't want to talk to him as he stuffed their bags with milk and eggs and Hamburger Helper; he knew what they were thinking. In his words: *Shut up, do something with your life, you're packing groceries.*

"To pack bags was a reality check for me," he said, "because I'm a go-getter. I like to get things done. I like to manage people. It really slowed me down."

But it wasn't long, nine months, before Nathan had worked his way up to what's called a category manager, with an office at Heinen's headquarters. Among his first categories were health and beauty (shampoos, deodorants, etc.), coffee and everything related (filters, creamers), and pasta sauces. Such managers are in charge of purchasing all the goods in their category. That means if one of your categories includes chips, you need to purchase not only the Lay's potato chips, Doritos, and Fritos, but also the I Heart Keenwah Puffs and Go Raw Sprouted Pumpkin Seeds, which Nathan discovered previously at Expo West. Not only do these good-for-you products help solidify the Heinen's brand, they have double the margin of the 20 percent earned on a bag of Frito-Lay chips. If you're in charge of cereals (cold), category #24 with revenues of $6.7 million, you have to make sure your shelves have a perpetual supply of all the varieties of Cheerios, Grape Nuts, and Special K, as well as "natural" alternatives to these, such as Kashi Organic Promise Sprouted Grains and Go Lean Crunch, and Nature's Path Flax Plus, as well as their Chocolate Choco Chimps and Gorilla Munch (organic, gluten-free, non-GMO, fair-trade alternatives to General Mills' Cocoa Puffs and Kellogg's Corn Pops).

If sports nutrition bars are your responsibility, you have to get your orders of Clif and Kind bars (available pretty much everywhere) as well as the Good! Greens bars made in Cleveland and the 18 Rabbits nut-free bars about to be discovered at Expo West.

Nathan's go-getter approach, combined with a natural facility for numbers and an entrepreneurial spirit regarding product development, quickly propelled him through the ranks. Eight years after managing cash registers, bagging food, and mopping floors, Nathan orchestrates the six category managers for all the center-aisle packaged goods, as well as, on the periphery, frozen and dairy. His actual title is Director of Packaged Goods, but it's more descriptive to note that when he was promoted to a category manager he was responsible for $25 million worth of product. Now he is, in effect, responsible for $250 million worth, or nearly half the company's annual sales.

Nathan has retained direct control over several categories (one of the managers he oversees is in charge of seventy categories), including coffee and tea, olive oils, and wellness products.

He is also in charge of all of Heinen's private labels, which means finding companies that make a superlative product and negotiating a deal with that company to put their product in a box or bag with the Heinen's label (such as Blount Fine Foods of Boston, which makes their private-label soups).

Heinen's has two different private labels. The Heinen's label is on some eight hundred different products, such as Heinen's corn chips, Heinen's cashews, Heinen's butter (which, as mentioned earlier, differs from Land O'Lakes butter in that it doesn't include "natural flavors" and is also less expensive), and Heinen's organic milk, which differs not at all from Organic Valley organic milk. In fact, it *is* Organic Valley milk, only sold in a Heinen's carton for a dollar less. "Organic Valley has the highest organic standards of all the organic dairy products," Nathan told me. So, whether you buy Organic Valley brand milk or Heinen's organic milk, it is the exact same stuff. (If you want to know where *your* store's private-label products come from, ask to speak with the department manager.)

The second private label, Two Brothers, is attached to just thirty or so premium or specialty products, such as Two Brothers gelato and Two Brothers deli meats. The brand has been surprisingly successful for the company, so much so that customers have asked, "Why isn't the Two Brothers brand sold at the Giant Eagle I like to shop at?" They have a killer barbecue sauce I always put in my cart when I shop there.

Nathan, along with his team of six, decide what new products Heinen's will put on their shelves and in their refrigerated cases. He is especially interested in those products that will help distinguish this small chain from the larger chains such as Giant Eagle. Some of these products he and the other members of the team discover at Expo West; others come to them, via cold calls from entrepreneurs, with whom he often works to create both products and packaging.

Back when I was shopping with my dad, in the 1960s and 1970s, the new products were likely to be new high-sugar cereals, such as Quisp, my favorite until Dad made the mistake of buying Cap'n Crunch. Of course, this was also a time when grocery stores carried fewer than ten thousand items.

Nathan's job is a double-edged sword, however, and he's well aware of it. Those center aisles he's responsible for filling are the ones the media warns us away from. I don't know who came up with this directive, but it's been effective in reaching a broad audience in its simplicity: Shop the perimeter of the grocery store for the most nutritious foods to fill your cart.

So, let's walk the perimeter of the grocery store. We'll start with produce, with all those refrigerated cases and misters to keep the vegetables from drying out. For obvious logistical reasons, these cool cases are typically located along a wall of the grocery store. Produce also needs to be near the refrigerated storerooms behind the walls. Not only do half the products need to stay moist and cool, much of the produce must be removed from the bins and shelves after the store closes and properly stored overnight, so the closer they are to the back storage coolers, the more convenient it is. This is why you will never find produce in the center of a store—it would be impractical.

Also around the perimeter are the other minimally processed foods that would go bad if not refrigerated—dairy, meats, and seafood. And near the meats, typically, is a deli and prepared-foods case, with staff to slice the Two Brothers ham, fill deli cups with potato salad, and, increasingly, weigh out barbecued spare ribs, green beans amandine, and panko-crusted orange roughy, all cooked and ready to reheat and serve.

Thus the perimeter of a grocery store is composed primarily of *things that go bad quickly*. This is what you want. Foods that go bad quickly do so in part because they are rich in volatile nutrients and are not processed. What food companies began doing beginning in the nineteenth century, but explosively so following World War II, was remove those nutritious elements from food that cause it to go bad, and also add preservatives, so that the food could sit on a room-temperature shelf indefinitely. (This is by no means the only way to create shelf-stable products. Properly canned and jarred foods keep indefinitely; this technique has been used by companies and households for hundreds of years. And food that is dried—for example, a properly cured ham or packaged beef jerky—likewise will not spoil.) Roller mills, which separated the germ from the rest of the grain as the miller crushed wheat into flour, came into widespread use toward the end of the nineteenth century. This resulted in flour that lacked the nutritious fatty acids in the germ and thus would not become rancid. Long before anyone understood the notion of vitamin deficiencies, this stripped-down form of wheat became a staple of the Western diet.

More accurate to say, however, is that food companies do more harm by what they add to food than by what they remove. And those things that may do the most damage to us fall under a single category: sugar. Whether it's in the form of maltodextrin, dextrose, sucrose, agave nectar, malt syrup, or the most vilified of the sugars we put into food, high-fructose corn syrup (HFCS), it's all sugar when it hits our blood-stream. That includes the "brown rice syrup" some good-for-you foods use as a sweetener (such as Bear Naked triple berry granola, a product so successful that Heinen's has its own private-label triple berry granola, made by Mint Brook Meadow in southern Ohio). Even ingredients such as cornstarch should be considered sugars. As should refined wheat and corn. Debates now center on whether HFCS is worse than regular fructose, dextrose, or glucose, or whether table sugar is worse for your children than a natural sugar such as honey or agave nectar. Nobody knows for certain.

What is certain is that those central aisles are fraught with peril. Here is where all the refined wheat and sugar products are, and the "sports" bars, and the canned soups and vegetables, plus the spices, cake mixes, vegetable oils, ketchups and mustards and vinegars, shelf-stable salad dressings, ethnic condiments, dried beans, and of course those long aisles devoted to breakfast cereals, chips, and soda. Grocery also includes pet foods and several aisles of non-edibles: plastics (bags, forks, cups), cleaning materials (soaps, sponges), paper (toilet, towels, plates), charcoal and lighter fluid, basic kitchenware, such as measuring cups and pie plates, as well as the products in category #105, listed on the Heinen's spreadsheet as INCONTINENCE CTGRY. There are hundreds of categories—magazines and mass-market paperbacks, candles and light bulbs, insecticides (admittedly a small category, but $31,000 annually nonetheless), and on and on.

And while these aisles are without question loaded with some nutritious foods, they are also filled with the most worked-over, processed, and heavily marketed products on earth. I can't repeat this enough: Nothing is known with certainty how such food affects our health long term, but the evidence is piling up that refined wheat and sugar are what's making us sick. Refined wheat and sugar are the number one and number two primary ingredients in too many products to name, from sliced bread to cornflakes. Move over to cereals such as Froot Loops and the sugar takes the number one spot. Look at the ingredients list of Lucky Charms and you'll see that the second one listed is neither a refined cereal nor straightforward corn syrup but, rather, marshmallows, which require their own parenthetical list of ingredients, sugar chief among them.

The dangers of which Nathan Perc, hulking through the many thousands of square yards of the Anaheim Convention Center with an eye out for new product and the thrill of the deal, knows well: As we discussed these issues at the show, he said, "Processed food has probably killed more people than cigarettes."

The breakfast bar shelves are almost exclusively given over to the heavy hitters: Nature Valley, owned by General Mills, and Quaker, owned by PepsiCo. These granola bars, fruit snacks, and Rice Krispie Treats are grouped together in the cereal aisle. "It's candy," Nathan says. "It should be considered awful. They make them smaller and smaller and smaller and charge more money for them. It's the American way: Charge more for less."

He does want to wedge better alternatives into these sections but, again, he has to weigh consumer demand for "cheap" and "good for you." And in the breakfast bar category the big companies have a lock.

For Nathan, his main challenge in selling these products, especially the bad-for-you products, is that they're all so alike.

"A box of Cheerios is a box of Cheerios, right?" he says. "No matter where you buy it. So it's the most price-sensitive [area of the store], because there is no differentiation. Price is the differentiation. Whereas you can preach your stories about different items in produce.

"We have a whole range, from non-GMO to vegan to shit products that have nothing in them," Nathan says. "[Breakfast bars are] a $2 million category. It's probably sixteen feet, and it's 95 percent Kellogg's, General Mills, Quaker. We need to find lower-tiered items that aren't selling and take some of the space back for higher-margin, specialty, unique items that our competition doesn't sell. I'd like to take that 24 percent margin to 30 percent. But when you deal with major national brands, there's more demand, there's more marketing, they're doing their own advertising. There's higher cost and you sell for lower retail because the competition all has it.

"But we also have the high-end customer looking for the good-for-you, organic, the non-GMO, the vegan, the gluten-free—though gluten-free is another issue, because they just replace the gluten with butter and sugar." He shakes his head over the gluten-free issue. "Sometimes I walk into one of these showrooms and want to say, 'Does *anyone* have *anything . . . with* gluten?'"

He walks through the thousands of yards of aisles of booths promoting new products with keen eyes: "I look at everything," he says. "We eat with our eyes, so I look at attractive packaging. Taste is important, but it's not everything."

We stop at a booth to sample a microwavable frittata. Nathan tastes it and proclaims it "pretty good," given that it's microwaved. I taste it and find it kind of disgusting, like food that comes back up on you, the texture of a curdled custard. But given the attractive packaging and the fact that it cooks in a couple minutes, I suppose he might have a point. Sort of.

He strides off with confidence. "Here, we're the big fish in the small pond." This is because, for the most part, the really big fish, such as Kroger and Albertsons, don't have as much of an interest in finding these specialty products, many of which couldn't possibly produce the quantities such chains require.

Nathan is on the lookout for beef jerky. When approaching the men at the Duke's Beef Jerky booth, who don't know the Heinen's chain, he says, "We're a twenty-two-store chain—eighteen stores in Ohio, four stores in Chicago. We're kind of a cross between Wegmans and Whole Foods." His intent is to convey the kind of volume they'd be purchasing in and the level of their clientele. This gets the Duke's people's attention.

Walking the vast expanses of Expo West is a bit like being at a farmers' market on a crowded Saturday morning, albeit indoors. You can only move so fast. Some booths are nearly empty; at others you have to wait in line for samples. Some people just glance left and right as they stroll; some stop at each booth. Over the course of three days, the Heinen's team will cover pretty much all of the 350,000 square feet of exhibition space.

Given so much space and so many people, I was bound to run into someone I knew in one of the big halls, which felt more like a carnival midway. It happened to be Marty McDonald, whom I hadn't seen in ages. We'd been derelict students at Duke in the eighties and even more derelict adults in New York City immediately after, when I was a copy boy at the *New York Times* and he was a student at the School of Visual Arts. Marty had moved into advertising in Seattle, then become interested in sustainability issues as this topic heated up nationally. He eventually helped create a brand development firm called Egg, working directly with companies making sustainable products, a hybrid advertising-design-social-interactive brand communications and product development company. A year earlier, he'd written to me for help in promoting a new start-up he and two colleagues had begun, Barefoot Provisions, an internet store offering all things paleo or, in their term, to avoid being pigeonholed without losing the message, "primal," their goal being to help you "eat as close to the past as possible," and urging you to "tap into your genetic heritage to maximize happiness."

After our West Coast hippie hugs, Marty asked, "What are you doing here?"

"Writing a book about groceries."

"Cool!" he said. With curly reddish-brown hair, square jaw, blue eyes, and a ready smile, he was always of a positive nature, and always sort of half-corporate and half-hippie once he left school.

"You?" I asked. "How is Barefoot?"

"Great. We come every year to see what's here, especially in the natural and organic channels."

This, of course, is yet another facet of our evolving food world: internet specialty food stores. It might be spiced crab apples or food for your hermit crab from Etsy, pastas and oils from Food52, or, from Barefoot Provisions, beef jerky, Caveman Cookies, raw organic Botija olives, or organic cinnamon red maca sprouted almond spread by a company in Oregon called Jem that makes a range of raw organic nut butters. Marty and a colleague are here to look for more products to sell on their site. Barefoot and other internet companies are an example of the continuing fragmentation of the retail food industry, and also a reflection of our culture's changing tastes and desires. And paleo foods seemed to be at their apex that year. He was also there to connect with people, visit the booths of some of the clients they do marketing for, and generally to understand "the greater cultural context" of this move toward natural and organic foods and what's driving it.

Later, in one of the smaller meeting rooms above the four massive halls, I peruse the booths with Chris Foltz. We stop at a booth offering samples of something called Hero kale-cashew bars.

A bald man in a chef's coat busily preparing samples pauses from his work when he sees me. "Mr. Ruhlman?" he says.

"Yes."

"I'm Walter Abrams. We met a while ago at the French Laundry."

"Of course!" I say. "Hi, Chef!" I've met so many young chefs at that iconic restaurant in the Napa Valley during my years of writing cookbooks with chef-owner Thomas Keller, I can't keep them all straight. But I am fascinated by Walter's trajectory. From young *commis* there, to cheffing at restaurants in Palm Beach, and now back in the Napa Valley making kale-cashew bars. He tells me about his bars and says, "I'm making them in Connie Green's kitchen!" Connie Green is one of the main wild mushroom foragers and purveyors in Napa ("gift from God mushrooms" she calls them, to distinguish her mushrooms from the cultivated ones at the grocery store); I wrote about her because she was such a big supplier to the French Laundry. Now kale-cashew bars were coming out of her house. (Many of these products actually do begin in home kitchens.)

Chris and I next approach a booth offering gourmet macaroni and cheese, behind which stands a man in a chef's coat preparing samples, Dan Stephenson. I thought he was of normal height until I realized he wasn't standing on a platform—a big guy, six-foot-seven, with straight dark hair. He is known in Nashville, where his company is based, as Dan the Mac Man. As we approach, he sees "Heinen's" on the badge hanging from a lanyard around Chris's neck.

"Heinen's!" Dan shouts. "I know Heinen's!"

"Yeah?" Chris says with a smile.

"Yeah! The Shaker store. We used to do cart races in the parking lot as kids! I love Heinen's."

We taste his samples—the rich and creamy Dan's Mac Attack with habanero-garlic sausage, Cheddar, pepper Jack, and Swiss cheeses on bowtie pasta was a relief after the mountains of kale and broccoli chips we'd been sampling—and he and I chat. He left school with a business degree but didn't like the world of finance. He'd always loved mac and cheese, since he was a kid. He and his brother would have mac and cheese making competitions. When he was in the corporate world, he'd come home and cook different kinds of mac and cheese with his girlfriend. Unfulfilled by his job, but completely fulfilled by making mac and cheese in his kitchen, he and his girlfriend began experimenting with various recipes in 2013. They began selling their mac and cheese at the Nashville Farmers' Market, and the product was popular. Dan's Gourmet Mac & Cheese would, within three years, be found in two thousand stores in thirty-five states.

But not in Heinen's, alas. The packaging evidently didn't catch Nathan's eye.

A shame—it would have been nice to have this passion come full circle and find a home where Dan, the mac-and-cheese-loving boy, once raced shopping carts.

Nathan knows that just about every booth wants his order, and to him, newbies are like deer in the headlights when he trains his blue-turned-green-eyed gaze on them. But I can no more follow Nathan's patter than I could that of an auctioneer at the Amish produce markets. "Okay, let me get a sell sheet from you" and "We're looking for distributor pricing" and "If I go out with two-forty-nine, what kind of margin am I looking at?" is about the best I can record in the strange vernacular of grocery store packaged goods. A sell sheet is a list of products and pricing. Distributor pricing means the price Duke's Jerky would sell to a middleman, a distributor of their product, rather than the retailer. ("No one should give you that," Nathan tells me on leaving the booth. "I'm not a distributor. But if you don't ask . . .") And on the question about margins he tells me, "I'm not looking to kill anyone on margins. I'm not Whole Foods."

Staying hydrated with a bottle of kombucha he finagled from the Health-Ade booth, Nathan finesses a deal with one of a dozen vendors he'll converse with. Again I try to follow the auctioneer-rapid transaction, with little success. Nathan strides off with sell sheets in hand, telling me, "I just got him to free-fill our store. That's $5,000. If we don't sell anything and it stales out, it costs us nothing. If you don't ask, you don't get anything."

Free-filling, Nathan explains, is one give-and-take method that a small company with an untested product can use to convince a store like Heinen's to give it some shelf space. A grocery store is full. In order for a new item to be added, something has to be removed. Why should a grocery store take a chance on an unknown product when their known products sell? Some grocery stores charge slotting fees for this reason, meaning they charge certain manufacturers for shelf placement; Heinen's doesn't do this.[63]

"The idea is that they are willing to give us a free case to ensure the item will sell," Nathan said. "With them backing it like this, it establishes that they have faith in their product and that it will sell, and for us to set up the initial space allocation on the shelf, they are willing to give us free product."

....

63 When I asked Jeff Heinen to confirm this, he replied: "We do not charge slotting fees per se, and I would argue that as a standard practice, the whole pay-to-play concept is way less prominent than it used to be. That being said, it still exists and can take many forms from straight cash to free stock to marketing monies." In the industry it's called "trade spend"—any money expended to the retailer or distributor—and it can eat up to 20 percent of a new company's budget, according to Shane Emmett, who recently helped found Health Warrior chia bars. So what Nathan was about to describe is, according to Jeff, a form of slotting fees, or rather trade spend. Slotting fees are typically written about critically because they had been used by huge companies to buy their way onto shelves and into consumers' kitchens, one of the many ways the big players squeeze out the small companies and manipulate the grocery shopper; here, though, was the opposite—a way for a new, small company to get its products into grocery stores.

But the reason Nathan likes the free-fill is not only that it allows them to test new product with little risk, but also, he says, "It's money in the bank."

Here's how it works. Nathan approaches a company's booth selling interesting organic, non-GMO pasta sauces in five different varieties: marinara, chunky marinara, garlic-basil, hot and spicy, and a creamy cheese sauce. Nathan has been on the lookout for organic, non-GMO sauces, so he asks for a price and learns that the company's wholesale price is thirty dollars per case. Nathan wants them in his store and the price is right. But he doesn't place an order. The first thing he asks is, "Will you free-fill me?"

If the vendor says yes, it means that the vendor will send a case of each style of sauce to each of Heinen's twenty-two stores. The math goes as follows: Five cases for each of twenty-two stores is a total of 110 cases. Nathan thinks they should make a 30 percent margin on this product, which adds nine dollars to the retail value of a case of sauces. If the sauces sell, 110 cases at thirty-nine dollars a case, then Heinen's has taken in $4,290 and risked only the expense required to enter the product in the computer and get it on the shelf.

"I ask that a thousand times a year," Nathan tells me. "If all of my buyers ask for free fill, we can add a million dollars to our bottom line, just for asking. Which is why I want to scream at these guys if they don't ask for free fills."

And what does the small, new company get in return for giving away $3,300 worth of pasta sauce? Well, if it's successful, as some of Heinen's specialty pasta sauces have been, they can sell three thousand bottles of each sauce a year for sales of more than $100,000 through Heinen's. And if they're successful at Heinen's, they have a shot at getting into twenty such chains. If so, then they're doing $2 million in sales. And if they then get into Whole Foods, their company is a seriously viable and growing concern. Of course if it is a superlative organic, non-GMO product, Nathan worries that they will get bought up by a multinational that will drive the quality down in search of savings.

Nathan names three such examples off the top of his head, companies that became successful for their uniqueness and quality, and then sold out to a big conglomerate that reduced the cost by diminishing the qualities that made the product desirable in the first place: "Honest Tea, organic, was bought by Coke, which changed the glass bottle to plastic when this company appealed to the tree-hugger type, and they were not happy about them moving it out of glass. Kashi, bought by Keebler [whose parent company is Kellogg]. Keebler has ruined the brand and its healthy-for-you image to the point that they are bringing back employees that they let go during the acquisition. Annie's Homegrown, organic, bought by General Mills—this is new, but don't be surprised if they mess this up."

There's one booth none of the Heinen's guys (and one woman, a new hire from Jo-Ann Fabrics, Diana Hurst, who would take over many of Nathan's categories) pass by: that of Revive Kombucha. Here the sales force doesn't simply pour samples into plastic cups—they have all eight varieties of this fermented, effervescent tea on tap. The booth has a convivial feel; it's like hanging out at a brewpub.

Here we all sample the company's original brew, the OG, created in Rebekah and Sean Lovett's Santa Rosa garage in 2010. In the beginning, they brewed kegs of it, bottled it, and sold it to Sonoma grocers and restaurants and at farmers' markets. By the end of 2014 they were selling $2 million worth of the stuff. The company expanded into a thirty-thousand-square-foot former bakery and now has eight different brews, including the caffeine-free Free Ride, the coffee-infused Up Beat, and Campfire, a green tea–style kombucha. The guys running the booth tell us they're now working on fermenting an alcoholic kombucha.

Five or six of us, with our Heinen's badges, stand around the taps, tasting. "Could I try that Tropic Wonder?" "A little more of the Solar, please?" Everyone is as thrilled by the tea—"The best I've had," Chris Foltz says—as they are by the tap itself, which the company had built for $8,000. Chris suggests they get these taps into their stores, set them up next to the beer taps and the wine-dispensing Cruvinets. Everyone loves this idea but is skeptical that Jeff Heinen would go for it. Kombucha nevertheless remains a huge growth category in grocery stores, as is anything that can be labeled "probiotic."

The term probiotics was coined in 1965 and began to be used more frequently in the 1980s. But the idea of it has been around since a Russian scientist named Élie Metchnikoff, who shared a 1908 Nobel Prize for his work in immunology, proposed that we could "modify the flora in our bodies and replace the harmful microbes by useful microbes," in his *Prolongation of Life: Optimistic Studies*. Probiotics connotes just this: that the more good bacteria we send to our guts, the less room there is for bad bacteria. The idea makes common sense. In my book *Salumi*, about dry-curing meat, I recommend using a mold culture in the drying room to ensure that the good bacteria, resulting in white mold, outnumber the bad bacteria (black mold) and prevent them from proliferating, and it works. In India, when one is suffering from the gastrointestinal blues, it's common practice to ingest only yogurt (teeming with beneficial bacteria) until the illness passes.

Thus fans of probiotics claim that foods with a lot of good, living bacteria can help everything from diarrhea and irritable bowel syndrome to high blood pressure and inflammation, and generally that they contribute to one's overall health.[64]

....

64 There's little scientific proof of any of this, but eating foods alive with good bacteria certainly can't hurt. My personal bias, based on no scientific evidence, is that if we eat a diverse diet of natural foods, we develop a gut terrarium crawling with the beneficial microbes that we ingest from all kinds of sources, from cheese and yogurt to organisms coating the surfaces of the raw food we eat. We were a lot healthier before probiotics were manufactured and marketed, but as noted earlier, pesticides may be poisoning our gut flora. So eating probiotic food certainly can't hurt and may help. Some cultures practice geophagy, eating dirt, for similar reasons. Recently a slew of articles have appeared suggesting that eating dirt bolsters the immune system and enhances gut flora. Maybe, maybe not. The bacterium that causes botulism grows there, too, as does a worm called *Toxocara*, which can make you very sick. But considering the amount of dirt consumed by normal kids who play outdoors, common sense suggests that a little bit of dirt doesn't usually hurt—and may even do some good.

Ever since Chris brought Todd Pesek on board as a health expert in 2010, the company has been eagerly pursuing products that can be promoted as probiotic. Anything that's fermented (sauerkraut, yogurt, salami) is by definition probiotic owing to the bacteria that do the fermenting, and anything containing naturally occurring live bacteria is considered good for the gut and good for you. Kombucha is a hip drink, in large part because it hits three top consumer hot buttons—it is probiotic, organic, and vegan—and it's shown phenomenal growth throughout the country (more than $500 million annually in 2015). Heinen's carries five or six brands. Their sales of the tea went from $294,000 in 2014 to nearly $900,000 in 2016.

"It's got an uplifting, bubbly feeling," Todd says happily. "And if we can get it fermented so you could get a little tipsy, that will be *awesome*."

Todd, age forty, stands six feet tall, is fit from tai chi, yoga, and running, and wears a black T-shirt and burgundy corduroys and a backpack to carry sell sheets and samples. He has an angular nose, large teeth, and green eyes, and his dark brown hair is pulled tight against his scalp into a short ponytail.

To all Heinen's thirty-five hundred employees, he is not Todd or Dr. Pesek. He is *Dr. Todd,* Heinen's chief medical officer, perhaps the first chief medical officer of any grocery store anywhere. "Pretty awesome, right?" as Todd would say.

13.

BETTER LIVING THROUGH ORGANIC TURMERIC, ASHWAGANDHA EXTRACT, AND HEMP SEED MILK

The first time I met Dr. Todd was in a conference room at the PNC bank offices on Euclid Avenue in downtown Cleveland. He and Chris Foltz had agreed to give a presentation on health and nutrition over a buffet lunch of "superfoods" prepared by Heinen's corporate chef, James Mowcomber, who had been lured away from his post at Lolita, Michael Symon's popular Cleveland restaurant. Dr. Todd was late. Chris shrugged and told me, "He lives on Indian time." Native American time, that is, and close to the ground. We were on the seventeenth floor, and Chris told me that Dr. Todd really doesn't like to be this high up.

Todd did eventually arrive, dressed in slacks and a dress shirt—uncommonly formal for him, I would learn. He noted that he could feel the building swaying. I got only an introduction, as Chris wanted to start the presentation to the fifty or so women, employees of PNC, who were already digging in to their kale salads and the like. Chris gave a brief intro and handed the presentation over to Todd, who described himself this way: "I'm an organic farmer. I'm also an Appalachian herbalist," before he named the universities where he earned his degrees. "There's so much food in our food system that isn't food," he told his audience, seated at a dozen round tables, then asked, "What is health to you? What does it mean?"

I was in a chair against the back wall, and the woman in front of me said, "Health is a vibrant, dynamic energy system."

"Beautiful," Todd said. "Health is a vibrant, dynamic energy system. Wow. That's awesome. That's kind of hard to follow."

He paced a bit, thinking, then said, "Here's my definition: It's the health of the mind, body, and spirit in the context of healthful environmental surroundings, or cosmos, right? And it's that environment that's missing from every definition of health out there. That context is overlooked. There is no human health without environmental health. The environment nurtures us, sustains us, entertains us. We're inextricably intertwined with our environment"—an environment, he would go on to argue, that is awash in toxins and filled with food that isn't food.

It was at about this time that I wondered both how a grocery store had come to hire a doctor, especially *this* doctor, and what a grocery store doctor actually did.

Chris Foltz explained later that Carla Iafelice, an associate in Heinen's wellness department, had looked into doctors practicing holistic medicine to help promote their vitamins and supplements. She found Todd Pesek online and called to ask if he'd be interested in doing an in-store seminar. Dr. Todd was a Heinen's shopper—"I love Heinen's," he told her—so he readily agreed. His seminar on longevity was so successful (with a hundred people in attendance) that Heinen's marketing director asked Chris to meet to see if they might work more with him. Chris is always open to new ideas; he also recognized that the wellness category had potential for growth, and was something he cared about personally. But the moment he saw Dr. Todd in the lobby of Heinen's headquarters, he thought to himself, *Well,* this *will be a short meeting.*

"He had a Peruvian pullover on," Chris recalled, "kind of like a combo sweatshirt/poncho, some baggy beige work pants like a mechanic might wear, and some of those hippie Sanuk canvas shoes." And, of course, there was the ponytail. A thirty-five-year-old hippie with a medical degree.

"Two hours later," Chris said, "we ended the meeting and were setting up our next. Three months later, we contracted with him to be our chief medical officer. That was five years ago."

His duties would be to build out the wellness category with the best vitamins and supplements available, coach the wellness managers so they could advise customers about the products and make recommendations, and enable customers to make salutary food decisions generally.

And he was at Expo West to look for new products that . . . *promote wellness.* I had a hard time typing those last two words. It's the "wellness" part. I don't have a problem with "promote." The meaning of "promote" is clear. Except when it comes to "wellness." To promote wellness—what does that actually mean? The words have an almost archaic quality, as if they were a phrase the Pilgrims used. "How fare thee, goodwife?" "Pray, I fare well; now sit thee down to the eggs I've roasted—they shall make thee full and promote thy wellness."

But try as I might to come up with an alternative, I could not. I first went to fitness. But that's a word that's been pretty well run into the ground. At its most basic, when it comes to characterizing people, it is Darwinian. Fit means one thing: the ability to produce healthy offspring. But by the mid-twentieth century, it had become associated with physical fitness, and brought to mind Jack LaLanne in his white exercise slacks and medicine balls. Physical fitness. We rarely refer to mental fitness or biological fitness. And still, fitness in my opinion is a more accurate way of describing whether or not you are in excellent health.

Because that's what we're trying to promote—good health. A "healthiness" department would be silly. So why isn't "wellness" just as silly? It is, which is why it catches in my throat.

Frankly, what is catching is not the word itself, but rather the need for it at all. We have to have a wellness center in our grocery store: a section of the store that sells products that will make you better than you are now, largely in capsule form. And we buy into it to the tune of $21 billion a year. You know what wellness center I spend most of my time in? It's called the produce department.

In a country whose relationship to its food is little different than its relationship to medicine, I suppose we're stuck with wellness. But why couldn't we use a word that's a little more fun and upbeat and less serious? We're so *serious* about wellness.

How about awesomeness? Why don't we have an awesomeness center in our grocery store? I know Dr. Todd would support it.

I asked to walk Expo West with Dr. Todd as a kind of counterbalance to the hard-driving Nathan Perc, after our breakfast of microwaved burritos and various forms of jerky. As I dressed to meet Chris and Todd that morning, I could see Dr. Todd from my window, on a rooftop deck of our four-story hotel, practicing tai chi. He looked like a Chinese action star battling an invisible foe in slow motion.

I found Chris down at the hotel bar drinking from a thermos of matcha tea and sorting through a plastic bag filled with pills, the exclusive Dr. Todd protocol that Heinen's wellness associates sell. It's designed to hit every part of your system, from your brain to your gut: a multivitamin, additional vitamin D, iodine, a probiotic, and DHA, an algae-based omega-3 supplement. Chris downed a half dozen or more capsules, including a couple filled with maca, a tuber that grows in the Andes and is the latest wonder-supplement. He admitted he was willingly drinking the Dr. Todd Kool-Aid.

One of the things Dr. Todd was able to do was source reliable multivitamins because, as Chris says, "You never know what you're getting because it's not regulated by the government." Todd found two companies, New Chapter and Garden of Life, that made vitamins with the specifications he wanted—raw, vegetarian, gluten-free, dairy-free, probiotic, and without binders and fillers. These companies, though, had recently sold out to industry giants Procter & Gamble and Atrium Innovations, respectively, so Dr. Todd could only hope the companies maintained their standards, given what so often happens when small companies are taken over by big ones.

At Expo West I was interested not in the myriad capsules and supplements, but rather in those natural foods that promise benefits beyond the pleasures of eating and drinking them. Many so-called superfoods make health claims beyond those of "regular" real food, such as an apple or a green bean, and boast anti-inflammatory, probiotic, and antioxidant properties. For example, the matcha tea Chris was drinking, according to a quick Google search, is something of a wonder drug: Not only is it loaded with antioxidants (equal to ten cups of regular green tea!), but it also enhances calm, memory, concentration, endurance, and energy; and it burns calories (so you don't have to!), detoxifies the body, fortifies the immune system, and improves cholesterol.

I'll have what he's having!

Todd is in the driver's seat as Chris and I get in. He shifts into gear and says, "Let's go to the show!" He's like a little kid heading to a candy festival.

Dr. Todd has been coming to this show for fifteen years, since back when this segment of the industry was represented by about ten booths. Now there seem to be hundreds. Small companies that once had a tiny booth, such as Go Raw, now rent space enough to set up an entire pop-up store with seating.[65]

It seems to me that the growth in this segment of the processed food industry is fueled by America's ongoing food-as-medicine mindset. If I drink this turmeric drink, it will enhance my body's anti-inflammatory response and help me be ready when the moment's right. So what if it doesn't taste as good as the sugar-laden Snapple—that must mean it's better for me, right? Because that's what we learned in our eat-your-peas-there-are-starving-people-in-Africa childhoods. I *kind of* like a good kale chip, but it doesn't come close to a Lay's potato chip, which I love. Sure, Go Raw's zesty pizza-flavored Flax Snax are good, but Planters Cocktail[66] Peanuts are more fun to eat, in my opinion. And those raw sprouted goodies come at a premium. The best deal I could find on the internet for a three-ounce pouch of Flax Snax was $3.65 (or nine dolllars on Amazon—yikes!), about what you'd pay for a *pound* of Planters peanuts. How about nutrition? Both products are real foods—no chemical additives, preservatives, or dyes. The humble peanut, a legume, is nutritionally dense, though high in fat. But raw sprouted flaxseed flavored with raw organic seasonings has about the same amount of fat, ounce for ounce, as cocktail peanuts. Does the fact that they're sprouted, which supposedly releases good-for-you enzymes, make them better? Dr. Todd would say yes. And apparently more and more consumers agree, and are willing to pay five times as much for the good-for-you option as for the mass-produced item.

----

65 Go Raw was created by Robert Freeland, who, distressed over the lack of raw "sprouted" snacks available to him as a seventeen-year-old, began making flaxseed crackers and selling them at San Diego's Ocean Beach Farmers' Market. According to the company website, they sold well, and he expanded to other markets. He got his certified organic stamp, and soon Whole Foods came a-calling. The company relocated north, to what is now a sixty-five-thousand-square-foot facility. It employs one hundred people and produces nearly three dozen different products.

66 Notice this little bit of Jazz Age marketing that hangs on from 1923, with America three years into Prohibition.

Most people have a general knowledge of where and how peanuts are grown. Fewer people, surely, know where flaxseed comes from, but it does have a health-food connotation, a good-for-you hippie vibe. Flaxseed comes from the flax plant, of course, which grows in cooler climates, such as central Europe. The fibrous plant is used in the textile industry, but the main value of the plant is its oil, called linseed oil, which is crushed out of its seeds. When I worked in a forge, we dipped finished hot steel in linseed oil, which kept it black and prevented rust. The oil is also an ingredient in wood-finishing products. The seed is indeed nutritious—and its oil can give a luster to that old cutting board of yours.

Is this what you think when you see a bag of raw sprouted Flax Snax on the shelf of your Whole Foods? Or what I thought when I added a half cup of flaxseed to the batch of granola I was making? No. I thought, *They're supposed to be good for you, so why not?*

Marion Nestle devotes a chapter in her book *What to Eat* to supplements—a multibillion-dollar industry in products for which there is no regulation and little evidence to support the validity of their claims or evidence of benefits. Indeed, supplements of fat-soluble vitamins (such as A and E) can be toxic if you take too much, as excess is less easily flushed from the system in the way water-soluble vitamins are.

Noting the lack of federal regulation, Nestle cites studies from ConsumerLab.com that found that many supplements contained little of what their label claimed, and some included lead or other toxic metals. And "nearly a third of probiotic ('friendly' bacteria) samples had less than 1 percent of the claimed number of live bacteria." She goes on to say without much exaggeration that, from a legal standpoint, "you can go into your garden, pick some spinach, dry it, pulverize it, put it into capsules and sell it in a Popeye-illustrated package labeled 'All-natural herbal supplement! Promotes muscle strength!'" When it comes to trials on herbal supplements, she writes, "The more carefully the research is designed, the fewer benefits it shows." And as for supplements: "Clinical trials rarely show much benefit from taking [them]."

I followed up with Nestle to make sure nothing had changed in the ten years since she published her book. Short answer: nope. But what about so-called "health food," flaxseed and whatnot? "Better for you is not necessarily good," she said, regarding all such supplements and foods. "Basically they are harmless and have powerful placebo effects. Whether they improve health is debatable."

I was especially interested in fish oil pills. Here is a $731 million industry with broad beliefs among consumers that it helps reduce triglycerides and thus prevents heart disease. What does Nestle think about them?

"I have lots of papers saying they perform miracles," she told me, "but the preponderance said fish is better."

"Is it safe to presume that when you want fish oil, you eat fish?" I asked. "You don't strike me as a fish oil pill person."

"No pills," she responded. "No good data on pills. Only fish."

And that seems to me to be the best advice, generally, regarding the whole supplement issue. Because it's possible that the body may not absorb the omega-3s in a fish oil pill but will absorb it when it comes in the form of a piece of salmon. The good Dr. Sukol had looked at my blood work after I saw her for my knee issue and noted a vitamin B_{12} deficiency, so at her urging, I started taking a precautionary B_{12} supplement. But I still would prefer to eat real foods rich in B_{12} than take a pill, just as Marion Nestle prefers to get her fish oil from fish, on the assumption that the body is more likely to absorb it when it comes in the natural form of food than it is when you take a synthesized pill. The best multivitamin treatment plan you can embark on is eating a diverse diet, filled with all kinds of different foods that you cook yourself.

And yet there's something in me that wants to believe everything Dr. Todd says, to drink the Kool-Aid right along with Chris. So I trail this enormously optimistic, energetic doctor through the halls of Expo West to a few of the booths offering products that particularly interest him.

"I try to pick out the innovators," he tells me, striding into the Anaheim Convention Center. "I've got to separate the wheat from the chaff. There's a lot of chaff out there."

The day before, he handed me a bag of "wrapped" cashews— cashews with their skin still on. They were delicious. Todd said, "These wrapped cashews are amazing. They are so much better for you because of all the polyphenols in the skin, and we are going to explain why and sell the *shit* out of them." And at the bar the previous night he gave me a knob of organic turmeric root and told me to eat it—it, and its juice, were, he said, "a rock star product" owing to their curcuminoids, which are powerful anti-inflammatories. "It's fat soluble," he explained, "which is why the ancients combined it with fatty ingredients like coconut milk and creamy curries."

And so he led me to Temple Turmeric, a company started by Daniel Sullivan, whom Todd describes as "a spiritual brother." Sullivan stands about mid–five feet and has abundant dark curly hair. He's dressed in a jacket and slacks, but all the beaded wristbands and necklaces suggest this is not his preferred attire.

Sullivan tells me he believes our bodies should be "sanctuaries of health and positive energy." Following a trip to India where he learned about the tenets of Ayurveda, an ancient, holistic healing system, then to Hawaii where he learned about the "life-changing and healing" powers of raw organic turmeric, a prominent ingredient in Ayurvedic recipes, he decided to use it to make health-giving beverages. He found a source in Kauai Organic Farms, started in 2004 by Michigan natives Phil and Linda Green on that remote Hawaiian island. He began making his elixirs and selling them from the back of a bicycle in New York City. Then he received a $35,000 loan from Whole Foods, which has a program for investing in small start-ups. Sullivan created a special blend called Turmeric Golden Milk that is proprietary to Whole Foods. It boasts thirteen grams, or nearly half an ounce, of raw organic turmeric. The main fluids are hemp milk (hemp seeds are soaked, then ground and strained to make a milky, nutty fluid) and coconut milk, and the beverage also contains cardamom, raw honey, bee pollen, chia seeds, vanilla bean, ginger, and sea salt. He gave me a bottle to taste. It was pretty good—like drinking a cold mild curry sauce. I wanted to pour it on some stir-fried chicken and eat it with rice.

Next, Todd takes me to Living Intentions, where a small pack of white guys wearing dreadlocks and face hardware are mixing all manner of smoothies, concocted from two dozen bins of powders, such as organic pea protein, organic freeze-dried kale powder, organic dehydrated açai powder, and organic wheatgrass powder.

"This is the future of the smoothie industry," Todd says excitedly. "I mean, this shit's off the hook!"

"Basically it started in my kitchen seventeen years ago," says founder Joshua McHugh. McHugh has vivid green eyes, brown dreadlocks that hang all the way down his back, and a scraggly beard. "Our goal is to create nutritionally dense food that tastes good first."

The company, which also sells whole nuts and seeds—the package for their pumpkin and sunflower sprouted seeds with Ayurvedic chili blend describes it as "an epic sprouted seed combination enhanced with potent medicinal botanicals and extracts, shilajit, ashwagandha extract, and turmeric extract"—now has sales of about $5 million.

Todd spots buttons on a counter and pins one to my shirt—it notes that I promise "to spread my radiant love."

The next booth we visit is Wildbrine, which produces raw fermented vegetable products—kimchi, sauerkraut, pickles. Todd found them several years ago, and the Heinen's account allowed them to grow. "Then Whole Foods took them on," Todd explains as we taste out of little paper cups, "and they said they could no longer supply Heinen's. I was like, what the fuck? They apologized, but it was Whole Foods." Four hundred seventy-five stores, that is, not twenty-two.

Then on to Rawpothecary, a raw organic juice company started by Stephanie Walczak. Her Skinny Greens mix includes fennel, cucumber, romaine, parsley, ginger, celery, and coconut water. "I made this stuff for myself, but it really touches people's lives," she tells me. She then laments that, as far as new products go, she picked the toughest category, the booming good-for-you beverages trade.

She points Todd to a company called Green Onyx, saying they are the future. Green Onyx is a new company developing a special juicer for a water plant called khai-nam, which they claim is exceptionally nutrient-dense, comprising protein, fiber, minerals, vitamins, and both omega-3s and omega-6s.

It was all enough to make my head spin. I was happy to get outside the crowded halls and sit in the sun with Chris Foltz, talking about what I'd seen.

"They're hippies," he said. "They don't *care* about making money. But they are going to make a *lot* of money."

14.

A WALK IN THE MEDICINE CABINET

When I contacted Dr. Todd several months later to ask if I could talk to him about grocery stores, he didn't ask me to meet him at the offices of his practice. He said, "Why don't we go for a walk in the woods?"

Given the stresses of the day, and the fact that it was July, a walk in the woods sounded like a good idea. Cleveland has a series of interconnected nature preserves called the Cleveland Metroparks, twenty-one thousand acres with hundreds of miles of hiking trails, referred to as the Emerald Necklace for the way this verdant, forested land surrounds the industrial and suburban city. Todd suggested the North Chagrin Reservation, where my soon-to-be ex-wife and I used to take our kids when they were young, a favorite family outing on summer weekends. A truly lovely place for standing under waterfalls and turning over rocks looking for crayfish. In fact, I hadn't been here since those more carefree days.

Todd arrives, only a little late, in his gray 2014 Jeep Rubicon. His last car was an Inca-gold Jeep Sport, which he called Old Yeller. He drove her without a top through all seasons for the last three years he owned the car. When he traded in the car with two hundred thousand miles on it, oak trees were growing in the backseat, acorns having seeded in the leaf litter.

He's wearing a black short-sleeved shirt, beige trousers, and his light gray Sanuks. He carries a brightly colored handwoven satchel, its strap knotted at the shoulder.

"Let's walk," he says, and leads me out of the parking lot and into the woods to an inclining dirt path about six feet wide and surrounded by what, before this walk, I would have called shrubs—forest ground cover and lots of tall trees. For Dr. Todd, I soon learned, it was a medicine cabinet. As we rise along the path, he explains why he asked me into the woods: "I wanted you to get a sense of who I am. *This* is who I am."

It is a weekday afternoon, we are alone on the path, and the only sounds are our voices and the birds. It rained earlier, so the path is muddy and the scents of the woods are rich. When the path we ascended levels off, Dr. Todd steps off it and into the ground cover beneath the canopy of trees. He holds out his arms and slowly rotates his torso to indicate a circle around him.

"Right here," he says, "where I'm standing is this incredibly complex ecosystem. It's a symphony, a harmony, both temporal and spatial and illustrative of the interconnections with everything within this ecosystem, of which we are a part. Mind, body, spirit, environment. We connect to the trees, we connect to the forest."

I have to admit, it is pretty lovely and relaxing to be in the woods.

He looks down and says, "This is spicebush." He picks some of its tiny green berries and asks me to crush them between my fingers. They smell like lime leaves. By fall they will be larger and ripe red and spicy, and Todd will collect and grind them as early settlers did for a seasoning akin to allspice. "And this is Solomon's seal," he says, stroking the long stemmy plant from which clusters of small, elongated white flowers hang like ornaments. The plant and its roots have been used for centuries as a healer for flesh wounds and taken internally as an all-purpose tonic.

He steps back onto the path and we continue walking.

"What happens is, picture this in the winter," he says. "It's snow. If you were living like our ancestors, the first thing that happens is the running of the sap. You drink the sugary goodness after a winter of nothing. And the first things that come up are the alliums, wild garlic, the ramps, wood leeks. Here are some seeds." He bends to pick ramp berries, or seeds, and hands them to me. "Alliums up-regulate your body's detoxification systems. They're rich in sulfides; they're antibacterial and a kidney and liver cleanse. Then you start to see the reducers—these are like the spring tonics. The toothworts, the diuretics, detoxifying." He spots a large patch of a low-growing plant with delicate lavender flowers. "Right here is one of the best—it's wild geranium." (Stops minor bleeding, mends ulcers, eases inflammation.) "And then you roll into the summer when food abounds." He pauses to quote Thoreau: "The fields and the forest are a table always spread."

"As you move into fall," he goes on, "antiparasitic plants abound, and then you roll back into the famine of winter. Your dietary focus shifts to mineral-laden root veggies, things that are underground and things you've gathered—tree nuts and seeds and dried legumes. Hickory, beechnut, acorns are all edible. Chestnuts used to be a staple, until the chestnut blight decimated the landscape and food supply. Our ancestors ate plants. And when in famine, they ate animals that ate plants, but that's more rare than people realize." He stops to look around. "Everything here has a purpose."

Dr. Todd grew up on a self-sustaining farm in rural Sweet Valley, Pennsylvania, thirty miles west of Scranton, and always refers to himself as an Appalachian root doctor rather than a medical doctor. "My grandmother's father was an Appalachian bonesetter of epic reputation," he tells me. "People would come from all over. He would always have the medicinal plants boiling on the fire and he would boneset and eat and heal."

Todd told me he graduated magna cum laude from Northeastern University in 1999 with a degree in biochemistry, then earned his medical degree from Ohio State University and the Cleveland Clinic. "I have traditional credentials to the hilt," he explained, "but I've spent all of my time and practice working hard to forget what modern medicine is. Because it's a non-sustainable way of looking at wellness." In 2008 he opened his holistic medicine practice, where he and four other physicians tend six to eight thousand patients (including Tom Heinen) each year. They also offer non-pharmaceutical chemotherapy. Dr. Todd created a line of his own supplements, Nutritional Roots, which include maca, made from a tuber that grows in the Andes,[67] and cat's claw, a vine that grows in tropical regions such as Costa Rica. But his overarching

....

67 This is the stuff Chris Foltz was taking at Expo West. When a friend told me she was anemic and had to see a doctor regularly to monitor her blood-iron levels, I told her to get over to the wellness department of her grocery store and eat some maca. Within a month, her doctor was astonished by the improvement. So who knows?

goal is to promote the idea that "health and wellness is possible without pharmaceutical drugs."

In his third year of medical school, Dr. Todd joined a Cleveland Clinic program on integrated medicine and had to present a paper to fifty or sixty doctors. He was terrified to be presenting to these august men and women in their long white coats. When he announced the title of his address, "Plants, People, and Global Healing," one of the doctors grumbled that he didn't have time listen to talk about plants—this was a hospital, after all—and left his seat. Todd, already nervous, was startled, but he recovered and called out to the back of the departing man, "Excuse me, Doctor." The doctor stopped and turned around. "When was the last time you prescribed morphine for a patient?" The doctor paused, sighed—morphine, of course, is derived from the seeds of the poppy plant—and returned to his seat.

Todd spots an empty potato chip bag on the trail, picks it up and puts it in his satchel, then moves to a small tree with a squiggly trunk. "Check this out," he says. "This is sassafras." He bends to examine some tiny sassafras saplings just emerging from the dirt. "These are delicacies, these leaves." He gives me one to taste. "It's got a nutty flavor—aren't they delicious? And all this around it, black cohosh, an important herb for women's health."[68] Farther down the path he stops to show me bloodroot, "a really powerful plant medicine."

He stops again to pick up trash, a large plastic Starbucks cup with lid and straw, and puts it in his satchel, saying, "People come here because they like it, and they leave stuff like this." A few feet away he sees another plant he loves, squats to scrutinize it, then carefully pulls off two vivid green leaves—spade-shaped, with serrated edges. "These are wood nettles," he explains. "It's strategic the way you eat them. You grab them from the top and you fold them." He demonstrates, turning the leaf into a tight bundle so that the nettled edges are concealed in the otherwise smooth leaf. "This is how the druids used to do it. Otherwise they'll sting the shit out of your tongue. But it's a beautiful flavor." I follow his

68 Black cohosh is used to treat symptoms of menopause, pre-menopause, hot flashes, vaginal pain, acne, and osteoporosis, among other things, according to WebMD.

folding instructions and chew—it does have an elegant leafy taste, with a spicy finish.

I recall a few things about Todd that Chris told me: "He's really smart—he must have a really high IQ. . . . He hears trees talk. . . . Did you know he's a shaman?"

All of which I am beginning to believe.

As we walk, he tells me his goals beyond his practice in Cleveland and work with Heinen's. He'd like to travel to mountainous regions where people live uncommonly long lives to learn from the native elders, traditional healers, and discover what grows in their region. He has been influenced by the work of the British environmentalist Norman Myers and his studies of "biodiversity hotspots," areas that have an extraordinary range of plant life, which are now endangered. Where they are least endangered is in mountainous regions, which, physically isolated, tend to sequester cultures and traditions. "I grew up in a mountainous region. I want to find other mountainous regions in the world and go there to meet the elders," he says.

He did just this in 1999, fresh out of college, with several doctors who traveled to the mountains in southern Belize, on the east coast of Central America. Trekking through the Maya Mountains with the traditional healers was perilous. They had no water for the first three days; they were chased by monkeys and had to be on the lookout for dangerous snakes. But they returned from the mountains with scores of indigenous plants used for healing.

They were able to create a garden in Punta Gorda, in southern Belize, amid the jungles and ancient Maya cities—ruins now, Dr. Todd explained, but still the epicenter of the Maya culture—to grow these plants so that the Q'eqchi' people who live in settlements with no access to nearby health facilities had some form of treatment.[69] "We gathered

---

69 In Central America, "medicinal plants continue to be the most economically and culturally suitable treatment for a variety of health conditions, including those related to women's health," write the authors of the study "Medical potential of plants used by the Q'eqchi Maya of Livingston, Guatemala for the treatment of women's health complaints," *Journal of Ethnopharmacology*, August 6, 2007.

these species, carried them out on our back, and grew them in a garden. And it now provides primary health care for most of the indigenous people of southern Belize."[70] He said the garden is now a model for others in the Peruvian Amazon and Andes and in Western Ghats, in southern India.

Dr. Todd continues to interrupt these stories to show me more plants: "This is squirrel corn. . . . Here's more Solomon's seal, the real one"—there's a false Solomon's seal as well. "Know chanterelles? These are not, these are jack-o'-lanterns; chanterelles don't grow on logs.

"This is jack-in-the-pulpit. This is a magical plant. There's a beautiful resonance. It's a plant medicine, but just as I was saying, it's mind, body, spirit, environment. There's energy, too. And these plants are soulful and healing on a lot of different levels. Think about it like this: Why is it that walking in the forest makes you feel better?"

And I did think about it. I felt more calm than I'd felt after months of personal difficulties. It was extraordinarily peaceful here—the birdsong soothed; the humid, rich-smelling air invigorated. I only *recognized* how glad I was to be here at his prompting, but my body was responding on its own.

"The plants themselves create phytochemicals," Todd says, "little compounds that make you happy and focused, give you entertainment and calmness of mind. The colors, the smells, the earth tones, the plants—the plants have a resonance, an aura. It's not froufrou airiness. There's science behind it."

We emerge from the forest on the other side of the park, and Todd's thoughts, as we head toward the parking lot, have turned to American medicine and, ultimately, the grocery store. "Here in America," he says, "the health care system is broken. Everybody goes straight to the

70 The 2010 study and a description of the trip, which Dr. Todd coauthored with other members of the team, "Sustaining Rainforest Plants, People and Global Health: A Model for Learning from Traditions in Holistic Health Promotion and Community Based Conservation as Implemented by Q'eqchi' Maya Healers, Maya Mountains, Belize," was published in *Sustainability* 2010, Volume 2, Issue 11. Todd would return many times after the first trip. He says, "I have spent cumulative *years* in the jungle with the bushmasters, healers, and elders."

pharmaceutical or surgical solutions first, for the littlest things. They've disconnected from this"—he indicates the forest.

"I see all the common ailments, all the diseases of civilization—high blood pressure, diabetes, those are easy [to address holistically]; inflammatory conditions, autoimmune conditions, those are easy. Fatigue, anxiety, depression. I tell people disease need not exist. If it does it's for one of two reasons, toxicity or trauma. And there are subcategories of each. Food toxicity, environmental toxicity. Plastics, PCBs, xeno-estrogens, pesticides, herbicides, larvicides, too much sugar, too much fat. The other side are the traumas and stress; we're not doing what our ancestors did.

"So, when people come to see me, I tell them what they need to do and they leave and are overwhelmed: Okay, I have to eat this way now, but how? And that's where the Heinen's partnership comes in perfectly. Now we can tell them to go to the wellness consultants and they'll teach you how to eat and how easy and delicious it is to eat healthfully. And they'll avail them of things like therapeutic, functional foods, certain medicinal plants and herbs. We have all that in the wellness center now. The grocery store, as an extension of the farm, is the doctor's office of the future.

"You have to farm it, get it from the farm to the grocery store, and from the grocery store to the consumer's kitchen, and teach them how to do that and why it's important. We're doing that at the grocery store."

We've reached our cars by now.

"What an amazing group of people," Dr. Todd continues. "We have this shared vision. What Tom and Jeff do, and Chris, really enables a lot. Those guys recognize that local and seasonal is key. That was our initial partnership bond, that they supported local and organic in an authentic way, not just lip service for customers. Seventy percent of our produce in spring and summer is local. That's legendary."

"But you still sell Cheerios and Wonder Bread."

"It's sad," he replies. "But it happens all over the developed world. You have two hospitals, public and private. People who can afford it go to the private, because the care is better. Same with the food supply.

There are people who can afford to eat healthfully and there are people who cannot. I'd say that represents a fundamental brokenness of our system and our food supply. It doesn't have to be like that."

"So, Todd," I say. "Describe for me the grocery store of the future."

"The supermarket of the future is going to be Heinen's," he replies at once. "It's going to be what we're doing. It's going to be a blending of food supply, farm, conscious consumerism, and health care. And all of it will be facilitating the food experience, how easy and delicious it is to eat healthfully. That's what I think."

"I hope so. Do you think things will change in our lifetime?" I ask.

"I think it's already started. And it's too big for one person's work. I just spend my time approaching things benevolently. Love each other, help each other, take care of each other. Hold no grudges. Benevolence. Teach, learn, and enable. It's really just love. Love and non-judgment and do the best thing you can every day."

"Are you a shaman?" I ask him.

"True healers don't identify themselves," he says. "The people around them do."

PART IV
THE PERIMETER

15.

THE FARMER WHO CAN'T FIND HIS ANIMALS

Brian Bean, owner of Lava Lakes Land & Livestock, maneuvers his white Chevy truck up the Pioneer Mountains in Idaho's Sawtooth National Forest, part of more than two million acres of protected woodland and pasture and mountains—many surpassing ten thousand feet. He pulls into a field and stops near a small hoop house–shaped trailer, white with a green wooden door and a small metal chimney tilting off the right side of the roof. Inside the ten-by-five-foot trailer, which looks to be from the 1940s, is an unmade mattress on a platform and a cooking stove. It's the home of Claudio Orihuela, one of Bean's four shepherds, three of whom are from Peru, one from Mexico. Bean has asked Claudio, who lives out here year-round, to take me and Tom Heinen to see Bean's flock of two thousand ewes.

Tom had invited me to travel with him to Idaho to meet with Bean, an investment banker turned rancher, to discuss Heinen's Lava Lakes lamb program. It's been working well for a few years, but Tom is concerned about their continuing to be able to supply enough of it. Bean's lambs graze this vast, unfenced wilderness rich with grasses and plants that are particularly nourishing to these animals, resulting in chops and loins that have a flavor that can truly be said to express this terroir. The flavor, combined with the fact that the animals are pretty much as organic as an animal can be—given no antibiotics or hormones, eating 100 percent wild grasses and plants, and raised according to their nature, pretty much the way lamb would have grown twelve thousand years ago when they were domesticated—is what the Heinen's customer wants, and Tom, who is a butcher at heart like his grandfather, wants to be able to provide it to them.

"People don't come to Heinen's to buy Wheaties," Tom says, stepping out of the truck.

Heinen's meat manager, Eric Besselman, had met Bean at a trade show, not unlike Expo West, only for buyers and sellers of meat. Eric was thrilled with the lamb and Tom agreed it was superb. He wanted to speak with Brian face to face, to see the operation himself and ensure that his stores can get enough of this very special lamb on a consistent basis.

Despite the Lava Lakes ball cap, jeans, backpack with extra water, and binoculars hanging from his neck (were we going to be bird watching as well?), Brian, sixty-three, looks professorial, with his trimmed salt-and-pepper beard and round spectacles. He warns us that we are already at a high altitude and will be hiking higher, so we shouldn't be surprised if we feel more winded than we expect. Then he turns and follows Claudio up the mountain.

Tom, who has an easygoing manner and what I consider to be an eminently respectable gut for a butcher/grocer, is dressed in a white Cleveland Country Club golf shirt, khaki shorts, white golf socks, and running shoes, not exactly high-altitude hiking attire (though, in jeans and sneakers, I'm not really dressed for a serious expedition either). But off we go on one of the most unusual tours of a modern-day ranch I've ever been on.

I'd tagged along because I wanted to see what this unique grass-fed meat "program" looked like, because meat in this country is linked to some of the biggest problems in the food industry—issues ranging from the environmental impact of ranching to the welfare of the animals to the effects on our health of saturated fat, the deadly *E. coli* bacteria, growth hormones in the meat we eat, and so on. And Brian Bean is committed not only to the proper raising of the animals we consume but also to the conservation of the land on which they are raised.

Tom and Brian's relationship is uncommon in a world dominated by commodity meat, and it's certainly not the kind of relationship a giant supermarket chain can cultivate. It's especially unusual for a grocer to go to such trouble for lamb, an item that represents only about 2.5 percent of all the meat sold and is diminishing generally throughout the country. Chicken makes up about 20 percent of the meat cases, pork 11 percent.

Beef continues to dominate the meat section, taking up 40 percent of the cases, and of that 40 percent, almost half is ground.

Loaders at Heinen's warehouse put twenty thousand pounds of beef and pork on trucks five days a week; on Saturdays it's thirty thousand pounds. Even a chain as small as Heinen's relies on larger producers, since they bring in, butcher, and distribute to their stores 130,000 pounds of beef and pork every week, or 6.5 million pounds a year. Beef: It's still what's for dinner.

Surely, no writer in America has described our industrial beef system better than Michael Pollan. He has not only reported clear descriptions of the massive feedlots and concentrated animal feeding operations (CAFOs), and how it is that thirty million cattle can be raised and slaughtered each year in the United States. He has also written thoughtfully on what the implications of this system are for the environment, for the animals, and for those who consume all that beef. And he has argued persuasively about what a really bad idea it is to raise beef as we do. "Growing the vast quantities of corn used to feed livestock in this country takes vast quantities of chemical fertilizer, which in turn takes vast quantities of oil," he wrote in the *New York Times Magazine*, for a story on beef production that he expanded in his book *The Omnivore's Dilemma*.[71] "So the modern feedlot is really a city floating on a sea of oil."

Moreover, he has helped us imagine this industrial livestock industry against a backdrop of the way we originally raised cows, which he describes with a kind of euphoric admiration for the simple logic of how animals and humans coexisted for thousands of years, the self-sustaining closed circuit of animals fed not by expensive oil but rather by sunlight.

"The reciprocal relationship between cows and grass is one of nature's underappreciated wonders," he writes. He notes how sun feeds the grass, the grass feeds the cows, and the cows fertilize the earth that grows the grass. About the grasses specifically, he writes that they "offer ruminants a plentiful, exclusive meal. For cows, sheep, and other grazers

---

71 "Power Steer," *New York Times Magazine*, March 31, 2002.

have the unique ability to convert grass—which single-stomached creatures like us can't digest—into high-quality protein" via numerous beneficial gut bacteria. Moreover, he says, "so long as the rancher practices rotational grazing, it is a sustainable, solar-powered system for producing food on land too arid or hilly to grow anything else."

Harold McGee, in *On Food and Cooking*, likewise calls attention to the power of sunlight when he discusses the humble chicken egg. "The yolk is a stockpile of fuel obtained by the hen from seeds and leaves, which are in turn stockpiles of the sun's radiant energy. The yellow pigments that gave the yolk its name also come directly from plants, where they protect the chemical machinery of photosynthesis from being overwhelmed by the sun. So the egg does embody the chain of creation, from the developing chick back through the hen to the plants that fed her, and then to the ultimate source of life's fire, the yellow of the sky. An egg is the sun's light refracted into life."

It's hard for me not to buy into the logic of this and even be inspired by it. Modern agriculture broke this natural chain when we introduced corn (89 percent of it genetically modified, according to the USDA) into not just beef but into too many items in a grocery store to count. The current system doesn't care that the corn that's fed to beef eventually makes the animals sick, which requires all kinds of drugs to treat all kinds of maladies. The current system cares only about speed: Cows that once took four years to grow to their optimal weight now reach that same weight in fourteen to seventeen months.

Pollan's writing has no doubt been one of the most influential factors in the now widespread availability of 100 percent grass-fed beef. Pretty much every respectable grocery store offers it today. Heinen's found a New Zealand company called PRE that sources grass-fed beef from around the world; Jeff Heinen says he personally prefers PRE over all their beef.

The desire for 100 percent grass-fed beef is particularly strong in the United States because most of our beef is raised on grain, and because of all the media surrounding the perceived benefits of grass-fed. Interestingly, in Europe, grass-fed beef is not in demand and is thus not a marketing issue; there, the focus is on non-GMO feed. I asked my friend David Lebovitz—a former Chez Panisse pastry chef, food writer, and long-time Paris expat—what the mood in Europe was regarding the superiority of grass-fed beef. He replied, "No one in France ever talks about grass-fed or what cows eat. . . . I've never seen anyone selling beef as grass-fed." [72]

One of my favorite Ohio farmers, Aaron Miller, raises some of the tastiest grass-fed beef that I've had. Miller explained that one of the critical factors is getting the cow to the correct weight, allowing enough fat to develop. Aaron sells all his meat (including pork and chicken) personally, making weekly deliveries to those who order it in Cleveland, about an hour and a half drive from his farm on Ohio's eastern boarder. He could probably raise enough cattle to supply a grocery store, his wife, Melissa, told me, but they would need significant lead time; Heinen's had been in talks with the Millers, but there were numerous obstacles, from pricing to processing and distributing, and discussion was tabled.

It's difficult to raise great grass-fed beef, though clearly beef farmers are learning and continuing to improve the quality of it, as Aaron's beef proved to me. For his *New York Times Magazine* article on industrial beef, written in 2002, Pollan compared grass-fed beef with grain-fed industrial beef, and he found the grass-fed beef "uneven." Too tough, he said, but its flavor was "much more interesting." Likewise, the grass-fed beef I've eaten ranges wildly in flavor and texture.

More intriguing to me was that in 2002, Pollan seemed to have had a hard time getting his hands on grass-fed beef—"Eventually," he wrote,

---

72 I traveled recently to southwestern Ireland, where the countryside is filled with lambs and cows grazing on the abundant grass. I visited Sean Murphy, an American who lives in Dingle and operates Murphy's Ice Cream, a fabulous small chain using raw milk from Kerry cows, a rare breed native to Ireland and one of the oldest in Europe. The farmer was making a delivery when I was there, pouring milk out of big, old-fashioned milk cans. It was some of the best milk I've ever tasted. The butter, too, is extraordinary because of the ways the dairy cows are raised. (Kerrygold sells their excellent butter in Ireland and in the United States. Tellingly, the butter sold here notes on the label that it comes from grass-fed cows; labels for butter sold in Ireland make no mention of what the cows were fed.) When I brought up the trend toward grass-fed beef in America with Sean, he chuckled and said, "I know. But that sounds ridiculous here. People here would say, 'What *else* would you feed them?'"

"I found a farmer in the Hudson Valley who sold me a quarter of a grass-fed Angus steer." He did say that hormone- and antibiotic-free beef was available at the time, but it was scarce. He noted that American regulators permit hormone implants, which speed growth, "even though measurable hormone residues do turn up in the meat." And he said that the use of hormones was an all-but-uniform practice in the industry. One of the ranchers he spoke with told him, "I'd love to give up hormones. If the consumer said, 'We don't want hormones,' we'd stop in a second. The cattle could get along much better without them. But the market's not there, and as long as my competitor is doing it, I've got to do it, too."

By the time *The Omnivore's Dilemma* was published in 2006, Whole Foods had already begun to change this dynamic, which may explain why the quote didn't end up in the book. Just four years after Pollan's article came out, rapid changes to our beef industry were well underway.

Tom Heinen is passionate about the meat he sells—pork, veal, Ohio-grown chicken, turkey, duck, elk, rabbit, bison, and pheasant. Heinen's works with a few companies to supply their pork, Indiana Packers being the largest, processing 3.5 million pounds of pork daily. Heinen's also sells Niman Ranch pork; Niman Ranch works with many hundreds of smaller farmers who raise pigs without antibiotics or hormones, and with a 100 percent vegetarian diet. Niman is viewed as one of the shining examples of large-scale meat production that can claim a genuine adherence to sustainable and humane livestock farming.

But beef is a kind of touchstone for Tom. He frequently notes that his grandfather began as a butcher, that Heinen's began as a butcher's shop, and he surely inherited some of those cutter genes. When Tom began at Heinen's in the late 1970s, the stores received beef the way they had been receiving it for decades: whole cattle sawn into quarters, hanging from racks in the trucks. The butchers at each store would heft the two-hundred-pound sections of beef one by one into the store and begin breaking them all down, a total of 475 for the nine stores they had at the time. Tom remembers at the store where he worked, store #04 on Green Road, they received more than a hundred cattle a week, or four hundred quarters. In order to use the whole animal, Tom said, "there was a lot of creative butchering." People don't want roasts in the summer; they want steaks. So they had to butcher steaks from what they had.

Beginning in the 1960s, packers began reducing the quarters to more uniform pieces that could be boxed. Hanging beef in trucks was an inefficient way to transport the cattle. Once reduced to boxes, called "cattle pack," more cattle per truck could be shipped. But they still delivered the entire animal. It just arrived in cardboard.

By the 1990s, "cattle pack" fell out of favor as retailers wanted the packers to do more of the butchering for them, and to be able to pick and choose the cuts they wanted. The major packers fulfilled this desire. Because of their scale, these operations could break down the beef more efficiently than a grocer could, passing on the cost to the grocer, who in turn saved money on labor. They would begin to send boxes of specific parts: boxes of rumps, of strip loins, of whole briskets. And stores could order less of the cuts they'd previously had a hard time selling (they could reduce the number of rump roasts in the summer, for instance), and order more of what they could sell when they needed it (standing rib roasts and tenderloins at Christmas time, when demand goes through the roof).

This is how Heinen's receives its beef. They employ their own cutters at the Heinen's warehouse to turn those huge rumps into roasts and the strip loins into strip steaks, porterhouse steaks, and rib eyes. The 92 percent lean ground beef arrives in ten-pound tubes. Heinen's will regrind much of this, adding various quantities of fat from the trim of butchering so that they can also offer 90 percent, 85 percent, and 80 percent lean ground beef, selling it loose and sending hundreds of pounds through a machine that shoots out patties with the sound of an air gun.[73]

....

73 I'd always wondered how a store could be so exact with the fat percentage. It turns out they use an Anyl Ray Fat Analyzer. Thirteen pounds of ground beef is packed into a cylinder and fitted into a machine that sends x-rays through the meat; mineral-rich meat absorbs gamma rays, but the fat does not, and from the amount of gamma rays not absorbed, the machine calculates the fat percentage.

Large whole cuts keep well, and the warehouse receives two deliveries a week. But once the beef is broken down into the various cuts, its shelf life begins to diminish. The cutters begin work at midnight, so that the meat that arrives at each store has been cut that day.

All this beef is broken down into an astonishing number of cuts: top round, thin top round, tri-tip, London broil, eye of round, cube steak, sirloin, tender roast, strip loin roast, beef fondue, beef kebab, flank steak, sirloin steak, bone-in tenderloin, Delmonico steak (thick and thin), chuck steak, chuck roast, English roast, Spencer roast, brisket, flanken, flatiron steak, beef shank center-cut bone-in, beef suet, family packs of strips, short ribs, porterhouses—seventy-nine different cuts in all on the daily order sheet, not including twenty-five different SKUs of ground beef, including a variety of value-added burgers.

We're still a nation of meat eaters, but our consumption of beef has dropped considerably. In the seventies, Heinen's was averaging forty-seven cattle per week per store. Today, they need about fifteen per week per store—a decline of more than two-thirds.

There are sixty packers in the United States that slaughter cattle for our beef hunger, but four of them control 80 percent of the market: Tyson, Cargill, National, and JBS USA, a subsidiary of Brazil-based JBS, the biggest meat purveyor in the world.

"It's a bizarre, dysfunctional system," Tom told me. "The beef industry is an example where the originator of the product has no connection whatsoever with the finished product. It's all about weight-to-grain ratio with no concern for how the finished product tastes." Typically a small rancher raises calves and sells them to the packers. While these ranchers surely care about the calves, they have no control over—and therefore little investment in—how the calf is raised once it leaves the ranch. The company that brings a cow to weight is primarily concerned with speed, the weight-to-grain plus time equation. "If the commodity system worked, I wouldn't need to find meat programs," said Tom.

All of Heinen's beef is "natural," so called because it's raised without hormones and without antibiotics for the last two-thirds of its life. About 30 percent of their beef comes from a JBS packer, which now has a no-hormones, no-antibiotics program, processed in Arizona and sold under the Cedar River Farms label. The rest comes from a single small packer, Brandt Beef. "Some people would consider us huge, but really we're a gnat on a rhino," Eric Brandt, managing partner of the company his father started, told me. He said they raise and slaughter thirty thousand cattle a year.

"And what would a rhino do?" I asked.

"Ooh, thirty thousand a day," Eric said.

That's a number hard to comprehend, one company slaughtering so many fourteen-hundred-pound beasts, processing forty-two million pounds of animal. Daily.

Tom is proud of Heinen's beef program, especially the Brandt operation, which sells a line of beef they call True Natural ("There are a lot of faux naturals out there," Eric said)—beef that has never had hormones and has been given no antibiotics after three hundred days, for the last two-thirds of its life, time enough for any residual antibiotics to have left the system. They give antibiotics only to sick animals; the animals aren't mass medicated as those raised in massive CAFOs routinely are. I called Eric to find out how their operation works. It seemed small enough to manage a specific kind of care for the animals as well as the finished product, and also to manage the impact that feedlots have on the environment in terms of animal waste and chemical fertilizers. But it was also large enough to deliver this more-cared-for beef to numerous smaller grocery chains of the kind I'd been focusing on.

Eric Brandt and his family raise a rotating herd of twenty-five thousand True Natural cattle at any one time on their ranch in Brawley, California, about a hundred miles east of San Diego. Southern California has one of the largest dairy concentrations in the country, he said. These dairy farms need only the heifers; they have no need for bull calves born on their farms. Calf nurseries developed around these dairy farms to take the male calves and raise them. Brandt works with one nursery that raises them to his specifications. After the calves have spent four months at the nursery and grown to about three hundred pounds, they are delivered to the Brandt ranch, which raises them in pens and feeds them a mixture they've developed of steamed flaked corn, delivered from the Midwest by train, along with local Imperial Valley alfalfa and Bermuda and Sudan grasses, which they grow. They compost the cattle manure and use this to fertilize the fields; they also sell this organic compost to nearby organic farms.

The steers live in rotating pens for a year, until they're ready for "harvesting." The cattle are then trucked to Harris Ranch Beef in Selma, California, a five-hour drive north. Harris processes the cattle to Brandt's specifications, puts it in boxes with the Brandt label on it, and trucks it to Heinen's once a week.

In the 1990s, concerns arose about the impact of bovine growth hormones in our meat and what it does to our bodies. And it was at about this time that Whole Foods was expanding throughout the country, continuing its mission to offer only natural products. Seeking to fulfill this demand, a company called Vintage Beef formed as a custom feeding company, wherein they gathered forward-thinking cattle feeders to raise animals to their specifications. The Brandts were among those raising cattle for Vintage Beef, which slaughtered Holsteins at a facility in Los Angeles for Whole Foods. Whole Foods ended up moving to their own natural cattle feeding program elsewhere and shipping the meat to their California stores. But other area grocers had found that their customers now wanted this hormone-free, antibiotic-free beef and needed to find suppliers. One of these grocers, Gelson's, then a family-owned chain much like Heinen's,[74] turned to another local packer and other local producers, including the Brandts, who, for a variety of reasons, were eager to continue to develop a hormone-free program.

Because Gelson's was big enough, but not too big, the Brandts could continue raising their cattle this way. Indeed, Eric says he learned an enormous amount from the Gelson's meat buyers in terms of what they wanted, the kind of quality they were after. So in this case, it was the grocer who was educating the rancher in raising and butchering cattle for the optimum quality the Gelson's customer wanted.

74 Like so many smallish, family grocery stores, it sold to a global private investment firm in 2014 and now has twenty-eight stores.

The Brandts ultimately invested in renovating the old National Beef plant, which is fifteen minutes from their ranch, meaning a less stressful (and less expensive) trip for the animal, and opened it in December of 2016. The animal handling area was designed by Temple Grandin, who has created what are considered the most humane systems for taking the animals from a pen to the actual moment of stunning and slaughter, reducing the stress on the animal. Brandt will process five to six hundred cattle a week at this new facility, but will also have the capacity to slaughter for their competitors—ranchers growing grass-fed beef, kosher beef, and others—when their new facility opens.

"I consider myself like a wine maker," Eric told me, about the raising of beef. "Just because you have great grapes doesn't mean you're gonna make great wine. But you can't make a great wine without great grapes. And we have some of the greatest grapes in the world, if you will. There's a craft that goes into it.

"One of the things we're trying to do is foster respect for the employees, building a team and culture, but also respect for the animals we're sacrificing. And then after it's slaughtered to treat each cut like it's filet mignon. It's not about how to get that meat into a box as fast as you can. It's how can we treat that piece of meat with the ultimate respect."

Tom Heinen found the Brandts a few years ago, after the all-natural beef vendor they had been using could no longer supply all they needed. Tom was pleased with the quality of the Holstein steer, with the way they were raised, and with the Brandt family itself.

"Heinen's is one of the few customers that gets it," Eric told me. "They know what they want and they have high expectations."

I was curious about this rancher's thoughts on corn, having bought into Pollan's persuasive corn-is-harmful-in-just-about-every-way argument, and knowing that Brandt operates a feedlot that uses corn, albeit mixed with plentiful roughage of alfalfa and grass.

"We've figured out how to do it naturally," Eric said, noting that their animals don't get the same grain-related illnesses found in the big feedlots. "I think corn has gotten a bad rap. Anything in excess is not a good thing. We eat too many Twinkies and doughnuts, it's not a good thing. There's nothing wrong with corn. It's more nutritious than grass.

"The argument that cattle were never meant to eat corn is a fallacy," he said. "You give cattle an option to go into a field of corn or to go into a field of grass, they're going to mow down that corn, because there's more nutritional value in the corn. In excess, is it a bad thing, yes. So you give them a balanced, rationed diet. It's just being good stewards, good animal husbandry. We believe in animal husbandry more than we believe in animal science. You take care of them and you don't need to add all these things."

I asked for Eric's thoughts on grass-fed beef.

"I respect it," he said. "I have friends who raise grass-fed beef, and we're going to process it [in the new facility]. It's just a different market. We cater to a crowd that wants to know that what they're eating is safe and good for them, but they want a good steak, a steak that's tender and juicy."

He also noted, without my prompting, his desire for more transparency in the industry generally, something everyone would like to see—from Pollan (who was not allowed anywhere near the kill floor when reporting his *Times* article) to animal activists to me.

"As an industry we've got to be more open," he said, when describing the refurbished facility in Brawley. "Because what we're doing is not bad. Because the industry is guarded and not letting people in, people make speculations. We've got to be more open so people can at least see what we're doing. It's nothing scary like these movies are portraying, what we're doing to beef. It's part of life, it's a part of nature."

Heinen's still takes pride in using as much of the animal as they can, and for this work, they get special pricing from Brandt. They still have to purchase extra strip steaks in the summer to meet this seasonal demand, and more rib roasts and tenderloins in December, but they do their best to stick with total utilization.

"Heinen's gets it," Eric said. "They take the majority of the animal, so we can do what we do and raise beef, and we're not just pulling tenderloins out. They utilize different beef cuts and that helps make *us* sustainable. So when people talk about sustainability, it's the chefs and the retail buyer just as much as it's us on the ranch utilizing the compost."

This notion of using the whole animal, and not just its finer cuts, is something everyone from Pollan to chef-author Dan Barber says is critical if we're going to raise animals sustainably.

In addition to the JBS and Brandt beef, Heinen's has begun a local beef program. This year, they'll bring in eighty-five head, according to Eric Besselman, head of meat at Heinen's, up from sixty-four last year. And they can do so only because Bob Boliantz runs a small USDA-certified slaughter facility about an hour southwest of the city, a rarity in America. Hoping to interest more Cleveland chefs in the local beef supply, I asked Bob if I could bring some friends to have a look. Unlike the big packing facilities that prevented Pollan from watching the actual kill, skinning, and evisceration, he welcomed us. We were able to watch the whole process from behind a large plate-glass window. A lack of certified slaughter facilities throughout the country is one of the main obstacles keeping local beef from customers who want it.

I believe it's important to witness a kill if you are going to eat meat. Those of us who think and care about food, cooking, and eating have made the ethics of eating meat an issue, and rightly so. Also, we are just now recognizing the environmental impact of eating meat—issues of pollution, greenhouse gas emissions, water use, and the amount of oil required for feed production and transportation in raising cattle. We kill sentient animals for our nourishment and pleasure. I don't believe we should do this blithely, but it's a fact that's easy to forget for people who throw a package of ground beef or two plastic-wrapped pork chops into their shopping cart. To witness a kill is to inform yourself about what you are eating.

It should be clear by now that I am an advocate of eating the flesh and organs of animals (and using their bones for stock and gelatin, their hides for leather). It may be a facile argument and one that Peter Singer, the most eloquent writer on the immorality of raising animals for food, would quickly undo. But there are good reasons for eating meat. As Karen Wise, my friend and copyeditor, pointed out in our discussions about this book, humans evolved to eat meat—healthy omnivores with sharp teeth. I would take it even further—that to refrain from eating in the manner that made us who we are is to distance ourselves from our own humanity (more later about how *cooking* this meat also helped define our humanity).

The meat, dairy, and eggs from livestock give us an abundance of what we need to be healthy; those who avoid these foods, Karen noted—vegans, for instance—have to be diligent in supplementing their diets in order to maintain their health. She and I both recognize that this is a choice that we human beings get to make for ourselves.

Also, I believe existence is an end in itself, and if we didn't raise pigs and chickens and cows for their meat, eggs, and milk, they would exist, if at all, only in the wild, a more cruel and unforgiving place than a farm or feedlot. We would likely get rid of them for being a nuisance, scarcely different than rats and mice, the lives of which most seem to have no moral qualms about extinguishing. Of course, if great numbers of us were to keep them as house pets, that would be a truly humane situation. When my daughter was young, she repeatedly asked if we could get a pig as a pet; I said, "Sure, if you can find one that can be potty trained." She produced an internet source, but I had to renege even on that. Pigs and cows as pets aren't practical where most people live.

We are so removed from the source of our meat, given our industrial food system, that we may not recognize the consequences involved in meat's being available to us. It's difficult to imagine an individual rib eye steak, in its Styrofoam tray wrapped in plastic, as part of an entire cow. I never truly understood the astonishing size of a cow until I saw a kill. The cow was stunned, hoisted, bled, and skinned; but the moment of understanding came when a worker unleashed the entire contents of its insides. The viscera filled a bin the size of an industrial trash can. These are enormous beasts.

A few years earlier, I'd bought two pigs from an Amish farmer, and I was able to visit the farm and see how they lived, what they fed on, where they slept. When they were ready for slaughter, I drove to the farm and helped herd the pigs into the back of a truck, which I followed to a man named Yoder, who agreed to slaughter them for me provided I didn't sell the meat; he wasn't USDA certified and served only his community. Mr. Yoder's was a wood structure, floor covered with hay. He stunned the first pig with a captive bolt, chained its legs, and hoisted it. He called me over with my orange Home Depot bucket (I'd asked for the blood as well, wanting to make proper blood sausage) and told me to ready it as he stuck the pig with a small knife, its blade thin from years of honing, and out the blood poured. When the blood had drained and the pig was still, Mr. Yoder maneuvered the block and tackle so that the pig hung before a gray plastic tub. He opened the pig up, and the viscera spilled out in all its reeking glory. I'd asked for the organs and wanted to harvest the intestines to use for the blood sausage. I'd also wanted the liver, but, as we examined it, Mr. Yoder pointed with his knife to various white spotty patches and said, "Parasites." The livers would be unwise to use, he said. The intestines were hot and full and it was every bit as disgusting as one would imagine. I was more fascinated than unnerved, though, and felt lucky to watch these slaughters, to witness the act that allows us to eat meat.

I often tell a story about Thomas Keller, chef-owner of the French Laundry and other acclaimed restaurants. When he was a young chef in the Hudson Valley in the 1980s, he asked his rabbit purveyor, "Next time, would you bring them to me alive?" The young chef figured if he was going to cook rabbit, he should know all he could about it. In short it was a hard and wrenching experience, killing that first bunny, and then recognizing he had nine more to go. But it taught him a lesson: He would treat this rabbit as well as he could; he would elevate his own skills to honor these rabbits whose lives he'd taken. They would be exquisite. He would waste nothing.

The most moving kill for me was of one of the smaller animals we cook for food: the chicken. Billions are slaughtered in the United States every year and we scarcely give it a thought. But do it yourself and things change. It happened on a farm in Medina, Ohio, along with a hobby grower, a record store clerk named Bradley Cramer, who held the bird upside down in a funnel so that it was disoriented and calm, its head sticking through the narrow opening. I pinched the skin at the throat as instructed, inserted the blade, cut the jugular, feeling the stiff windpipe behind which it ran. And soon the chicken had been bled out. My heart hammered against my ribs and I was shaking.

I went on to learn from Bradley how to eviscerate the chicken, placing it backbone down and making a small slit in the belly, just below the bottom of the rib cage. I squeezed my hand through the opening, surprised by the heat, and pulled out the innards. This was the first time it looked like the chicken I was used to seeing on my cutting board at home. A few moments later it was in an ice bath to chill completely. I made sure to identify it so that I could bring home "my" chicken, the one whose life I'd taken, to roast it properly. I never took such care in roasting a chicken as I did that bird.

The actual cutting of the chicken's throat, I won't forget. The adrenaline, my racing heart, the deep unease at the visceral sense of wrongness of the act along with the intellectual understanding of the necessity of it if we choose to get our nourishment from meat. I'm sure I'd get used to it if I did a hundred a day, but the first one made its impact, and I would urge anyone who intends to eat meat to do it yourself in order to appreciate the magnitude and meaning of eating something as pedestrian as a chicken Caesar salad or as sublime as a perfectly roasted chicken at home.[75]

All of the above—my understanding of industrial meat, our ethically conflicted beef production system, Tom Heinen's devotion to offering high-quality meat to the hundreds of thousands who shop at his and Jeff's grocery store—are the reasons I flew out to Idaho to see Brian Bean and the Lava Lakes lamb. Tom and I arrived in Boise the day before our

75 I filmed the evisceration process and wrote about it here: ruhlman.com/2012/06/how-chickens-are-processed. Vivian Goodman, a reporter for NPR affiliate WKSU, came along for her own story: wksu.org/news/feature/quickbites/32846. The experience wasn't fun, but it was deeply instructive.

trek into the Sawtooth National Forest, along with Chris Sutliff, sales and marketing manager for Mountain States Rosen, a Denver-area lamb and veal company that processes Bean's lambs, as well as those of about 130 other family ranchers. Bean's wife, Kathleen, met us at the airport and drove us the hour west to the Sun Valley Inn near Ketchum. On the drive, Kathleen, age fifty-six, trim, attractive, with shoulder-length auburn hair, told me their story.

Brian was an investment banker in the Bay area (though I noted in his Copper Creek Capital Group bio that he had a dual major in botany and molecular biology at Pomona College before heading to business school), and she was a fund-raiser for the Nature Conservancy. They loved heading east to the mountains of Wyoming, so they began to look for several acres to buy near Jackson Hole. But Kathleen discovered that they could buy five thousand acres in Idaho, two hundred miles west of Jackson Hole, for what it would cost to buy five acres near that tony city. So they looked into it and began buying up ranches in Idaho, realizing they could have an impact on the conservation of this pristine land. Some of these ranches happened to have a lot of sheep on them. "We wanted to leave the landscape better than when we came," Kathleen said. "And, we fell in love with sheep."

So they became sheep ranchers. And rather than hiring a trained rancher to oversee daily management, they hired a conservationist and had him trained as a rancher. Beginning in 1999 they bought twenty-four thousand acres. But, more important, they knew they could lease huge swaths of the nine hundred thousand acres of national park land as part of the Land Conservation Act, more than enough space to graze several thousand sheep.

The lambing happens in January and February, ideally south of here near the Snake River, where it is warmer, Kathleen told us. Their two thousand ewes birth three thousand lambs in an average year. The baby lambs are never weaned. After four months, they are simply turned out onto pasture, where they naturally begin feeding on spring grasses. During the course of the next several months, they head north, grazing and traveling more than a hundred miles into the Sawtooth National Forest.

Midway through our drive, Kathleen pulled off the two-lane highway to show us a fifty-foot wooden suspension bridge about a yard wide, the kind of bridge whose rails you hang on to tightly the moment you skeptically set foot on it. "You should see it when thousands of lambs cross this," Kathleen said. "It's an amazing sight." And it truly did bring to mind the days of Wild West ranching. Though crossing the two-lane highway after the bridge was a considerably more modern affair.

The lambs graze until July, when they are trucked sixteen hours to the nearest slaughter and packing facility outside Denver—the lack of slaughter facilities is a regrettable fact of the meat industry generally. But till that day, she says, these lambs live the way they evolved to live, presumably in bucolic contentment and ease, not to mention protected by the shepherds from the wolves and coyotes that roam these hills.

That evening we met Brian, and the five of us dined at a Sun Valley restaurant that serves Lava Lakes lamb.

Wine poured, Brian having recounted their story, Tom said to Brian, "I just want to tell you what an amazing thing you've done, creating this brand from scratch. I've never done a *seasonal* meat product."

"I really appreciate that," Brian said.

He sensed that Tom understood the dysfunctional meat system in America and went on to talk openly about his goals and struggles in the lambing business. Of the latter, it was a matter of finding more land where more ewes could give birth. Winters were too cold here, and they needed more land farther south. In order to be truly viable to grocery stores, he believed he'd need twelve thousand ewes, he said, not two thousand, a goal he was working toward.

That evening, I saw how a grocer develops a personal relationship with the producer of a specialty meat for his grocery stores, a product that is extremely difficult to manufacture, as it were. The lambs must be guided through hundred-mile treks and rickety bridge crossings, and protected from wolves, animals that want them even more than a grocery store shopper with tons of meat to choose from. And I also saw how a rancher gains a new understanding of what a grocer needs and why, and how much work a grocer puts into creating "brand awareness" of a special product and gets the story of that product into the world. I witnessed the forging of a genuine connection between the man who births and raises meat and the man who sells that meat to customers thousands of miles away—a rare circumstance in both the grocery business and the livestock business.

Tom went to great lengths during the meal to describe how Heinen's advertises the Lava Lakes lamb, creates compelling signage announcing it, conveys the story of Lava Lakes—and how successful it has been. They receive more lamb from Sutliff's company under the brand Shepherd's Pride. This lamb sells fine, but the Lava Lakes sells out because of their marketing and, of course, the quality of the product. "The choices have never been greater," Tom said to Brian, "so stores need to explain the story to customers." The story does two things: It personalizes the product, and it also identifies the source of the product and its maker for the increasing number of people who want to know where their food comes from.[76]

Brian said he had no idea Heinen's did anything of the kind. He presumed they simply put out the Lava Lakes lamb with the rest of the meat. He seemed genuinely surprised and pleased to have this new appreciation for what a grocer can do for his product.

After our return to the Sun Valley Inn, Tom and I stopped for a drink at the bar before turning in. I asked his thoughts about Brian and he said he liked him very much, was impressed by his intelligence. He took a sip of his whiskey and said, "But believe me, before I leave here, I'm going to address the question of whether or not he can supply me the lamb I need on a regular basis." He paused. "Otherwise he'll just be one more blowhard promising what he can't deliver."

And indeed Tom did just this, first thing the next day. Brian joined Tom, Chris Sutliff, and me for breakfast at the inn. Pretty much as soon as Tom's egg-white frittata and Brian's eggs Benedict arrived, Tom said

....

76 Heinen's uses a third-party verification company called Where Food Comes From for many of their products (wherefoodcomesfrom.com).

to Brian, "I've got to have animals or I don't have a program. I don't care how long the season is. Up in Alaska, the Copper River, they manage that incredibly well. They count them and they turn it off," he said, referring to the state's quota, "and when they do, that's it. So I don't care how long the season is, I just need to know in advance that I'll have a season every year. Because if you can't guarantee I'll have lamb each year I don't have a program."

Tom said he'd need twelve hundred head. Chris told Tom he'd need six thousand head to fill his own current demand for Lava Lakes lamb, or more than double what Brian is able to raise now.

Brian said, "We have to grow. I understand what you're saying and I appreciate your candor."

Chris knew this was a problem and said, "I've had to short some of our regular customers."

"Really?" Tom said. "Short them?"

"I've had to tell some stores you're not going to get any Lava Lakes lamb," Chris said.

Tom looked at Brian and said, "Well, that can't happen to us."

Brian nodded and broke the yolk of his second egg.

Soon we were on our way in Brian's truck up into the Sawtooth National Forest.

The four of us follow Claudio from his tiny trailer home up a crest along the edge of a range of Douglas firs. The forest is fragrant and cool as we follow Claudio, up and up. Brian stops to point out various plants, a wild rose, wild geranium, a mustard-like plant. "The biodiversity is very high," he says. "We believe that [the lambs] take on the flavor of the plants they eat." He stops to pick some huckleberries for us to taste. He spots a rubber boa, a rare find as these docile snakes prefer dusk and dark. "There haven't been a lot of rattlers this year," Brian says.

After about forty-five minutes we are out of the forest and into the bright day, blue skies with a few cirrus clouds high overhead and rolling hills of sage scrub and brambles, tall brown grasses, nothing but hills in every direction. We'd hike up one hill, tall enough to prevent any view, only to get to the top and see another taller crest in front of us. And down we'd go, Tom's shins bleeding from the brush and brambles. It's hot and dry—this *is* rattlesnake terrain. One hundred species of birds are also at home in this national park, and these grassy hills and forest glades are home to black bears and mountain lions.

Up and up we climb. And then down steep declines toward an even higher hill, which Claudio has already reached; turning 180 degrees, he is scanning the landscape looking for the sheep. At the top of each crest, I can see for miles and miles. A carpet of tall golden grasses before me dropping off to nothing and beyond, hills of more golden grass, tree-filled valleys and more hills beyond that. At about the two-hour mark of our hike, after traversing innumerable crests and valleys, we pause for a breather and a drink of water. Brian removes his cap, scratches his head, looks around, and says, "I hope we find them." He puts his cap back on and says, "We may not be able to." And he starts down a steep slope.

I think, *Wait a minute. I've traveled two thousand miles to see a rancher and his animals, and we may not be able to* see *the animals?* And then I think, *Well, we're on nine hundred thousand acres—I guess it's a possibility.* And then I think, *I have been following for two hours a rancher who has no idea where the animals he's raising are.* I had never encountered this before. Every farm I've been to that raised animals, you could pretty much point to them. If it were a bigger place, you might have to take a short drive, and then point. This is why we have fences.

"Sheep don't like fences," Brian tells me.

Tom breathes heavily behind me.

In one gulley, Claudio tells us to wait as he hikes up the next hill to determine if he can see anything before making us climb up. He walks the crest and motions us forward. Not that he sees anything. By the two-and-a-half-hour mark I'm ready to head back. But on we hike.

Claudio is short, in the mid-five-foot range, with an oval face of a light brown, almost reddish, color, broad nose, dark eyes and eyebrows. He wears a heavy cotton shirt of faded lavender, sleeves rolled down and buttoned even in this heat, jeans, and a Lava Lakes cap. He speaks no English that I heard. He is Brian's lead guy out here.

Around the time I am ready to give up, I see Claudio squat in a patch of dirt. He stands and points and speaks to Brian in Spanish. Brian tells us that Claudio has found a hoof print. And on we trek, Claudio following the shepherd's horse's tracks. Tracking Old West style. I imagine the sheep on the run from us, looking back and saying to each other, "Who *are* those guys?" Claudio is searching not for the sheep but for the shepherd, a fellow Peruvian, Leone. Leone is a new hire. The usual shepherd, Mario, is on vacation. It is Leone's job to look after the sheep, so if we can find Leone, we can find the sheep.

We descend one steep crest and ascend another. And another. And then Claudio makes out a small dot on a crest about a half mile off. Brian says, "He sees Leone's horse." To himself, with what sounds like concern, he says, "But where's Leone?"

At last we reach the twenty-seven-year-old mare, who will not budge from her spot. Some Border Collies gallop up around the horse, and suddenly I don't feel as if we are lost. And I sense the lamb are close.

Scanning the valley with his binoculars, Brian says, "There they are." (It turns out they are sheep binoculars, not bird binoculars.) Barely visible is a gray patch way down in the valley. We begin a careful descent through grass and brambles, sideways, one hand on the ground because it is so steep.

And there it is, a flock of sheep, grazing in a small damp pocket behind a cove of aspens, baaing and munching grass.

Claudio returns eventually, having located Leone. Leone had realized that a large group of sheep had split from the flock in the night and he'd had to find them. He would mount the old mare and with the dogs help them rejoin the flock. How does a shepherd know from looking at what should be two thousand sheep that some are missing? Most of the ewes are light gray, but the rancher puts one black ewe for every hundred light ewe into the flock (along with a couple of studs to initiate the breeding). If the shepherd counts only seven black sheep in the flock, he knows a large number of ewes have gone missing. One of the reasons this happens is wolves and coyotes. Brian, a conservationist, is opposed to killing animals that might prey on his sheep and so uses a variety of tactics to protect them.

Foremost are the Pyrenean Mountain Dogs, or Great Pyrenees, big animals that ward off the wolves. In addition to dogs, there are several ways to protect the sheep without resorting to shooting the wolves. Sheep will bed down for the night in one spot, close together, and the shepherd sleeps with his flock. He will urinate all around the flock's "bed ground," which repels wolves. In areas where wolves are known to be prevalent, they may put up temporary fencing with red flags around the flock to deter wolves. The herders carry powerful lights that scare the wolves. And they have a variety of noise-making devices, such as starter pistols and air horns. Sometimes two herders will bed down with the sheep. And they carry satellite phones to call for reinforcements, though these are not always reliable in the mountains.

Having observed the contented ewes, and with Brian satisfied that the errant sheep will be returned to the flock, we all head back toward Claudio's trailer. We have hiked more or less in a circle, as it turns out, and descended into the valley, so it is then a short mile hike on flat land.

"The more we learned about our food system, the more we hated it," Brian says, when I ask why he does what he does, given that he was perfectly successful in the business world. "It's grotesque. All the antibiotics in feedlots, resistant bacteria, strep, staph—it's a shit show. Part of me believes that it's people or outfits like Lava Lakes in our own small way that can have an impact on our food system."

We walk in abundant sunlight, light that feeds many kinds of plants and grasses, some beneficial to lambs, some toxic (lambs instinctively find the most nutritious ones on their own and avoid the toxic or even benign plants, Bean tells me). The ewes we found were eating these plants, feeding the bodies that would in the coming winter bear lambs—thus turning the pure wild grasses of a protected national park into flesh.

"There's a huge amount of talk about that now," Brian continues. "But before Michael Pollan wrote that article, people didn't know. People just ate what was sold. You look at it now fourteen years later, there's a revolution that's happening. When I look back, the one legacy I'm most passionate about is selling a high-quality product [from] a high-integrity outfit that is trying to do the right thing for the animals and for the environment."

Back at the farmhouse, Brian rolls out the maps of the territory, shows us his acreage, and also the land farther south by the Snake River where the winters are milder. He badly needs to increase the number of ewes who could give birth in January, and sheds to shelter their off-spring. His acres are simply too cold at that time of year for birthing.

To no one in particular, Brian Bean concludes with a remark about Tom: "This gentleman is going to make us a better lamb producer."

Almost exactly a year after my trip to Idaho to visit the lamb farmer, in mid-July, I happened to be eating lunch at the bar at Jean-Georges, one of Manhattan's four-star restaurants. The kitchen sent out a lamb chop to me. It was delicious, and I asked my server where the lamb came from. She returned from the kitchen to say, "This lamb is from Niman Ranch," and then, with evident excitement, she added, "But in two weeks we'll be getting in Lava Lakes lamb!"

I asked to speak with executive chef Mark Lapico, when he had a moment to break from a busy lunch service. I told him about my trip to Idaho. He said he was out there a few years before and did virtually the same thing I'd done, after a New York City purveyor had turned him on to Lava Lakes. We immediately compared photos on our iPhones. It had been a fabulous trip, he said.

What, I asked, impressed him?

"You can't deny the integrity of the person who owns it," Mark said of Brian Bean. "He has no ulterior motives. It's sort of crazy, and bless him for it. He allows the lambs to live a genuinely free-roaming life, the way they were intended to live their life. They have hundreds of thousands of acres of land to feed off of, and they have three saints who make sure they won't get attacked by a wolf."

"Why do you like the lamb?" I asked.

"The lamb had a distinctive flavor that I couldn't pinpoint till I went there," he explained. "And when I went there, as I was hiking through the mountains, everything I smelled when a breeze would come by is exactly what I could taste when I ate the lamb. I've never really been able to have that kind of connection with a product before. I mean, you have it a little with vegetables, but to have it with meat is very special, genuine terroir. I get blackberries, and people come up with all kinds of descriptions. But here you couldn't deny what you were tasting and smelling. Amazing. The twentieth will be the first day we get it in. It's expensive and it's not for everyone. It's the most expensive lamb we've ever bought."

The Lava Lakes lamb arrived half a week late, but Mark was pleased with it. "We only purchase the rack, then remove the breast and confit it," he told me. "The rack is roasted and served with crispy strips of the confit breast as well as a cucumber relish and crunchy garnishes. All in, this is my favorite."

I made a note to return to Jean-Georges before it was too late.

I called Brian to follow up. Was he growing? He must be if his lamb is reaching New York City. How had things changed?

I reached him in Colorado, where he was to tour the Mountain States Rosen processing plant, whose business would be expanding as they take over JBS lamb (JBS was reportedly getting out of the lamb business).

"Do you remember our hike?" I asked.

"I do!" he said. "Very distinctly. It was a great hike, you guys were in great good spirits, and it was *bizarre* to find the horse standing all alone with no herder."

Had he been able to acquire more ewes? I asked. Alas, no, he said, but he was working on a deal to acquire three to four thousand this year and land by the Snake River, where the winter was warmer. He had also gotten into the grass-fed beef business, for which he said there was enormous opportunity, especially given the seventy-eight thousand certified organic acres for raising it on. But growth, while simple in principle, was proving harder than he'd anticipated.

I told him about my Jean-Georges experience, which delighted him. Then I asked if he'd be able to supply Heinen's this year. His response was oblique:

"My objective is to supply more," Brian said. "We want to get a phone call from Tom that says, 'Stop it already, we can't take any more lamb.'" He paused. "I feel like I've let him down. We're in the lamb business for God's sake, we need to supply lamb. If you want to change the food system, you don't do it by reducing your production—you do it by increasing your production."

A couple of weeks later, I contacted Eric Besselman, Heinen's meat manager, who was happy to report that their first shipment of Lava Lakes lamb would arrive on July 31. And it was a healthy order: a few hundred pounds for each store of racks, loins, legs, shoulder cuts, and ground lamb.

16.

THIRTY-TWO THOUSAND POUNDS OF CARROTS, EVERY WEEK

The average American grocery store takes in $516,000 weekly, according to the Food Marketing Institute, or about $26.8 million annually. Multiply that by the number of grocery stores in the United States, roughly thirty-eight thousand, and we get an estimate of what we spend on groceries each year: as much as $1 trillion, which is a number too big to mean anything. But one can try to put it in context. This country's gross domestic product, the value of all goods and services sold in America in a year, is about $16 trillion—so imagine all the products, from boots to pens to cars, and services, from restaurants and hotels and spas to advertising agencies and FedEx and flower deliveries and, well, everything. Groceries make up one-sixteenth of it all. Another way to look at how big this number is this: If you were to count to one trillion, averaging a digit per second, it would take you thirty-two thousand years.

I can begin to wrap my brain around the amount of cereal we produce, or fudge-dipped pretzels—that's a factory-production issue. And America is capable of producing more food than we need. According to Marion Nestle in *What to Eat,* "There is far too much food available— 3,900 calories per day for every man, woman and child in the country." So the processing of more food than we should be eating is not hard to imagine.

But for me, produce is a different story. How is it that I can walk into any of the thirty-eight thousand grocery stores in the country and buy a pound of pea pods or broccoli or green beans 365 days of the year?

The short answer is that in winter the pea pods come from Central America, and as the seasons change, Heinen's supply will come from Mexico, then up into Texas and so on, until it's full-on summer and they can buy local. "We look at it like a clock," Terry Romp, head purchaser of local and organic produce, said, referring to the earth and its seasons.

One grocer I spoke with put it even more succinctly: At any given time of the year *some*body *some*where is growing asparagus. This is the nature of commodity crops.

Heinen's, one small family grocer, brings in eight hundred pounds of snow peas every week, week after week. Just making rough estimates, we can guess that the chain controls 10 percent of the market in this midsize Midwestern city. This would mean that about eight thousand pounds of snow peas are brought into Greater Cleveland every week, all year long. American grocery stores, roughly estimating, then, order and receive something like 1.4 million pounds of snow peas a week. That's nearly seventy million pounds a year.

The volume boggles the mind. Broccoli: Heinen's trucks about three hundred bunches of broccoli to each of its twenty-two stores every week; extrapolating, eleven million bunches of broccoli are distributed to grocery stores across the country. Every week, all year long.

Broccoli is nutrient-dense and high in vitamins C and A, and contains calcium and iron and both omega-3 and omega-6 fatty acids. A child growing up in the early twentieth century probably didn't know whether he or she liked broccoli, because it didn't really exist in America. Thomas Jefferson is said to have brought seeds back from Italy, where it has grown for centuries, and planted them here in 1767. But American farmers didn't start growing it until the 1920s. And major production didn't begin until after World War II. Now we each eat on average nearly six pounds of it a year.

Today the United States grows about two billion pounds of broccoli annually, primarily in California, but also in Arizona and Texas, and sells it for $750 million.[77] China grows nine billion pounds.

Mario Grazia is in charge of buying all the nonorganic broccoli Heinen's sells. He receives it in bins that each hold sixty heads; forty of these bins arrive two or three times a week at their warehouse, an enormous room kept at 40 degrees Fahrenheit. All day long a dozen men on pallet-lifting trucks whiz and zip around the warehouse, taking pallets

---

77 "Broccoli Production," Michael D. Orzolek et al, Penn State Extension website.

off trucks and delivering them to their designated aisles and shelves. It can get so busy in this vast, chilly warehouse, you've got to be careful you don't get run over.

The farms that Heinen's buys broccoli from are out in Salinas, California, and Yuma, Arizona. But thanks to Terry Romp, hired by Heinen's ten years ago specifically to begin sourcing local vegetables, they now have Ohio farmers who will grow broccoli for them, enough broccoli to supply all of Heinen's stores from September (it's a cool-weather crop) through the fall and sometimes up until Christmas, depending on the weather.

Another major crop produced year-round almost exclusively in Salinas and Yuma is lettuce. Of the 3.6 billion pounds of lettuce harvested each year, Salinas accounts for about 70 percent and Yuma about 20 percent. In the early twentieth century, ice shipping became possible, so that lettuce could be carried by train from Salinas throughout the country. Because leaf lettuce was considerably harder to ship, the stuff that arrived in Chicago and Cleveland and New York was head lettuce. Known as Crisphead, the heads of lettuce were loaded onto cargo cars, which were then topped with mountains of ice. When they barreled into Midwestern train stations in the 1910s and 1920s, the train cars looked like rolling icebergs, which is apparently why head lettuce is referred to as iceberg lettuce.

Thus, up until the 1980s, salads were composed of head lettuce. This was the primary lettuce available at the grocery store, and stores sold a ton of it. As well as bottled dressings to pour over it.[78] Joe Calori, one of Heinen's store managers, recalls that a single store would sell a pallet of iceberg lettuce every other day—well over two thousand heads a week. Heinen's also carried some bulk green leaf lettuce, Bibb lettuce,

....

78 According to the Association for Dressings & Sauces (yes, there is apparently an association for just about every group and trade), the first bottled salad dressing was created by Joe Marzetti, who opened a restaurant in 1896 in Columbus, Ohio; in 1919 he began packaging his popular dressings to sell to customers. In 1912, a New York delicatessen owner, Richard Hellmann, sold his mayonnaise in wooden boxes; a year later, owing to its popularity, he began to put it in jars. Mayonnaise quickly became popular and, in 1925, the Kraft Cheese Company (which began in Chicago in 1903, when James Lewis Kraft began buying cheese wholesale to sell to local merchants) purchased several regional mayonnaise makers, and soon got into the pourable salad dressing business with what it marketed as French dressing.

and romaine. And they would create some of their own mixed salad sold in foam trays (this was before plastic clamshells).

"Today we sell, at our store, about five cases per week [or 120 heads]," Joe told me. "Bag salads are king now. Iceberg lettuce is almost obsolete compared with bag salad sales. I can remember when bagged salad first came out. We carried three varieties: garden (iceberg, carrots, and red cabbage), Caesar (romaine, croutons, Caesar dressing), and European (romaine and radicchio). I remember saying to another produce manager, 'Who in this world would want to buy this stuff?'"

Joe soon found out: Sales in 2015 at Heinen's for iceberg lettuce totaled $697,624; sales for bagged salads totaled $7,166,740.

Today two companies dominate the bagged-salad market: Fresh Express and Earthbound Farm. Both companies claim to have offered the first bagged salad in the 1980s. Fresh Express, a family-run business begun in the 1920s, was sold to Chiquita in 2005 for $855 million.

Earthbound Farm was started on a few acres of land in Carmel, California, by Drew and Myra Goodman, who were determined to farm organically. When the local chef who had been their main lettuce buyer moved, they were left with an abundance of greens. Myra had made a practice of bagging a week's worth of salads for their own consumption and had found that the lettuce held up well all week. They decided to do the same with their new abundance, washing and bagging a mix of greens and selling the bags to food retailers. Business grew steadily. They were soon washing so much lettuce they needed a gentle-cycle washing machine designed by Myra's father to get the work done. Then, in 1993, Costco placed an order, soon to be followed by Walmart, and that changed everything. The Goodmans had to partner with conventional growers who knew how to grow and pack in the volume required by these major stores.

"The prewashed salad business became one of the great success stories in American agriculture during the eighties and nineties, a time when there wasn't much to celebrate, and the Goodmans are directly responsible for much of that success," wrote Michael Pollan in *The Omnivore's Dilemma*. The Earthbound processing plant in San Juan

Bautista is, according to Pollan, "a 200,000-square-foot refrigerator"; workers there wash and pack 2.5 million pounds of lettuce each week, an extraordinary volume. "They helped dethrone iceberg," Pollan wrote, "which used to dominate the Valley, by introducing dozens of different salad mixes, and innovating the way lettuces were grown, harvested, cleaned, and packed." Once again, it was not the ability to produce the food that led to industry-wide changes, but rather innovations in what to put it in and how. In this case, the solution was specially formulated bags pumped with inert gases—carbon dioxide and nitrogen, with a little oxygen left in to ward off the anaerobic botulism bacterium. These "pillow bags" both prevented spoilage bacteria from growing and stayed inflated to protect delicate lettuces.

In addition, Pollan noted, through partnerships with industrial growers, "the Goodmans have helped to convert several thousand acres of prime Salinas Valley land to organic." Today Earthbound Farm works twenty-five thousand organic acres and is the country's largest producer of organic salads. It began with three acres and took thirty years of work—but there's a lot of money to be made in lettuce if you do it right: In 2014 a company called WhiteWave Foods, which owns Horizon Organic and several other food companies, bought Earthbound Farm for $600 million.

Carrots are near and dear to my heart, in part because of their flavor, fiber, and nutrition, but also because they remind me of my dad. When I took the podium at his memorial service, before I said a word, I removed a carrot from my suit jacket pocket, took a bite, held the carrot aloft as I chewed, then returned it to my pocket, confusing just about everyone there but those who had worked with Dad at the ad agency.

Heinen's buys thirty-two thousand pounds of carrots a week, about thirteen thousand of which are organic. That's a lot of carrots for just one grocery store chain (again extrapolating for a general order of magnitude, this would mean about sixty million pounds arrive at grocery stores around the country, every week of the year). Pretty much all the carrots sold in the United States are grown in, or in the vicinity of, Bakersfield, California, about a hundred miles north of Los Angeles, by two companies, Bolthouse Farms and Grimmway Farms. Heinen's buys all their whole carrots from Grimmway,[79] a farm started in the early 1970s by Rod and Bob Grimm. Rod and Bob originally used carrots as a rotation crop, in between corn harvests, at a time when carrots weren't in the demand they are today. They moved to Bakersfield in 1981 to focus full-time on carrots, where the climate allows for two crops a year in what are clearly ideal conditions for carrot growing.[80]

Then, in the mid-1980s the "baby" carrot was invented by Mike Yuro-sek, one of the three main carrot growers in Bakersfield.[81] Frustrated by the percentage of carrots that were too short or misshapen to sell, he began to experiment with vegetable peelers to figure out a way to make the stubbies salable. It eventually worked, and he was able to sell the mini carrots to a West Coast supermarket chain, which immediately begged for more.

Sales grew steadily but incrementally and then rocketed in popularity in the early 1990s. "In just a few years, these mini carrots have achieved a popularity that speaks volumes about lifestyle and dietary changes in America," Donald Woutat wrote in 1993 in the *Los Angeles Times*. This was at a time when Americans were counting every fat gram, and these convenient little good-for-you snacks were beloved by both kids and their moms, for themselves and also for the way they so easily filled a school lunch bag. In the 1970s, Americans ate about six pounds of carrots per person per year. By 1997, that number had increased to more than fourteen pounds. Twenty years later it has stabilized at about eight and a half pounds.[82]

79 They also get some processed carrots, such as bagged shredded carrots, from Bolthouse.

80 Carrots are one vegetable Terry Romp can't find locally for Heinen's, even in the summer—Ohio soil, he said, is too dense for carrots. "They're too stubby," he said. I'd learned this as a boy trying to grow them, along with corn, behind my garage in Shaker Heights. (Ohio corn is some of the country's best, but I couldn't grow that either.)

81 "The Carrot Kings: Bakersfield Triumvirate Is Tops in the Field," *Los Angeles Times*, August 15, 1993; "Profiles in Doing Both: Mike Yurosek, Father of the 'Baby Carrot,'" *Forbes*, November 4, 2010.

82 I retrieved much of my vegetable intelligence from the Agricultural Marketing Resource Center website. I spent hours reading entries on produce and found them filled with concise, fascinating details about any vegetable or fruit I was curious about; I highly recommend it for the produce inquisitive.

I don't see a lot of men eating "baby" carrots. I don't think men have anything against them; they just don't tend to choose them. I know my carrot-loving father didn't eat them, likely for two reasons. First, regular commercial bagged carrots are cheaper, which would have been all the reason he needed; he didn't want to pay for work he could do himself. But more significantly, baby carrots are not easily accessible when kept in a suit jacket pocket.

I do know why I have never bought them: because they aren't really baby carrots. They are the core of the carrot, the least tasty, least nutritious part. But worse, I feel the makers are duping a gullible consumer into thinking they are something they're not—that is, tender young carrots. I wouldn't mind so much if they were called carrot cores, though I still wouldn't buy them. I love good carrots and probably eat a couple of pounds during the course of a week's lunches.[83] But I don't like the very fat carrots with the woody, flavorless core. Which is often what those early "baby" carrots were.

No longer, apparently. Yurosek sold his business to Grimmway and the brothers Grimm not only began to invest heavily in processing and marketing the baby carrots, they also found a variety that was naturally thin and able to grow in dense clusters. This way they could grow in larger volume, harvest them more quickly and with minimal waste, then cut them to length to be "polished," the term they use for tumbling the cut carrots on coarse rollers till they look like miniature carrots.

Scouring the internet for baby carrot trivia, I came across Erika Kerekes, a marketing consultant, food blogger, and self-professed food- and produce-processing geek based in Santa Monica, California. She toured Grimmway Farms and their processing plant with a group of food bloggers and wrote an informative post[84] about how they work and

83 This is when I'm at home working, which I am at least half the year; this means, I realize only now, that I consume at least fifty pounds of carrots a year, which would not have impressed my father, but certainly ought to put me in the running as a paid spokesman for the carrot industry or at least deserving of an honorary mention in the World Carrot Museum—a virtual museum curated by a guy named John Stolarczyk in Skipton, England.

84 Visit inerikaskitchen.com and search "How Carrots Are Made."

how their carrots are processed. She learned that carrots not the right size are used for juice; that the sludge left over from carrot "polishing" is sold for cattle feed; that the greens are tilled back into the soil; that the baby carrots get a chlorine bath (for which she is grateful, having once had a child sick from salmonella); that even big farmers are still farmers with a farmer ethic. Ultimately, she writes, "There's just no way to get your head around the quantity of carrots they deal with."

When I contacted her to ask about her trip, her description of how she saw one of the company's carrot fields gave me the best way to get *my* head around it. Rather than drive to where the carrots were being harvested, they had to *fly* to the farm. And then fly to the processing plant.

She admitted she had no idea where she was when they got to the carrot fields, beyond being somewhere in the southern part of the San Joaquin Valley, the fertile belly of California. This valley stretches from Los Angeles up to Sacramento, where it segues into the Sacramento Valley, which goes even higher up in the state. The region produces 25 percent of the country's table food on 1 percent of its farmland, according to one government report. That's how fertile it is, but only if there's enough water—agriculture here uses 80 percent of the water available to it (the rest is for commercial and residential use), and that water is now gravely threatened by drought.

"All [Grimmway's] operations are in the middle of nowhere and hard to get to," Erika wrote to me. "All their people travel by plane. The company keeps three to four planes and pilots, each of which holds about fifteen people, and operates them like commuter shuttles. People book rides to get to meetings. Each of their operations has a little airstrip with a hut where the pilots hang out."

That is how big a carrot farm needs to be to feed half the country.

"They have many different orchards/tracts, not all contiguous, I believe," she wrote. "They have bought up many smaller and medium-sized family farms in the Central Valley and have been much criticized for it because in the process they also bought up water rights for much of the Central Valley, too. You know they also grow almonds, pistachios, tangerines."

Grimmway began their expansion into other crops such as citrus in 1991, and bought Cal-Organic Farms in 2001 to feed the nation's growing appetite for organic carrots. Erika's comment that these vast tracts of land aren't contiguous is also an important part of understanding how enough produce gets to all the grocery stores in America. These big farming companies can expand only by buying more land on which to grow more produce.

For instance, Terry Romp initiated a relationship with a company called Stemilt Growers, which grows apples, pears, and cherries in Wenatchee, Washington. Kyle Mathison, son of the founder, is crazy about cherries. As Mario Grazia put it, "He makes Dr. Todd look normal." Mathison even bought an orchard in Chile so that he could vacation in winter without giving up his passion for growing cherries, even though he doesn't sell these cherries in the United States—not yet, anyhow. (When I tried to reach Mathison during cherry season, I was told it may be difficult because he spends almost 100 percent of his time in the orchards. A spokesman for the company called him "one of the most famous cherry growers in the world.")

One of the Mathison family's orchards grows on the eastern edge of the Cascade Mountain range, at twenty-five hundred feet above sea level. The company says no cherries on earth grow closer to the moon. They call them moon cherries, because Mathison believes the moon has a lot to do with their flavor. "The lunar gravitational force pulling the flavors, the carbohydrates, sugars, acids, aromatics from the tree right into the fruit," Mathison says in a video the company made on this cherry. "They're mystical, like the moon."

In the summer of 2015, when I'd begun looking into where our produce comes from, the high heat and dry conditions in Washington led to serious wildfires raging throughout the region, burning homes and buildings (though not orchards; fires will burn only a couple of rows, if any at all, owing to the heavy irrigation, and orchards are an effective fire block for that reason).

Stemilt's packing facility was burned to the ground and Heinen's felt the impact. When I sat down that October with Vinnie Latessa, head of produce for Heinen's, and buyers Mario Grazia and Terry Romp, to listen to their rundown of the week's produce issues, they remembered the cherries. After the fires, their cherry supply dried up.

"Right now there is not a cherry on the planet," Terry told me later that fall, "and there won't be until December." That's the time cherry season in the southern hemisphere begins.

The cherry crop coming out of Washington was dented by the heat and fires but still produced an enormous supply, just not as bountiful as the previous year. In 2014, cherry growers there shipped about 460 million pounds of cherries. The following year, growers shipped 360 million pounds, a 22 percent drop owing to acts of nature.

"Weather is the great unknown in this business," Mario said. "And water is the linchpin in the whole thing."

Heinen's works with about 180 produce vendors, but Stemilt is a special client given the volume they do and the quality of their product, as well as their ethos. "They share the same values as Heinen's," Terry told me. "When we are rolling with them in the apple season, we get two to three loads of apples a week at twenty thousand pounds per load. This doesn't include other varieties of apples that we don't buy from them, so it's only part of our business."

Forty to sixty thousand pounds of apples per week for Heinen's alone, every week through the winter. Did you ever wonder how you can still buy apples even after the fall apple season? Apple companies hold their apples in vast warehouses filled with a mixture of oxygen and carbon dioxide, which, in industry parlance, puts them to sleep. The companies "break the room," in Terry's words, as needed to ship the apples. This means that if you're buying a "fresh" American apple in August, it was harvested late last year.

This obviously affects quality, said Vinnie, but it's the only way to ensure a year-round supply for grocery stores throughout the land. "It doesn't eat the same if it sits around for a year," he admitted. His produce managers start clamoring for newer apples come summer, when Heinen's will buy them shipped from New Zealand and Chile. Heinen's sells about ten varieties of apple—there are so many that you have to limit what you buy. "The big dog is Honeycrisp," Vinnie said. "They can sometimes sell for one hundred dollars a box. People are looking for the next Honeycrisp. Stemilt has Piñata, that's proprietary. Lady Alice is proprietary. You have to also have Jazz. Three or four organics."

Heinen's stocks as many local apples as they're able to in the fall. They can't do local organic because this part of the country is too moist and has too many pests that create spots, and customers won't buy spotty apples. They get some Honeycrisp from Nova Scotia and New York, but the majority come from Stemilt.

Stemilt has about sixteen thousand acres of apples, pears, and cherries, according to Roger Pepperl, marketing director for Stemilt Growers. The company ships about five hundred million pounds of apples, eighty-eight million pounds of pears, and seventy-two million pounds of cherries each year. Roughly 25 percent of this volume is organic.

Sixty-two percent of American apples are grown in Washington State. Stemilt, like other major apple growers, uses atmosphere-controlled warehouses to hold each year's harvest. The technology has been in use for decades, Pepperl noted, but the quality has improved, as has the quality of the apple itself. Some apples that don't hold well, such as Honeycrisp, remain seasonal, but Pepperl said they were working on refining the Honeycrisp variety so that it could be stored all year. "You should see Honeycrisp store into the summer in five years," he said.

But fires, which have plagued the western United States, aren't the real worry to the Mathison family and other farmers. Climate change is. "The warm weather records we have been setting from global warming have been an issue," Pepperl said. "Our crops are earlier from early bloom. It also can affect fruit quality if stressed from the heat. The cherry crop was two weeks early this year, which is incredibly strange. It is the earliest crop in the history of the state."

Of all the grocery store departments, the produce section may be the most radically changed over the decades, at least in terms of variety, quality, and availability of product. It's also one of the most important from a business standpoint for Heinen's. With 40 percent margins, it generates more revenue per square foot than any other area and accounts for about a fifth of the company's annual sales.

I sit down with Vinnie, Mario, and Terry at their weekly Wednesday meeting in the lunchroom of the produce warehouse, concrete block walls painted a drab yellow, rows of tables and chairs against one wall, a coffeepot on the counter, to hear them talk and ask them about changes in the industry. Vinnie has been working produce for thirty-seven years and has seen those changes firsthand. "Blueberries," Vinnie says. "Now you've got blueberries from Uruguay. Have you ever heard of Uruguay? What the hell is going on there?"

Many former "third-world countries" now have the infrastructure and technology to grow, pick, and ship produce efficiently, Terry adds.

Wednesday mornings are slow, as they've already "gotten all their buys in," so they can take a breath and see where they stand, and discuss with me the state of produce, pricing, and sales. Produce moves in and out *fast*. It's perishable, so the quality always varies; the volume and turnaround time require many people to work efficiently.

"It's important that they run with the same mentality and process that I do," Vinnie tells me. "Like Peter"—Peter Ross, in charge of receiving—"he's going to reject all these clementines today because of a lot of seeds in them. He cut the whole bag. A customer who buys a seedless clementine or wants some clementines, they'd be pissed if there were like five seeds in it, right? They ate good, but we don't want 'em. Two or three pallets. Now, problem: We don't have clementines." For filling holes, they use Cleveland's produce terminal. This was the only place where people who retailed fruits and vegetables could buy produce in decades past; it was where Joe Heinen went when he introduced produce to his original supermarket. Most large cities have a central distribution center for commodity produce, but more and more grocery stores these days buy direct and use the terminal only to fill holes.

"Now, here it comes down to vendor relations," Vinnie says. He's rejecting three pallets of fruit, not paying for them or their shipping;

the vendor will have to eat the shipping costs[85] and try to unload the clementines at the food terminal downtown. "Because," Vinnie explains, "the vendor can say, hey, I want a Federal on them. I'm not eatin' all this freight, all the pallets." In this case a USDA inspector is called to the warehouse to check the specs on how many seeds per fruit per bag are acceptable. If the inspector says they pass, then Vinnie is required by law to accept them. But Vinnie would then say to his supplier, "Are you going to tell me I *gotta* take 'em? Okay, I'll take 'em. Have a nice day. See ya. That's your last sale."

Vinnie says produce is the most complex section of the grocery store in terms of ordering, receiving, and distributing. "People making quick decisions," he says. "It's not a pallet of Campbell's soup. It's gotta move. And *we* have to move, and if I don't move and I wait, and the store is selling what they've got, what happens? They deplete. Where's your reload? Coming in a few days? No. I need this *today*. So, yeah, it's fast paced."

Vinnie, age fifty-five, with an oval face and short, light brown hair, has brought some stone fruit to taste because Tom hasn't been happy with it. Mario is forty-nine and has a helmet of thick, dark hair. He's been working in produce at Heinen's since he was fifteen and now buys the commodity fruits and vegetables, so he has nearly as many years in the business as Vinnie. Terry Romp, fifty-four, the fourth generation of his family to work in the produce world, had his own business, Danny Boy Farms, before Jeff hired him eleven years ago specifically to source local produce. Between them these three men have a combined century of produce experience. And they speak in a strange produce vernacular that's sometimes hard to follow.

Discussion begins with which items to highlight in their weekly ad, both online and in a newspaper insert. This week, for instance, Terry tells them they've got a lot of green bell peppers coming from Bainbridge, Ohio, not far south, and they can offer these for ninety-nine cents a pound. But once they've got these items listed, they move into

---

85 A truck from California to Ohio costs about $8,000.

the trouble spots, beginning today, in mid-July,[86] with blueberries. Their main supplier, and the country's main supplier, Driscoll, has no blueberries. In the winter Heinen's will get blueberries from Uruguay if necessary, but they prefer to stay in the Mexican highlands, because South American blueberries travel by boat and then truck, weeks after having been picked, whereas Mexican blueberries reach Heinen's in ten days by truck. But it's summertime in North America and there's a blueberry shortage.

This is unusual, as the California-based Driscoll strives to have all berries all year long. They do so by working with family farms throughout the Americas, from Baja California to the Pacific Northwest, from Florida to North Carolina to New Jersey. Mexico is a huge berry-growing area for them, and they also use farms in Chile and Argentina. Go to just about any grocery store in America and you're likely to see the Driscoll name on all the blueberries, raspberries, strawberries, and blackberries.

But this month, they'll have to watch their blueberry supply carefully or, as Terry puts it, "Blues, we gotta tighten up, you know? Driscoll, no blues until mid-October."

"So we have *no* blues until October?" Vinnie asks with concern.

"No, we got plenty of blues out of Michigan. But since they're the only gig in the country, the price is just stupid. I got a lid from Driscoll on this." A lid, or ad lid, is a price that a company will guarantee on a specific item for the length of an ad they want to run, so that the grocery store can advertise their own sale price without fear that the vendor will suddenly up their price and give the store a loss.

"What was the lid?"

"Thirteen."

"Wow."

"And they're twenty-six out of Michigan"—that is, double the

---

86 They'd recently come off a good July 4 weekend, one of the biggest corn weekends of the year: thirty-six thousand ears of corn sold in a weekend. Aside from the obvious Thanksgiving turkeys and Valentine's Day strawberries, another "holiday" for which we buy more of a single item than at any other time of the year is Super Bowl Sunday. Heinen's will sell twenty-eight thousand avocados that weekend. It's estimated that America could fill that Super Bowl stadium with guacamole, we make so much.

price—"so that's why I put a note on it. We have product, we just have to tighten up on everything. We got plenty of raz, plenty of black, no issues there."

"What about on straws—winding?" Vinnie asks, meaning are strawberries winding down?

"Straws, we're going down. Only one pound, no twos"—companies are shipping only in one-pound containers—"fruit size is way off, so the volume is way down. They are no longer packing twos until the fall crop and it cools off out there."

Vinnie says, "Usually we can make it through Labor Day."

"Crazy heat," says Mario.

"Watermelon," Vinnie says to Terry. "Local coming in?"

"We have local forty-fives—these are actually Indiana thirty-sixes—and we got another load coming Friday." The numbers refer to the number of melons per box and therefore indicate size.

"What about lopes," Vinnie asks, regarding a fruit I eventually gather is the cantaloupe.

Mario says, "We're fine after this week. The heat. They're small. We saw small ones mixed in with the twelves. It's the heat and the lack of water. Prices are going up."

Vinnie says, "They had some brown spots, too."

"Really? I didn't see that. But we've got plenty."

"What about grape?" Vinnie asks, and turns to me, adding, "I mean if we're just buying green grapes, shame on us."

Terry says, "Grape, we have plenty. Friday I'm going to start loading with Giumarra. The Sweeties are ready." To me he explains, "They're the sweetest grape in the industry." Giumarra Vineyards, based in Edison, California, just east of carrot-central Bakersfield, grows, packs, and ships fourteen varieties of green, red, and black grapes. The Sweeties are an intensely sweet green grape with a crisp bite.

Grapes are an example of how technology can lead to a better product, as the grower can take a brix[87] reading to know the exact sugar

87 "Brix" is short for degrees brix; sugar content is measured in degrees relative to the mass of the fruit; 1 degree brix means 1 gram of sugar per 100 grams of fruit.

content, so Terry can ask for and get varying levels of sweetness. Green grapes may average a brix of about six, whereas some of the varieties they can find brix at fifteen or sixteen.

Heinen's also gets grapes from a specialty purveyor, Melissa's Produce, that sells a grape developed from Lambrusco, a red wine grape. They've registered it as Cotton Candy, because it tastes like cotton candy—and I mean *exactly* like cotton candy. It's remarkable. They also offer Jelly Drop grapes, Moon Drop grapes, and long, skinny purple Witch Finger grapes, all of them deliciously sweet. Heinen's also buys most of their exotic fruits from Melissa's, such as jackfruit, horned melons, Buddha's hands, finger limes, and cactus pears. These may not sell like bananas and apples, but Heinen's feels that offering such exotica is a draw for many of their customers.

"Tom was in my office," Vinnie says, holding up one of a few peaches and nectarines he'd brought, "and he said he hasn't eaten a good peach yet from us. He says mealy, and blah blah blah."

"Tell him to quit buying it in Chicago," Terry says. "Tell him to buy it from here, one that hasn't sat on the counter."

"I haven't heard any complaints," Vinnie says. He's obviously taking this personally.

"Peter told me that the Family Tree peaches that we've had the last three weeks have eaten better than anything else all summer long," Terry says. "We had one week of homegrown. We'll have more on Saturday. We've got homegrown in Chicago, and we're the only store in Chicago selling local peaches."

"Talking about stone fruit, what about white flesh?" Vinnie asks. "Another—what, two, three more weeks?"

"I have 'em going in the twenty-sixth ad," Terry says, "and then I was going to pull them after that? And then let 'em wane out until Labor Day? Probably after Labor Day we might just go to organic peach, nectarine only out of Washington State. It's the same price as conventional. California is just about done."

"Why carry two? That's fine."

Mario asks, "What about the pluots?"

"We'll just start thinning that out so maybe have one black plum," Terry responds.

"Isn't that program going till the end of September?" Vinnie asks.

"You know, we always say, 'Why can't we sell this good stuff?'" Mario says. "But people switch to school mode and . . ."

These men watch people's eating habits and note that most of us seem naturally to eat seasonally. Meaning Heinen's may still be getting great stone fruit in the second week of September, but by then, people are ready for apples. That, combined with the fact that cut apples travel better than cut stone fruit in a youngster's school lunch bag, causes them to reduce the quantity of stone fruit they buy come fall, no matter the quality.

"Yeah, it turns off," Vinnie says. "Okay, should we go to the normal stuff?"

Normal stuff would be all those items Mario is responsible for: the commodity broccoli, cauliflower, green beans, asparagus. None of which is a problem in the summer, as Terry can get most of what they need from right here in Ohio, relying on three Ohio produce auctions.

Later that month, I drove an hour southwest of Cleveland, down to the County Line Produce Auction, in a part of the state composed solely of flat, straight roads and farmland as far as I could see, to meet with Isaac Kein, an Amish farmer and a bishop in his community. It was, as Terry had promised me, "like going back in time." Most of the farmers are Amish; scores of horse-drawn buggies were parked behind the twenty-seven-thousand-square-foot covered, open-air auction barn.

I found Kein in a group of buyers, a tall, robust sixty-six-year-old in a broad straw hat and round spectacles, and sporting a bushy gray beard. He carried a five-by-seven legal pad divided into columns to keep track of his orders, as well as a knife for tasting, as he strolled with a dozen other buyers past pallets of tomatoes and cucumbers and squash, listening to the rhythmic chanting of the auctioneer, making some purchases, letting others go. He's got to be particular because Peter Ross can reject a delivery of watermelons just as he did the clementines. Today, as on every Monday, Wednesday, and Friday all summer, Kein will fill a fifty-three-foot semi rig, sometimes two, with produce that will arrive the following morning at the Heinen's warehouse: fifty boxes of heirloom tomatoes, fifty of Roma tomatoes, two hundred boxes of grape tomatoes, eighty bushels of eggplants, one hundred boxes of cucumbers, twenty bushels of onions, ten enormous boxes of watermelons.

Kein has eight sons and six daughters who work his eighty-five acres of cabbages, peppers, eggplant, and broccoli. He also has about four thousand maple trees on his property, which will yield fifteen hundred gallons of maple syrup. Starting at daybreak that day, his family and workers picked one hundred bushels of bell peppers, all of which will go to Heinen's. In fact, just about everything he grows goes to Heinen's.

About 250 farmers in the region sell at the County Line Produce Auction, for a total of about $60,000 worth of produce a day, all of which has grown within a ten-mile radius of the market.

"It's really helped our community out," Kein told me of his ten-year relationship with Heinen's. "You can make a living for your family on ten acres."

When Vinnie, Mario, and Terry sit down for their Wednesday morning meeting the following March, they're discussing entirely different issues than are likely to come up in the summer. For instance, cold weather has created a shortage of many vegetables, such as lettuces, broccoli, and cauliflower.

"We're getting what we need, but supply and demand costs went sky-high," Mario tells Terry and Vinnie. He typically buys a box of nine heads of cauliflower for eighteen to twenty-two dollars. That winter he's been paying forty-seven, or more than five dollars a head. Which is why Heinen's, and grocery stores around the country, are charging seven dollars for a head of cauliflower.

But it's also a time to reflect on the wonder of greenhouses and hydroponics. "Who'd have thought strawberries?" Terry says to the group. Lettuces are one thing, but to grow the complex strawberry was something else. A company called Sunset Produce, in Ontario, Canada, figured out how to do it. "Eight years ago, when we went up there, it was very secretive," Vinnie recalls, wondering aloud how much time and money went into figuring out how to grow such a fruit without soil.

Sunset, owned by Mastronardi Produce, can claim that it's the only greenhouse in the world that produces strawberries hydroponically, and in Canada's most frigid months no less. Fifty years ago, the idea of growing strawberries in March in Canada would have been unimaginable. But in Canada, and specifically Ontario, and even more specifically the city of Leamington, greenhouses and hydroponics are a booming business. Vinnie calls Leamington "a city of greenhouses." In all, Ontario has about twenty-five hundred acres of food growing indoors, tended by two hundred farmers. And it's from these greenhouses that Heinen's gets much of their lettuces, herbs, vine-ripened tomatoes, eggplants, cucumbers, and bell peppers in the winter months.

According to Vinnie, greenhouse growing declined in the 1970s and '80s, but then picked up steam in Holland with developing technologies. Canada improved these technologies, and the movement began heading south. Sunset opened a sixty-acre greenhouse in Coldwater, Michigan, and the Canada-based Nature Fresh Farms is building a 175-acre greenhouse in northwestern Ohio, which will allow Heinen's to put a grown-in-Ohio label on this produce, an effective selling tool.

Heinen's was one of the first to carry the hydroponically grown lettuces of Great Lakes Growers in nearby Burton, Ohio. They are able to display these lettuces in water-filled cases, so that the lettuce roots remain in water until the customer puts them in their cart, an excellent bit of merchandising that actually improves the quality of the food. Heinen's was the company's first retailer, and the volume Heinen's brought in allowed them to expand. Great Lakes Growers now moves three to four million heads of lettuce and bundles of herbs a year to more than a hundred grocery stores throughout the Midwest.

Urban, vertical, and rooftop growing is expanding as well. Gotham Greens has 170,000 square feet of greenhouses in Brooklyn, Queens, and Chicago. BrightFarms operates greenhouses in Virginia, Illinois, and Pennsylvania on its quest, the company writes, "to bring commercial scale urban agriculture to the market, take our farms and the industry to the next level, and change the way we eat as a society." They're so innovative that they've partnered with McCaffrey's Food Markets to build greenhouses on the rooftops of the stores.

Continued growth of the hydroponic industry is all but assured as technology improves and demand for high-quality produce year-round increases. Hydroponic greenhouse growing has many advantages over traditional agriculture; I don't see how it can fail to expand. It's the most water-efficient method of growing, as the water can be recirculated. Traditional agriculture worldwide uses 70 percent of our accessible freshwater supply. Hydroponic growing requires no soil, which itself needs feeding on a traditional farm. Because the atmosphere is controlled, it requires few if any pesticides, resulting in cleaner food and eliminating the chemical runoff of traditional agriculture, perhaps the biggest single source of environmental pollution. With hydroponics a farmer can also grow more food in less space. The sterile environment virtually eliminates the possible contamination of the produce by such pathogens as salmonella and *E. coli*. Many of these greenhouses are solar powered, and thus energy efficient. They are not affected by global warming or by the drastic weather shifts we've been seeing with almost spooky regularity, such as the extreme heat in California. They are not as vulnerable to natural disasters such as the fires in Washington. They require minimal acreage within buildings, unlike the endless fields required for traditional agriculture, so that if one had a power outage (their biggest potential danger) only a small amount of food would be lost. If a carrot blight hit Bakersfield, carrots would all but vanish from the grocery store. This won't happen with more fragmented indoor farming. And perhaps most important of all, hydroponic growing means we can grow food all year long.

One company, Freight Farms, specializes in converting old cargo containers into greenhouses. Theoretically, these containers can grow food anywhere in the world in any climate. This might one day include the back parking lot of your neighborhood supermarket. After all, we have restaurants with elaborate gardens, such as that at the French Laundry in the Napa Valley. The restaurant has a full-time gardener/horticulturist, Tucker Taylor, and the chefs harvest produce mere hours before they serve the dishes. As grocery stores become more like restaurants, can grocery store gardens be far behind? These are unlikely to handle the volume grocers sell, but supplemental gardens are being experimented with.

It's important to recognize how young this movement is. Hydroponics have been around since William Frederick Gericke pioneered the idea at the University of California, Berkeley, in the 1930s, and I began hearing about hydroponically grown lettuce in the 1990s. But growing hydroponically on a commercial scale is a relatively recent development, due in large measure to the high start-up costs involved in creating a building and infrastructure to grow such an inexpensive product. Terry Romp concurs: "Hydroponics really only came into their own about four years ago."

And the quality only gets better. Vinnie and his team love the flavor of the vine-ripe tomatoes now grown hydroponically year-round. "We haven't had a Florida tomato in twenty years," Mario says. "They're terrible—they taste like cardboard." Florida tomatoes are picked green and ripen en route north. Of course, if you pick a tomato when it's green, it's bound to taste different from one that has used all its ripening time on the vine, soaking up the nutrients that make it taste good in the first place.[88] (The same is true of bananas, almost all of which arrive in the United States hard and green.[89] I was on a magazine assignment several

....

88 I'd be remiss if I didn't mention here Barry Estabrook's superb *Gourmet* magazine article on the Florida tomato industry ("Politics of the Plate: The Price of Tomatoes," *Gourmet*, March 2009), which includes information on how that industry works—"Between December and May, as much as 90 percent of the fresh domestic tomatoes we eat come from south Florida"—but most importantly sheds light on the appalling living conditions of the people who pick the fruit. He expanded the story for the book *Tomatoland: How Modern Industrial Agriculture Destroyed Our Most Alluring Fruit.*

89 Bananas are a fruit that, once ripe, will quickly go bad; thus they're picked green and shipped from Central America in cargo containers. They will not ripen once picked and must be treated with ethylene gas. Heinen's bananas, mostly from Costa Rica, arrive in Philadelphia, then are trucked to Cleveland, where a wholesale produce company, Sanson, puts them in a chamber that fills with ethylene gas and ripens them to varying degrees before sending them to the Heinen's warehouse. Americans eat a lot of bananas, an average of twenty-six pounds per person per year, more than any other whole fruit. And because they have such a brief window of ripeness, Heinen's sells them in varying stages of ripeness, from pale green to bright yellow, knowing that many customers buy bananas to eat later in the week.

years ago in Suriname, a small country on the north coast of South America, and bought a bunch of bananas on the street. I couldn't believe the flavor. It was like tasting a banana for the first time.)

The prominence of hydroponic and greenhouse growing in the northeastern quadrant of the United States and in Canada couldn't be more important right now, as the biggest swath of traditional American agriculture, the San Joaquin Valley, faces dire water shortages. Regardless of the water supply, simply from a commonsense point of view, hydroponic and greenhouse growing is critical as the world's population continues to expand. The United Nations predicts the earth's population, currently at about seven billion, will increase by nearly 50 percent, approaching ten billion, by mid-century. So we *must* create more total acreage and grow ever more food.

And we are. And not just with indoor growing. As Vinnie notes, high-tech companies are creating farms in developing nations. And regions that have generated food of erratic quality in the past, such as Mexico, are getting better at it.

"There's more technology," Vinnie says. "And better growing practices. Once you have technology you have more time to do other stuff. Drones, for example, going out and checking where they can't get to by foot. These little improvements allow them to grow a better product." There's increasing competition in the market, which also results in a better product.

"Believe it or not, Mexico is probably going to outdo California," Vinnie says. "They have everything you need to be successful and they don't have the water problems California has, they don't have the labor issues California has. And the quality of the product they're producing is good."

Vinnie notes that the consumer still doesn't like to see a "Product of Mexico" sticker on a piece of fruit, though, and still thinks of Mexican produce as being inferior and more likely to be contaminated. "It's still that old shit—'They're peeing in the fields,'" he says. "In the old days, you got in product from Mexico, you didn't know what farm it was coming from. But things have changed, really changed. These are

American growers, American technologies. They're moving shop is all they're doing."

Of all the departments in the grocery store, produce seems to me to be the most hopeful, with many innovations on the horizon. In 2008, at a food conference in Napa, I met Dickson Despommier, a professor of microbiology at Columbia University, who presented a case to the audience for vertical farming, an idea that began in one of his classes. He said that not only was the planet soon to host ten billion people, but more to the point, 80 percent of that population would live in urban areas. He argued that one solution to feeding all these people is to grow food where they live by creating farms in skyscrapers. A process called plasma arc gasification could be used to eliminate all human waste and landfill with the usable byproduct of potential energy in the form of gas and sterile building materials. If we could do this on a worldwide scale— grow a substantial amount of food vertically, and turn our waste into energy-producing fuel—we could give back the land we took. Farming isn't natural, he noted. It's a human invention, and one that degrades and pollutes the land and is a major factor in global warming. If we grew our food vertically, and let wide swaths of land lie fallow, the earth would naturally repair all the damage humans have done to it.[90]

Greenhouse and hydroponic growing were not yet advanced enough to do this on a commercial scale when Dickson and I spoke. And they still weren't quite there in 2010, when Despommier published his book *The Vertical Farm: Feeding the World in the 21st Century*. But we're very nearly there now, or at least well on our way, if we can afford to build such structures.

At a TEDx talk in Chicago, Despommier presented his ideas and displayed a list of all the produce that can now be grown hydroponically:

....

90 This was one of Dr. Todd's points, made during our walk in the woods. Referring to the writings of the scientist E. O. Wilson, he noted that if suddenly all bacteria or all insects vanished, the landscape would collapse and die; but were all humans to vanish from earth, the planet would flourish. To which I would add: flourish as it had been doing until humans invented farming.

blueberries, strawberries, raspberries, cranberries, huckleberries, green beans, tomatoes, coffee, grapes; vine vegetables such as squash, pumpkins, okra, cantaloupe, and watermelons; peanuts, beets, carrots, onions, potatoes; critical grain crops such as barley, corn, wheat, and rice; and of course dozens of leaf lettuces and even more herbs.

Of course, we're not likely to see hydroponically grown stone fruit or apples or anything that grows on trees anytime soon; you can't raise cows hydroponically, or chickens or fish. But we can grow more than was imaginable fifty years ago, so who knows what the future holds as we press toward 11 billion people?

The New Jersey–based AeroFarms already has what it describes as a thirty-thousand-foot vertical farm, in what was a paintball arena in Newark, and is building a seventy-thousand-square-foot greenhouse in the same neighborhood. Their five-year goal is to be operating twenty-five such farms throughout the world. The company stresses that they use 95 percent less water than traditional farming and half the pesticides—and they don't require soil or sun.

AeroFarms has put a small hydroponic farm in the Philips Academy Charter School in Newark to begin teaching America's kids about this kind of agriculture. (Not to mention introducing them to the vegetables themselves.)

This is a promising innovation, bringing the growing of food to schools. It was begun twenty years ago by Alice Waters when she helped found the Edible Schoolyard, establishing a garden at a school in her neighborhood in Berkeley, California, home of her seminal restaurant Chez Panisse. It became the model for other such schools in Los Angeles, San Francisco, New York, and elsewhere. It's all part of a broader effort to inform children about food generally, especially those in low-income neighborhoods, some of whom don't regularly see basic commodity produce.

The layout and scale of the American grocery store reflects our culture's general attitudes when shopping for food. The very fact that the produce department is often one of the busiest, if not the most shopped, is a promising sign. We want our vegetables.

Produce is a growth industry!

17.

"NOBODY KNOWS HOW TO COOK—
IT'S MIND-BOGGLING"

I'd arrived mid-morning at store #05, the one in Pepper Pike that I love, on the day before Thanksgiving to watch a store satisfy our needs on the biggest food holiday in the country. It's our only holiday that is centered on food, that celebrates our bounty, and, as it's not a religious holiday, one that is celebrated by all Americans. The day before Thanksgiving is actually not the biggest *shopping* day of the year, though. That is traditionally the Tuesday before Thanksgiving. Everyone thinks that on Wednesday they will contend with nightmare crowds, so they all try to beat the rush by shopping Tuesday. And that Tuesday at store #05 was no different, registering sales of $219,000 in a single day, nearly half of a typical week's sales.

And on Wednesday, when people tend to shop for the last-minute items—flowers, the sage that someone forgot, the decaf coffee because Grandpa Henry can't have caffeine past noon—the store looked pretty much the way it did on a normal Saturday, and there were not a lot of high rings at the register.

But it was busy enough for James Mowcomber, not even a year into his job as Heinen's head chef. I'd met James a couple of years earlier when I entertained some food writers visiting Cleveland by taking them to dinner at Lolita, where James was the chef de cuisine. The restaurant was originally Lola, where I'd spent months writing about Michael Symon, one of the country's most talented chefs, for my book *The Soul of a Chef*. And I loved its reincarnation as a casual restaurant selling wood-fired pizzas and a Mediterranean-influenced menu. I wanted to impress out-of-town food people, and Symon's restaurants never failed to impress.

Lolita is popular, and I had to pull strings with Michael to get us a four-top. He said, "You gotta meet James; he's an amazing cook." Indeed, the food didn't disappoint. After we finished, I found James at the pass. He was tall, more than six feet, solidly built, short dark hair and dark eyes in a round face. I introduced myself as he fussed over the finishing garnishes on a plate, said thanks for the meal, and mentioned that Michael said I had to meet him. He said hello, you're welcome, and went back to the plate he was working on. He wasn't being unkind. He was, like so many chefs I know, a man of few words and, of course, in the middle of service.

So I was intrigued that Heinen's had hired this talented restaurant chef away from Lolita, and curious how and why he made the move to becoming a corporate chef.

The day before Thanksgiving may not be the busiest day in the grocery store's front of the house, as it were, but back of the house it's crazy. James, now age thirty-nine, and his staff have to prepare scores of complete Thanksgiving dinners for families throughout this tony suburb. When I passed through the refrigerated hallways and back rooms, which the day before held more than a thousand turkeys stacked along walls up to the ceiling, into what looked like a restaurant prep kitchen, there was James breaking down a line of roasted turkeys on a cutting board on a long stainless steel table.

"I roasted more than fifty turkeys," he told me, not looking up as he deftly removed both legs and sliced one half breast off the carcass. "And I've got to get *home* and cook Thanksgiving dinner." He intended to roast one last turkey there and do other prep tonight so that he wouldn't have to work hard tomorrow.

One of the services Heinen's offers, as do most grocery stores, is the preparation of Thanksgiving dinners to order. Most people who order prepared dinners want the turkey broken down. And many orders are only for partial turkeys. An order that one of James's cooks worked on from a seemingly endless list comprised three pounds of white meat, one pound of dark meat, and one whole leg. Another of the four cooks working this kitchen might finish off the order with two pounds of mashed potatoes, one pound of roasted sweet potatoes, a quart of gravy, a pint of cranberry sauce, and two pounds of green beans. Just keeping track of them is difficult, but the cooks also have to find a place to put the finished orders, in large covered foil trays, and to be able to locate Mr. Smith's order whenever Mr. Smith arrives to pick it up. The refrigerated halls were lined with tables stacked high with the foil trays, an order sheet taped to the outside of each.

Meanwhile, a cook named Dan pulled two-gallon bags of soup, sent from the central warehouse, out of the combi oven where they had reheated, cut them open, and spilled their contents into a steel insert that would go out into the prepared soup station near the cafe area. White chicken chili, beef barley, tomato basil bisque, broccoli and Cheddar, crab and corn, and Buffalo mac and cheese soup.

"The Buffalo mac and cheese is really good," Dan said, explaining that the company that makes the soups pours a lot of the sauce made for the Buffalo wings right into the soup.

After he got the soups out, Dan began frying chicken because even though it's the day before Thanksgiving, the staff still have to function as a normal grocery store crew, loading the salad bar and the deli case with prepared foods, clerks restocking shelves with cereal and cat food, and of course the endless refilling of the terra cotta bins of green beans and broccoli and pea pods, replacing lettuces in the misting racks.

All this activity—the complete Thanksgiving dinner, the fried chicken, the soups, the scalloped potatoes, the quinoa salad and two dozen others in the salad bar—represents one of the most dramatic changes in the grocery store, one that seems to have begun decades ago, then exploded in the 1990s: prepared foods.

We shoppers now arrive at any grocery store expecting to be able to buy a range of cooked and ready-to-reheat foods if we're not in the mood or don't have the time to cook dinner.

"It's gone mainstream," said Carin Solganik, who was hired three years ago to take over Heinen's expanding prepared foods operations. "Everyone has some form of prepared foods. Even Walmart has prepared food." She seemed amazed by this, but everyone wants a piece of this $30 billion pie, one that only shows signs of growing.

"Right now prepared foods account for 4 to 6 percent of our sales," Carin told me. "In Chicago, that number is 8 percent. And I expect it will see double-digit growth, which is unheard of in any other department."

"What accounts for the growth?" I asked.

"The driving force is women in the workforce and how much time people have," she said. This seems intuitive, but her second reason for the growth was, to me, ominous. "Also, nobody knows how to *cook* anymore. It's mind-boggling. Some women don't even know how to hold a knife."

"Interesting that you single out women," I said. "Why is that?"

"Because, like it or not, women are still the ones who are mainly responsible for the meals at home."

For better or worse, and notwithstanding my own concern about the state of cooking in America, Carin's prediction of double-digit growth in grocery store prepared food seems inevitable.

To understand how the prepared foods explosion began, I asked Tom Heinen, who was there for the birth of it at his stores in Cleveland. It likely began sometime after World War II, when many women joined the labor force, and escalated slowly throughout the 1950s and 1960s as the country's social dynamics changed.

"My grandfather," Tom said, "hired Otto Mauf, a Statler Hotel chef who lost his job, in 1966 to help develop the new departments that were called the barbecue departments."

So, while little has been written about when prepared foods entered the grocery store, it's likely that it was around this time that most grocery stores began selling prepared foods, as they all tracked the industry to know what their competitors were up to. And small family chains would have been more likely to do so, given that their size afforded them a kind of agility that a big chain such as A&P did not have.

"Fried chicken, rotisserie chicken, and sandwiches," Tom said, when I asked what was the state of prepared foods when he began his career at Heinen's in 1979. "It pretty much started to take off when I started in the business."

And at Heinen's it seems to have begun with chickens, followed by lasagna, and branched out from there in a way that couldn't have been more haphazard.

One of Tom's first jobs, I recalled, was frying chicken, but I asked if there were rotisserie chickens before he began working in the mid-seventies.

"We were doing rotisserie chickens when I came to work here, and had been for many years, based on the condition of some of the rotisseries I inherited," he said.

Heinen's did a thriving business in cooked chicken until Church's franchises started popping up in town. "Took literally half our business," Tom said.

As the young man in charge, Tom now had ovens that had once cooked and kept the chickens hot, but now he needed only half of them. "So I said, 'What are we going to do with all these units?'" Tom told me. "And someone said, 'Well, you know, I make a pretty good lasagna, and I've got some other recipes we could do.' So our first recipes were people's *moms'* recipes. But they were good. We were making good food. And we couldn't make enough. Sales outweighed our ability to control it. We thought, 'Shit, the more we make, the more we sell.'"

There's an important *but:* "It didn't make any money," he said. "Never. We had no cost controls or anything."

Grocery stores at the time and throughout their history up to this point were only merchandisers. Yes, they broke down beef quarters and cut up fruit in the store, but generally they'd receive food, put it on shelves or in a case, try to make it look good, and sell it. But now, almost by accident (and, in Cleveland, due to the advent of a chicken franchise), the grocery store made its entry into the manufacturing arena, bifurcating and complicating its business model. And because the customer now expected it, the grocer had to deliver.

This is a common story in the industry, Tom said, whether it's fresh-squeezed orange juice or value-added cut produce. Once a customer wants it, you've got to get it for them or risk losing all their business to a store that *will* carry the item. "But you put a pencil to it," Tom said, "and we were getting killed. We were taking a supermarket mentality instead of a restaurant mentality. We didn't understand the labor component of prepared food. No one ever said, 'You know, food cost should be 25 percent.'"

Eventually they hired chefs, but this didn't work out. "We hired the wrong people," Jeff told me. "They were great chefs, but most chefs are shitty businesspeople and can be shitty *people* people.

"I can't tell you how much money we've lost in prepared foods," Jeff went on. "Oceans. *Oceans.* We make no money. Why do restaurants only make money if their bar is successful? Because it's *hard*." Especially given that, as former restaurant chef James noted, "People expect grocery-store prices, not restaurant prices."

Despite the financial drain, though, Jeff, Tom, and Chris all believe that investing in prepared foods has been the right move because of the implications of a new term that emerged in the grocery business in the 1990s: "share of stomach."

"It's a good buzzword," Jeff said. "You can only eat so much. America is testing that a bit. But you can only eat so much food. And people want it differently than they did thirty years ago, twenty years ago, ten years ago." Indeed they do—I don't think I'd ever heard of kale ten years ago, or wanted a quinoa salad. "They're not going to eat more food," he continued. "What's going to change is how they eat it, and how they get it. And that was the beginning of prepared foods. And everybody went into it."

Again, that's part of the nature of the grocery business. If somebody walked into a Fazio's on Van Aken Boulevard in 1979 and asked for lasagna like they have a mile in the other direction at Heinen's, you can be pretty sure Fazio's would start offering lasagna as well.

It's not just that it's hard to make money in prepared foods, it's all but impossible to *know* whether you're making money on them. Everyone cooks their numbers differently depending on how they allocate infrastructure costs, such as utilities, and labor. Most grocers I spoke with told me that of course their prepared foods department made money. But Jeff doesn't buy it.

"We've lost money in bakery and food service for longer than I care to think about," Jeff said. "Everybody does. If they account for it. One thing we're good at is facing the facts."

When grocers get together, they have these kinds of discussions.

Jeff to a fellow grocer, say, at a conference cocktail party: "You've got a nice bakery."

Fellow grocer: "Thanks. We work hard at that department."

Jeff: "Do you make money?"

FG: "Yes, we do."

Jeff: "All those ovens use a lot of energy. Do you account for that in bakery?"

FG: "No, we figure that as percentage of sales, about 3 percent."

Jeff nods, but thinks, *Bakery energy is a lot more than 3 percent.* Feigning interest so that it looks as though he's trying to figure out how *his* bakery department can make money, Jeff asks, "Do you charge the labor to bakery?"

FG: "Oh, no. We charge it to grocery."

Jeff nods politely and changes the subject to something more objective, such as where did they find those nifty anodized steel misting racks.

"We're kind of a plodding company," Jeff concluded. "A one-trick pony. We're stubborn. So even though we were losing money, we knew we had to do it. It was Tom's area for a while and we were losing our ass. Then it became my area because I was frustrated. We lost our ass. It became Chris's area. We lost our ass."

Then Carin Solganik called Tom Heinen. A diminutive woman, then fifty-nine, with short blonde hair, talkative but in a no-nonsense manner, Carin had known Tom for more than twenty years in the grocery business and considered him a friend. She explained that she was tired of working at Jungle Jim's International Market,[91] where she'd been

---

91 This Cincinnati landmark has elevated the grocery store to the level of theme park with, according to its site, 150,000 products spread out over 200,000 square feet. It's so big they have an "American Groceries" section, which carries the forty thousand or so products you would expect in a normal grocery store. On their website, they have a "Plan your trip" link, which recommends a two- to four-hour initial visit. Be sure to use the map, available at all the entrances. And you might consider bringing a sandwich, water bottle, and perhaps a change of clothing as well. The owner, Jim Bonaminio, told *Good Morning America,* "People get lost. We're ready to give people beepers here, like a restaurant. They get lost for days." He opened a second store in 2012, just a thirty-minute drive away, handy if the flagship is out of the African hot sauce you'd been after—though surely one of their 1,499 other hot sauces could satisfy.

hired to work in the prepared foods recipe development department. She asked Tom to let her know if he heard of any openings anywhere.

Tom said, "You should come up and talk to this guy, Chris Foltz."

She did. And while Chris certainly didn't say, "We can't figure out prepared foods—all three of us have tried and we've all lost our asses," he did say, "You're hired." A 1980 graduate of the Cornell University School of Hotel Administration, Carin had front-of-the-house restaurant experience, beverage director experience, and twenty years in groceries. And Chris knew that prepared foods represented a great opportunity for the business if they could make the financials work.

"Carin Solganik is why we're finally beginning to turn [prepared foods] around," Jeff said.

I first met Carin at Heinen's headquarters in a large boardroom. Chris had invited me to a tasting of potential menu items for an in-store cafe they were planning for one of their new stores. Carin, chef James, and a man who in the restaurant business would be called his sous chef, Jay Larkin, were presenting dishes for the approval of Tom, Jeff, Chris, and a few managers. The dishes had to be tasty, had to look good, and had to be able to be prepared or at least finished without the use of a stove—all they would have for cooking equipment was a TurboChef, which uses both microwave and radiant heat and looks like a giant microwave. We tasted a charcuterie board, a cheese platter, a variety of flatbreads, and pan-roasted mussels in a chorizo broth, the last of which was so good I could have eaten it all day long.

This seemed to me very much how a chain restaurant would operate, with corporate chefs presenting food to company execs for approval. But it wasn't long before it became clear to me that this represented a relatively new phase in the evolution of the grocery store, as they begin to function more and more like restaurants. I'd already seen this at my local Whole Foods Market, where I could sit at a counter and order off a menu, and a chef would cook a hot lunch for me right there, beer and wine available by the pour—and a very decent menu and meal at that. I ate at the counter in between the cheese case and the wine racks, with a view of the store's impressive seafood cases facing the center grocery aisles.

At the Whole Foods in the Time Warner Center in New York City, there's a sit-down sushi bar and a pizza station cooking wood-fired pies all day long, in addition to a hundred feet of prepared foods behind cases and five tables filled with food in steam-table hotel-pan inserts, a beer and wine section, and seating if you wanted a proper restaurant-like meal. And the checkout line for those buying prepared foods seemed to be the longest wait in the store.

When I visited the Whole Foods in Austin, Texas, where Whole Foods began, on a Saturday afternoon, I saw crowds at the back of the store drinking craft beers. What's more, that area of the store had the vibe of a restaurant and bar, not a place where you buy cereal and milk and dish soap.

Wegmans, a family-owned grocery chain lauded nationwide for the caliber of its prepared food and quality of its service, has several different styles of restaurants within their stores. They've opened four burger bars and ten in-store restaurants called The Pub. Each of their eighty-nine stores includes a market cafe—pizza, subs, sushi. And they are the only grocery chain I'm aware of in the country that has opened a stand-alone restaurant, across the street from their grocery store in Pittsford, New York, outside Rochester.

Heinen's itself was designing a new store in Chagrin Falls, Ohio, with an area of the store that would act exactly like an upscale artisanal pizzeria, complete with wood-fired pizza ovens.

The prepared foods at all these grocery stores are just a step away from restaurant-style cooking.

What Carin could bring to the table was a knowledge of how food service works in both a restaurant and in a grocery store. She knew that some prepared foods have to be treated on the ledger like restaurant food because of high labor, while other items can be treated like groceries because they come ready-made, and that the trick is in balancing all the moving parts.

Prepared foods have myriad paths from the source of the food to the deli case and salad bar. The soups I'd watched Dan reheat and empty into steam-table inserts were made in Boston by Blount Fine Foods. Blount shipped all their soups in these two-gallon bags to the Heinen's warehouse, and Heinen's trucked them to their various stores with the other refrigerated foods ordered by each department. (Blount also makes the Heinen's private-label soups, delivered in pint containers with the Heinen's label already on them.) Another company, Sandridge Foods, in Ohio, also sells them soup. As for chili, Heinen's makes that themselves at the central warehouse, as a way to use trim from the meat cutting—just like at a restaurant.

But Heinen's doesn't always simply heat and serve the soup they buy from other companies. Some soups arrive more as a base to which Heinen's adds its own ingredients. The tortilla soup comes as a base, and unsold rotisserie chicken is shredded by Heinen's cooks and added to these soups, as a way to reduce waste without compromising the product. Or the Heinen's cooks might add sausage to the black bean soup or pasta to the fire-roasted vegetable soup.

They have a strong rotisserie chicken program—selling around forty-five hundred a week for $7.99, pretty much the same price as an uncooked chicken—using the same antibiotic-free, vegetarian diet–fed chickens from an Ohio chicken farm. Carin notes that they have a rigorous protocol that requires all rotisserie chickens to be pulled from the shelves and blast-chilled if unsold after two hours. These would go into the soup. But not the pulled chicken, one of the most popular of their prepared foods. For this, they roast whole chickens and pull the meat while it's still hot. Then they chill it.

This, of course, is one of the main differences between prepared foods and restaurant foods. Everything has to be chilled after being cooked, and cooked so that the food finishes to the right doneness at home. Some items, such as the breaded orange roughy, are undercooked for this reason.

Hot food looks better than cold food, and if it doesn't look delicious in the case, no one will buy it, so developing these dishes is tricky. For instance, olive oil congeals, so no matter how delicious the olive oil may be when the roasted salmon is finished at home, James and his crew can't cook or finish that salmon with olive oil. This food, unlike restaurant food, has to look delicious cold. And because many of the dishes are being prepared in the store, rather than coming from the central warehouse, they've also got to be simple enough to replicate, because twenty-two stores have to make them as consistently as possible, and no two cooks are alike.

Because this food is cooked, chilled, and reheated, I've always thought of prepared food in the grocery store as high-end leftovers. Carin didn't like it at all when I called them leftovers, but I maintain that that is, in effect, what they are. You've cooked dinner at home, breaded chicken breasts, say, but you made extra just in case. When dinner is over, the remaining chicken, cooled to room temperature, is put on a plate, covered with plastic wrap, and slid into the fridge. The next day, or even the day after, the chicken is reheated in the toaster oven, the breading re-crisped, and it's almost as good, if not equally as good as it was the first time. Certainly beef stew that has sat around in the fridge for a few days is better than it is straight out of the oven, as any chef will tell you (all braises improve with time). Again I use the words "sat around" to make a point of how careless one can be and still have delicious food. But if I were to rephrase it to sell you on the idea that if you're serving beef stew or braised lamb shank at a dinner party, it's best to make the dish several days in advance, I'd explain that in fact it's not really "sitting around," it's ripening, like a duck confit. Flavors transform, and as a rule, the longer something takes to cook, the longer it will last.

Flavors transform for the worse, as well. Sauces are a good example. An excellent sauce, a simple pan jus, for instance, is best right out of the pan. Anyone who drinks coffee already knows a perfect example of the volatility of flavor: Freshly brewed coffee or pour-over coffee drunk immediately is a considerably different experience than coffee drunk after it has sat for three hours and been reheated.

So when a grocery store creates dishes, it has to keep these facts of cooking in mind. And being a restaurant chef, as James Mowcomber has been for twenty years, prepares you well for this kind of thinking, because at least half of what you eat in a busy restaurant other than the protein—that is, the meat or fish—is cooked ahead of time, chilled, and reheated. It's not always the case, but it's mostly the case. It's the only way four cooks behind the line can put out three hundred elaborate meals in the span of five or six hours.

When I worked as a cook for a short time at a high-end restaurant in Cleveland, part of my afternoon was spent cooking green vegetables (asparagus, sautéed spinach with garlic). Properly prepared, cooled, and stored, these items could be served over the course of three days. It was prepared food. I'd make big batches of scalloped potatoes that could last four days. Plus, once the potatoes were chilled, I could then use a ring cutter to make perfect discs for an elegant presentation, reheating them on a sizzle platter in the oven. And of course my veal osso bucco only got better after a few days in the cooler. These are lessons that any home cook should know in order to make the daily meal more convenient.

Because one of my chief goals in writing about food is to encourage people to cook their own food, I was fascinated by the grocery store's prepared food program. I became fixated on one of Heinen's signature dishes, their chicken Romano. It's just breaded chicken, fried and blast chilled. And it's delicious. Heinen's has been selling it for more than twenty years, so long that no one remembers who came up with it.

In all likelihood, a chef at one of the stores was responsible (most dishes twenty years ago were created this way). It probably began as what is referred to in-store as "value added" meat, which essentially means prepared in some way but uncooked—marinated shish kabobs, say, or a stuffed and rolled flank steak. Chicken Romano began as an uncooked item, breaded chicken breast. A meat department associate mixed some grated Romano cheese with bread crumbs. He dusted the chicken breast with flour, dipped it in egg wash, dredged it in the bread crumb mixture, and put it in the meat case. Then some stores began to cook it and chill it as they began to sell more prepared food. It sold really well, so this store kept making it and the recipe was shared with other stores. Everywhere it was a hit. In fact, stores were selling so much of it, it was eventually taken out of the individual stores and given over to the central warehouse, which now cooks this dish for all the stores.[92]

Heinen's currently cooks and sells eighty-five thousand pounds of it yearly, or about seventeen hundred pounds every week all year long.

Chef James came up with another popular item, grilled shrimp with a sriracha-honey-lime sauce. This dish is cooked in individual stores. This is another no-brainer, easily prepared by a variety of chefs at twenty-two stores, and a dish that cooks quickly and reheats well. They move through fifty-one thousand pounds of this offering every year.

Its popularity required Carin to use another strategy to handle the volume. She outsourced the sauce to a Cleveland company, which makes it in big batches; the sauce became so successful they are now preparing to bottle it under the Heinen's label, so this one dish created its own stand-alone product.

Other dishes in their rotating prepared foods lineup: twice-baked potatoes with bacon and Cheddar cheese, pulled pork, baked salmon with Two Brothers seasoning, zucchini and feta cakes (one of James's most popular creations), sautéed mixed vegetables with garlic and herbs, grilled asparagus, penne pasta with creamy pesto sauce, Tuscan kale and potatoes, teriyaki flank steak, barbecued chicken with bourbon-bacon sauce, Thai chicken and vegetable salad, nut-crusted tilapia filets, kale with toasted walnuts and Parmesan, corn casserole, and seared cauliflower with turmeric, ginger, and garlic. To name a few.

This doesn't include the thirty sandwiches they offer (chicken Caesar wrap, grilled eggplant sub, and so on). Nor the seventy-five different salads. They don't offer them all at once, but they offer a lot—you can choose from twenty-four different salads at larger stores. This is yet another emblem of the transforming American diet. America wants convenient food and, increasingly, nutritious, good-for-you food. Thus the emergence of the salad bar.

---

92 It's very easy. The standardized recipe for the breading is one part grated Romano, four parts panko bread crumbs, some granulated garlic and dried parsley, and some olive oil to moisten the mixture. The boneless chicken breasts are floured, dipped in a milk-and-egg wash, dredged in the breading, and pan-fried. Try it at home!

I remember the first salad bar I encountered. It was in the late 1960s, when I was still a tot, and my parents took me to a Cleveland steak house chain called the Brown Derby, unrelated to the Hollywood landmark. I know that I was seeing the salad bar close to its origins, which most sources date to restaurants in the late 1950s or early 1960s,[93] because I remember being annoyed when I picked up my plate (the plate invariably piping hot from the dishwasher) and found that for the first time I had to contend with a large Plexiglas obstacle between me and the chopped lettuce, dreary tomatoes, chickpeas, chopped hard-boiled egg, sliced red onion, sliced mushrooms, crunchy bacon-flavored bits of unknown substance, and four crocks of dressing. My dad—who wrote ads for the restaurant: "Thick steaks, thin prices"—explained that these were "sneeze guards" that had been mandated for sanitation purposes. Anyone born five years after I was, in 1963, may not know that these guards didn't exist at the beginning of the salad bar era (signaling, perhaps, another change in the American psyche, the beginnings of our fear of germs, which has gotten so out of hand that reputable media outlets are recommending that we don't rinse our chickens before cooking them because, these new articles argue, splattering water gives the entire kitchen a potential shower of salmonella bacteria[94]). I remember thinking that being able to serve myself was a nifty invention if only because it meant I didn't have to eat the raw sliced button mushrooms my mom liked to put in our salads at home.[95]

....

93 The *New York Times, Washington Post,* and *Los Angeles Times* all offer the leading contenders for the inventor of the salad bar, which may go back as early as the 1950s, suggesting that one of its early creators was restaurateur Norman Brinker in the 1960s, and may well have been vaulted into popularity when Rich Melman, CEO of the Chicago restaurant company Lettuce Entertain You, created a salad bar featuring dozens of items to choose from. But such history is difficult to pin down precisely.

94 See my blog post on this topic: "Bacteria! Run Away! Run Away!"

95 Thinking about the salad bar has unearthed a cherished childhood memory, as food can so easily do. I love my mother for any number of reasons, but this event is chief among them: On one visit to the Brown Derby, my parents and I, aunt and uncle, and two cousins had all passed down the salad bar, making plates of our own personal salad preferences, and were back at the table digging into them. A waiter stopped by the table and asked, "How

Today, the salad bars of yore are less and less in evidence. In fact, had I been transported from the 1970s to the salad bar of today, I'd have scratched my head, perplexed. Quinoa? Kale? Farro? *Blueberries*, in *salad*? And what the hell is edamame?[96] But in fact the primary way the salad bar has changed is that the bins do not contain individual ingredients to mix and match but are filled with an array of already composed salads. We have, in our constant quest for convenience, taken even the guesswork and choice out of composing this most simple of dishes, the salad. No longer the agonizing series of choices that Rich Melman's forty-item salad bar forced us to make. We simply choose the wheat berry salad with asparagus, fennel, and oranges, the curried chickpea and fennel salad, or the cranberry-almond quinoa salad. The salad category is so vast that Heinen's list is broken down into numerous categories: protein salads, pasta salads, bean salads, grain salads, and, my favorite category, the "Dr. Todd Approved" salads, five out of the seventy-five.

One of Dr. Todd's approved salads is called the "Detox Salad." Kale, broccoli, cauliflower, shredded carrots, golden raisins, sunflower seeds, and diced red onions, all dressed with Dr. Todd–approved Cindy's Carrot & Ginger Dressing. It's a damn good salad. And its components are trucked to Heinen's central warehouse from the Ohio company Freshway Foods, then delivered by Heinen's semi rigs to all the stores, which combine and dress the salad daily. The stores originally dressed it with a Freshway dressing until they realized the dressing contained high-fructose corn syrup. Being "clean-label" conscious, as Carin puts it, they now use the dressing from Cindy's Kitchen, a Boston-based company that sells dressings both wholesale and retail.

---

is everyone enjoying their salad?" All nodded but for my mother. She glanced up from her salad to the waiter standing over her right shoulder and, with withering scorn, said, "My salad is . . . *despicable*." The waiter was so dumbfounded that my mother deplored a salad she herself had made, he simply apologized and departed, as my father doubled over in laughter. It would live on as a family catchphrase when commenting on the quality of a salad for decades.

96 Why aren't they called soybeans? According to Merriam-Webster, the word "edamame" derives from combining the Japanese words for branch and bean, and usually denotes soybeans that have been cooked.

"It's all about relationships," Carin said, echoing what countless restaurant chefs have said to me regarding their own purveyors.

Here is a clear example of consumer demand leveraging the unrecognized power and influence of the grocery store. Because American shoppers want tons, literally, of salad, the grocery store had to find a way to provide it; whole companies transformed themselves to fill the requests of the grocery store, to produce and deliver not only massive quantities of bulk composed salads, or their component parts, but also soups and stews and any number of foods that can be prepared in massive quantities, chilled, packaged, and shipped, for the woman (usually) of the house to serve to the family. Freshway Foods, Cindy's Kitchen, Signature Sauces in Cleveland, and Sandridge Foods are just a few of the half dozen or so manufacturers this grocery chain relies on to supplement their prepared foods.

This has happened, in one form or another, in every department of the grocery store—consumer demand translates to grocer demand, which creates new businesses or allows them to expand. It's important to note that it is a company the size of Heinen's—or Festival Foods in Minnesota and Wisconsin, Bristol Farms in California, and Roche Bros. Supermarkets in Massachusetts—that is most likely to drive such changes in the way we eat because of their unique volume. A Kroger or Albertsons— like the A&P of old, which was very slow to make changes—doesn't have the corporate agility to initiate the kinds of changes a smaller chain can (such as Carin's switching out a dressing containing high-fructose corn syrup for one without that sugar, or Chris's investing in a small company's product discovered at Expo West). The big chains tend rather to respond to those changes in the industry that prove to be successful.

From the moment it opens its doors till the lights go dark, section by section, the grocery store hosts a continuous stream of shoppers entering, pushing carts through the produce section for a bag of carrots, a few apples, some lettuce, and a bunch of bananas, past the dairy for milk or soy milk, yogurt, and eggs, stopping in the cereal aisle, picking up a chicken, a couple bottles of wine, a plastic clamshell filled with Dr. Todd–Approved Sesame, Kale, and Ginger Salad, a pound of sliced ham, a bag of chips, and the popular Talenti Sea Salt Caramel Gelato, and maybe, on the way out, a case of bottled water. At this store each of the 2,250 shoppers each day usually hands over forty to fifty dollars. I did see some monster bills when I was bagging—$400, even $500—and I myself have personally spent more than $1,000 during a single grocery store run when cooking for a large group over the course of a week at the Publix in Key West. I once filled four whole shopping carts, twice what my dad would buy in the 1960s to feed a family of three for a week.

The river of food courses down the conveyor belts all day long, every day of the year—food that increasingly doesn't even need to be cooked at all.

18.

THE COOKING ANIMAL

Is this a good evolution—the increasing amount of food we eat at home that doesn't need to be cooked? The social food researcher Harry Balzer noted without prompting that Americans are not cooking more, they're simply eating more meals at home. It might seem that the steady growth of prepared food is good. But a conversation with the chef Dan Barber made it clear that even he—someone who cooks for a living so others don't have to—worries about what all this convenient prepared food presages.

Barber, chef of Blue Hill in Manhattan and Blue Hill at Stone Barns north of the city, has written widely about the importance of agriculture and our food supply. I called him to ask for his thoughts on the grocery store, and one of the first things he brought up was prepared foods.

"I was in a Whole Foods the other day," he said. "The produce section seems to be shrinking and, like, 85 percent of the store was prepared foods and private vendors. I mean, if that's the future of the grocery store, then . . . *fuck*."

Why the expletive?

For about the first decade of writing about food, I tried to distance myself from the designation "food writer." I was a *writer*, not a *food writer*, which I somehow believed was a lesser species. And yet I didn't cover wars in Iraq or explore corruption in government, let alone attempt the more risky and difficult search for art through poetry or fiction.[97] I was instead writing about veal stock and *sauce Robert*, how to clarify a consommé or whip up a hollandaise.

....

97 I feel no shame in noting, these many years later, that during my time at Heinen's, I did in fact publish fiction, a collection of novellas called *In Short Measures*—no shame, that is, because the book sold, I believe, all of fourteen copies.

But by the mid-2000s, my thinking began to change. First, that I had been successful in writing about food all this time meant there was an audience for it. Indeed, the country's obsession for all things food-related had snowballed since the 1990s, and that huge ball was now accelerating downhill, unstoppable. People were interested in food in ways they hadn't been before.

Then two important books arrived on the scene in the first decade of this century, Eric Schlosser's *Fast Food Nation* (2001) and Michael Pollan's *The Omnivore's Dilemma* (2006). Both addressed the industrialization of our food supply—Schlosser by way of our fast food industry, and Pollan through agriculture and three differing food chains—and both were chilling in their implications of the impact of our industrialized food systems. While the books are wide-ranging, what seemed to grip our imaginations most strongly was the way American ingenuity and commitment to capitalism, combined with the consumer's demand for ever cheaper food, had created such a bizarre and dysfunctional, even mortifying, food system, one that seems guaranteed to trash the environment on which everything we eat relies. It pollutes our soil, rivers, and oceans, and at the same time debases the food itself. Most of all, it makes us sick.

Pollan called his introduction "Our National Eating Disorder," apt words for a country that seems to require investigative journalists, certified nutritionists, physicians, and professional chefs to answer my father's favorite question: *What do you want to eat?* Shouldn't be difficult. "As a culture," Pollan writes, "we seem to have arrived at a place where whatever native wisdom we may once have possessed about eating has been replaced by confusion and anxiety." And almost nothing seems to have gotten better in the decade since he wrote those words. The subjects of that confusion and anxiety may have changed—gluten has replaced carbohydrates in terms of what to avoid, paleo has replaced South Beach in terms of eating strategies, for instance—but we are no less confused and anxious when charged with *choosing* what to eat, a choice that is most acute when we enter a grocery store. It's one thing to order food at a restaurant or scan a takeout menu and make a selection from twenty or thirty options. It's quite another to stand in the vast expanse of a grocery store before forty thousand different things to eat, the majority of which must be prepped and cooked, or at the very least heated, and make that same choice.

Three years after *Omnivore* arrived, a third book came out that helped clarify my thoughts about the reason for America's food obsession/confusion: *Catching Fire: How Cooking Made Us Human* by the Harvard primatologist Richard Wrangham. In it, he proposes that it was not the control of fire or a genetic fluke that pushed our hominid ancestors to evolve into the *Homo sapiens* we are today, but rather the cooking of food. That is, he believes that the key evolutionary mechanism responsible for creating the most successful species on the planet was a shift from eating raw food to eating cooked food. Yes, as we've long suspected, diet[98] is important, but just how important it is we may not always recognize.

How and why humans evolved as we did is surely complex and came about as a result of numerous factors, a perfect storm of biological and environmental circumstances, but we were one of a dozen upright species two hundred thousand years ago—why did we survive while others died out?[99]

Wrangham argues that once we began cooking food, our hairy, barrel-gutted ancestors could consume huge amounts of calories in a very short time, as opposed to their raw-foodist brethren, who spent six to eight hours a day masticating plants, which was how long it took to ingest enough calories to thrive—a solitary activity, not a shared one, I should note.

Once we learned to cook food, we could also eat a wider variety of foods. The abundant calories and nutrition made us uncommonly

....

98 For those to whom derivations matter, this pedestrian and simple-sounding word has meaningful origins: Diet comes from the Greek word *diaita*, "a way of life." In this sense, maintaining a healthy diet has some meaning.

99 Indeed, recent genetic evidence suggests that all humans today evolved from a *single* population in Africa fifty to eighty thousand years ago: "A Single Migration From Africa Populated the World, Studies Find," *New York Times*, September 21, 2016.

healthy, and our genes spread rapidly. Our guts shrank (we no longer needed food in that volume), our jaws shrank because we didn't have to chew so hard for hours, and we lost much of our hair so we could both hunt and travel long distances on the hot savanna without overheating. We became the "naked ape," spreading genes in greater distances than before.

More important, our brains grew. Brains are voracious calorie consumers—a two-hundred-pound man uses up to 30 percent of his calories to feed the three-pound mass inside his skull.

But in order to take advantage of the calories and nutrition cooked food provided, we had to do something we didn't necessarily have to do previously: work together. Cooking *was* work, as it is today, and so we had to share in the labor. Some members of the tribe had to go out and hunt and forage, while others stayed home to tend the children, protect the homestead, and prepare the roots and tubers, which required long cooking, in the event that the hunter-gatherers returned empty-handed. We had to *cooperate*. We became tamer and calmer, perhaps even empathetic. Because eating was now a group effort, you couldn't be an asshole or you'd risk being alienated from the group and denied food.

Wrangham goes so far as to argue that the cooking of food, and the behavior required to take advantage of it, created a sexual division of labor, was the basis for marriage, and resulted in the formation of communities.

Wrangham doesn't write about cooking's impact on the development of language, but when I reached him by email, he said it wasn't unreasonable to speculate that because we were no longer swallowing pounds and pounds of raw vegetation, our esophagus, like our jaw and gut, shrank as well and thus allowed for the development of more complex vocal anatomy that could produce the broader range of sounds required for something as nuanced as language. A common language is of course a useful component of cooperation and would come in handy when strategizing ways to overcome competitors and to protect a community against attackers.

So, cooking food made us smarter, healthier, and more agile than competing species. The practice forced us to work together and possibly facilitated and encouraged the development of spoken language, which would be far more effective than signal-based communications. Eating together also tamed us and taught us restraint as we shared meals around a fire. And ultimately, as many from Brillat-Savarin to Claude Lévi-Strauss have observed, cooking gave us culture.

Wrangham bolsters his argument further by noting that there are no records or stories of any group of humans who can exist for long on a completely raw diet and how difficult it is to get enough calories and nutrients for those who try.

We are the only animal that cooks. We are the cooking animal.

By the early 2000s, another cultural phenomenon began to be recognized and written about. While Americans were increasingly interested in food—watching cooking shows on television, posting photographs of their meals to Instagram, turning restaurant chefs into media stars—we were also cooking less and less, a fact confirmed by food researcher Harry Balzer.

Indeed, we had been cooking less and less for decades, a change that seems to have begun after World War II, then increased in the 1950s and 1960s as women entered the workforce in significant numbers, food manufacturing companies created more and more ready-to-heat foods, and life generally felt busier with each passing year. The decision not to cook became increasingly easier, thanks to McDonald's and to food manufacturers, and the grocery stores that sold their food.

It seems to me that all these factors—from the industrialization of our food to the belief that cooking for our family is a chore rather than a fundamental luxury with unrecognized benefits for the people we love—are directly responsible for our food-related diseases and illnesses, and what will ultimately drive our need to turn our food confusion into knowledge and our anxiety into assuredness.

This I believe: When we cook our own food, and share in both the work of it and the pleasures of eating it together, our bodies are healthier, our families are healthier, our communities are healthier, and our environment is healthier. There are even underappreciated benefits to the smells of food cooking in a house. Everyone knows the experience of walking into a house where something good is simmering on the stove; we cannot help but remark, "Smells good in here!" There's a reason for this. Smells are received in the most primitive part of our brain, one linked directly to our sympathetic and parasympathetic nervous systems; the latter regulates, among other things, anxiety and stress. I believe that when we smell good food, it immediately reduces stress.

There's a reason Pollan opens his book by asking the reader to consider the supermarket from a naturalist's point of view: "Your first impression is apt to be of its astounding biodiversity. Look how many different plants and animals (and fungi) are represented on this single acre of land! What forest or prairie could hope to match it?" A naturalist evaluates the health of a landscape by the extent of its biodiversity; in this regard, the American supermarket is the healthiest landscape in existence.

That is, of course, except for the edibles it contains that we suspect are making us sick, all the heavily processed food composed of refined wheat and sugar, items so culturally beloved and so pleasurable to eat that they're difficult to let go of—our Wonder Bread, our cornflakes and Cocoa Puffs and breakfast bars, our Doritos and Fritos and my own beloved Pringles, our Pop-Tarts and cake mixes. In this respect the only landscape more dangerous than the American supermarket is the American fast food restaurant.

But what of the increasing number of prepared foods? It is surely a good thing, no? A range of nourishing, all-natural, good-for-you dishes that require no more preparation than a frozen dinner. Perfect for the busy dual-income family that has little time to devote to cooking. But it also means we have even less reason to cook. We have no need to share the work of preparing the food because someone else can do it for us. But with work comes a heightened appreciation of that work's result, so when we bring home prepared food and heat it in the microwave or on the stovetop, there's no one to thank or be grateful for, there's no deeper appreciation of the food other than whether it tastes okay, and the house is without the relaxing aromas of food cooking.

Ultimately we must consider this question: *At what cost convenience?* Convenience isn't free; it involves a trade-off. With the convenience of prepared food, I give up the benefits of cooking food in the home in order to ensure that the family at least gets to eat together, or to take advantage of more time to do something else—attend my son's soccer game, put in some overtime on an important project at work, watch television. It's all a matter of time allocation.

Cooking food at home is important, and we get the food we cook primarily at a grocery store. Thus have grocery stores become, to my mind, even more important than I'd originally supposed.

19.

FROZEN

Growing up in the 1970s I ate a lot of green beans, because that's what Mom cooked while Dad was outside grilling the steaks. But I don't think I ate a fresh green bean until I was an adult, even in the summer. My mom grew up eating fresh green beans all summer, as her mom tended a large vegetable garden behind their suburban Detroit house. Her mom didn't grow vegetables because they tasted better than the stuff trucked in from California and Florida or frozen in a cardboard box or canned by the Jolly Green Giant; she grew them because they were basically free food; she and her husband had four kids and not a lot of money and were shell-shocked for life by the Depression, during which squirrel was not an uncommon ingredient in their meals. My mom pulled excess vegetables in a red wagon, selling them door to door.

But those memories of eating freshly picked green beans didn't translate for my mom into a desire to cook them as an adult. Perhaps it was in part because Mom wanted to distance herself from her lower-middle-class roots (growing your own food and selling it to neighbors was an emblem of those roots, not the mark of prestige it might be today). Or maybe it was because Grandma Spamer cooked the bejesus out of those green beans. I think there's a reason green beans cooked to a drab olive color are unappealing—it indicates that half the nutrition is gone, as is all the flavor. But most likely, it was just plain easy for Mom to drop a block of frozen Birds Eye French-cut green beans out of the cardboard box and into a pot of boiling water.

Times have changed dramatically: Mom wouldn't think of buying frozen green beans now—instead she buys fresh haricots verts, the slender and tender green bean, available year-round at her local Publix. And as an adult, I was the one reaching into the frozen vegetable case at the grocery store for the rock-solid peas, because that's all my kids would eat. I considered getting the kids to eat anything green a triumph, and frozen peas were an easy, inexpensive, reliable victory.

There's no comparison between frozen peas and fresh shelled English peas, of course, which are available all summer long both at the grocery store and at our farmers' market in Cleveland. Frozen peas are starchy, dimpled, and dull; fresh are light, with a crisp bite and a sweetness absent in frozen peas, given that the sugars haven't had time to convert to starch. I even love the meditative work of shucking fresh peas, the textural sensation as my thumb pops them rat-a-tat-tat off the funicles attaching them to the pod and into a bowl. Frozen peas depress me, because I know how a fresh pea can taste.

Frozen peas nevertheless are one of the most popular frozen vegetables, and have been since Clarence Birdseye discovered in the 1920s that peas quickly blanched before being frozen result in a vividly green pea.

Birdseye was the father of frozen food, the man most responsible for what is now a $240 billion global industry. As with so many of our food innovations, frozen food arose from the unpredictable mix of an eccentric, adventurous, inquisitive mind, a man's serendipitous move through the world (his interest in frozen food was rooted in fox farming in Labrador, in northeastern Canada, a place that gets mighty cold in the winter), and advances in technology and in packaging during the 1920s that allowed new ideas to find their physical realization.

Birdseye's influence was no small matter. As Mark Kurlansky writes in his book *Birdseye: The Adventures of a Curious Man*, "Undeniably, Birdseye changed our civilization. He created an industry by modernizing the process of food preservation and in so doing nationalized and then internationalized food distribution." Moreover, Kurlansky writes, Birdseye "greatly contributed to the development of industrial-scale agriculture." Once we could stockpile produce that previously would have gone bad, we could grow more and more food and keep it indefinitely.

As a young man seeking adventure in the early twentieth century, Birdseye was offered a chance to work for a celebrated medical missionary in Labrador. There he found a land rich in animals valuable for their pelts, and abundant sea life—lobsters, halibut, cod, and seals. Inhabited by fur trappers, fishermen, and Inuit, Labrador routinely experienced temperatures that could drop below –30 degrees Fahrenheit. Survival required him to learn all methods of preserving food—salting, drying, and freezing. And with freezing, he paid particular attention to the size of the ice crystals relative to the way the fish or meat was frozen. He recognized that when the crystals were large, a result of slow freezing, they damaged the cell structure, the meat leaked juices, and its texture became mealy. He experimented with freezing vegetables and caribou meat, simply as a matter of ensuring he had enough to eat.

On returning from Labrador, he took a series of jobs, eventually landing a position as the assistant to the president of the US Fisheries Association, a lobbying group for commercial fishermen that worked to improve the fishing industry. Kurlansky notes that "the decision in 1920 to work for the fisheries was another one of these serendipitous moves that so often directed Birdseye toward his destiny."

Now engaged in work that joined two of his passions, wildlife and food, he turned his attention from the fisherman to the fish itself and the problem of getting fish to market before it went bad. Thus was born his first idea: a change in the way fish was packaged.

Birdseye developed an inexpensive container that was better insulated than what was currently used, and kept the fish chilled during transport to markets. The fish was better, but still not comparable to what it was at its source. Birdseye knew this was due to spoilage, and he considered his packaging a failure. It was a problem he kept working at in the back of his mind.

Frozen food had been around forever in frigid climes, but it had also made inroads into America as ice became plentiful. The quality of frozen food, however, was terrible. Most of it was frozen in bulk portions, whether whole sides of beef or great blocks of strawberries. The first patent for freezing fish was given in 1862. But because the quality was so bad, frozen food was largely frowned upon.

Then Birdseye recalled a traditional method he'd learned from watching the Inuit: fast freezing. "My subconscious suddenly told me that perishable food could be kept perfectly preserved in the same way I had kept them in Labrador—by quick freezing!"

He needed to find a way to re-create it in the United States, so he convinced an ice cream company to let him experiment in their plant. He left his job with the US Fisheries Association and embarked on a new adventure, creating in 1923 his first frozen foods company, the General Seafood Corporation.

His first major invention in freezing food, of some two hundred inventions during his lifetime, was the development of hollowed metal plates filled with an ammonia-based refrigerant that kept the metal between –20 and –50 degrees Fahrenheit. Two-inch-thick cartons were filled with food and pressed between the plates (not unlike the block of green beans my mom dumped weekly into a pot of water). Multi-plate freezing, as it was called, would be used for decades.

The next leap for Birdseye was to change those metal plates to belts, chilled with a calcium chloride spray—food could run continuously between the belts and the space between the belts could be adjusted. More food could be frozen faster than ever before.

But while he would invent various tools for the actual quick freezing, Kurlansky writes, "The originality of Birdseye's work was as much in the packaging as the preparation of food." Here again, as with the tin can and cardboard box, food innovation began with packaging. This packaging had to eliminate air pockets, and the material had to be waterproof, as moisture condensed on the packages. Waterproof ink had to be used. Cellophane, a French invention, was relatively new. Birdseye wanted to use it for packaging fish but found that it disintegrated when used on moist fish. So he persuaded DuPont to create a waterproof version of cellophane.[100]

Harvey Levenstein, in *Paradox of Plenty*, notes that many methods of freezing predate Birdseye, "but they were used primarily to preserve foods that were already going bad from deteriorating further; this had

....

100 For a time Birdseye was the only customer for the product. "Then cigarette companies bought it," Kurlansky writes, "and cigars started to come wrapped in it, and soon cellophane wrappers were a standard feature of American consumer goods—another little-known Birdseye influence on our world."

fostered a connotation between freezing and low quality in the public mind." In other words, one of Birdseye's major contributions was to convince a skeptical public, via savvy packaging, that this frozen food was high quality.

Birdseye could now freeze enormous quantities of food. In the summer of 1927 he froze 1.6 million pounds of seafood. And this abundance resulted in a problem that had to be solved. What to do with all of it? There weren't trucks or trains that could keep the food frozen during transport. There weren't warehouses with freezers to store the food. And retail stores didn't have freezers. But there was now a need for them, and they would soon follow. The first retail store freezer became available in 1928 and, while expensive, it allowed some stores to stock frozen food.

Thus it was that America would become the country where commercial freezers and frozen food developed and also the country that would lead the world in the manufacture of refrigerators and freezers.

In 1929 the new Birds Eye company began working at capacity, freezing and storing twenty-seven kinds of food from meat to fish to berries to peas and spinach, and would launch with major advertising to introduce to a country suspicious of frozen food a brand-new product called "frosted food." It promised unparalleled convenience, the luxury of eating vegetables out of season, and fresh-tasting seafood to the middle of the country, but the infrastructure required for its success didn't exist. It wasn't until after World War II that frozen food came into its own. Within a decade, frozen foods would be a $50 billion dollar industry in the United States, and $300 billion worldwide.[101]

This was due in large part to the proliferation of larger and larger supermarkets in the late 1940s and 1950s, the great spinning wheel of

....

101 It's worth noting exactly how forward thinking Birdseye was. Again from Kurlansky: "Birdseye always believed in the central concept of agribusiness, that through technology hunger in the world would one day vanish. . . . Birdseye also believed in hydroponic farming. Plants grow by extracting nutrients from the soil, but if they are provided these nutrients in water, they have no need of soil, which means that fields are not necessary for growing crops. . . . Birdseye envisioned a New York City whose produce needs were locally supplied by rooftop hydroponic farming. He predicted that 'eventually we shall learn to manufacture food from sunlight, as plants do.'"

American commerce and technology accelerating, advances in one product fueling advances in others to feed a growing, prosperous country. Once relegated to the perimeter of the store, aisle-long stand-alone freezer cases—referred to as "upright multi-decks"—are common and have become more energy efficient. At my favorite Heinen's, these cases run about seventy-five feet at the rear of the store, one of which contains a single category: a seemingly endless array of ice creams, sorbets, sherbets, and gelatos, and variations for every diet-restricted lover of cold confections.

The frozen offerings are staggering in their variety. Eggo pancakes and waffles sit below Heinen's all-natural organic mini waffles, Red's turkey sausage bacon burritos, Jimmy Dean's version of the Egg McMuffin, and another labeled "Smart Ones" (a name perhaps suggested by the Snackwell's guy), Special K flatbread with breakfast sausage, cinnamon rolls, monkey bread, bagels, strudel.

Piecrusts await, along with puff pastry, phyllo dough, ready-to-thaw-and-eat cookie dough, potatoes in every form and shape—even frozen mashed potatoes, crushed ginger, chopped basil, garlic, veggie fries, veggie burgers, spicy basmati rice with edamame, steam-in-a-bag microwavable vegetables of every kind, raspberries, blueberries, strawberries, and speckled butter beans and black-eyed peas.

There are several cases labeled "Natural and Organic," with enchiladas and burritos, egg rolls, General Tso's chicken, pot stickers, chicken tikka masala, Stouffer's fettuccini Alfredo and macaroni and beef, red wine–braised beef with polenta, Lean Cuisine five-cheese rigatoni, White Castle sliders, Hot Pockets, pizza rolls, Hungry Man TV dinners, bagel bites, chicken and turkey potpies (which I ate for dinner pretty much every time my parents went out on the weekend, which was every weekend of my youth, unless they themselves were entertaining), chicken nuggets shaped like pterodactyls ("600 mg of omega-3s, 100% all-natural and organic" its label announces to prospective parents), gluten-free corn dogs, Healthy Choice meatloaf (again, the name—let's choose that one, obviously!), T.G.I. Friday's potato skins, mozzarella bites, Super Pretzels, whole turkeys, breaded cod and shrimp, challah, cheese blintzes, bourekas, falafel, and gefilte fish.

Then ten whole cases filled exclusively with pizzas, gluten-free English muffins, dinner rolls, pretzel rolls, pizza rolls, frozen pasta, frozen marinara sauce, pierogies, and potato dumplings. And chicken: wings, breasts, nuggets, patties, and "whole lean chicken wing sections" (sections?), breasts stuffed with broccoli and cheese, gizzards, feet, gravy— I could go on.

And I would, if any of it were any good. But it's not.

In my opinion.

The berries and corn are passable, peas when the kids were young. When I find myself eating alone these days, I'll sometimes pick out an organic frozen enchilada or some Thai noodles in their little cellophane-sealed cardboard container. These take hunger away after five minutes in the microwave but aren't particularly fun to eat, and seem to me more an emblem of sad solitude than convenience.

"Frozen food has really leveled off," Jeff Heinen told me as we strolled past case after case of frozen dinners. This jibed with food marketing researcher Harry Balzer, who told me, "The frozen dinner, the Lean Cuisine or the Healthy Choice—it needs a new explanation, it needs to be rebranded."

This is ironic in that it was, according to Harvey Levenstein, Lean Cuisine that pushed frozen dinners into the future in the early 1980s. By the 1970s, the frozen dinner and the TV dinner had become emblems of mediocrity. It took Stouffers,[102] capitalizing on America's disastrous low-fat mania, to reinvent the frozen dinner in the form of my father's go-to weekday dinner. Noting that frozen dinner sales had been in decline since 1972, Stouffer's introduction of the Lean Cuisine found whole new markets. "Within a year of its introduction," Levenstein writes in

102 Stouffer's was something of a Cleveland institution. It began as a creamery in Medina, Ohio, then opened a shop in downtown Cleveland, which became a restaurant. The restaurants expanded to locations as far away as New York City. In 1946, Stouffer's entered the frozen food business. In Cleveland grocery stores, Stouffer's lasagna was ubiquitous. Their frozen foods flourished in the 1970s and 1980s (though they had already been sold to a bigger company in 1967, which in turn sold them to Nestlé). Stouffer's is the brand for you if you're looking for the kind of food you'd find in a school cafeteria circa 1975: turkey tetrazzini, creamed chipped beef, meatloaf, Swedish meatballs, creamed spinach.

Paradox of Plenty, "it had almost single-handedly led sales of lo-cal items to jump from 7 to 17 percent of the frozen entrée market."

Today, though, while Stouffer's has its aging following,[103] it clearly needs to take Balzer's advice. "I think about Stouffer's," Jeff Heinen told me as we stood before the multi-deck freezer stocked with Stouffer's frozen lasagnas and Salisbury steaks. "We still give it space, but it doesn't sell. They're struggling. I think they got stuck in things that were successful, but they haven't changed. As a kid we ate a lot of this stuff. And as a young single adult I always had four or five packages in my freezer just in case. But I haven't bought Stouffer's frozen food in—we haven't had it in our house in I can't tell you how long, or even any frozen food." He guessed that the rise in prepared foods in the deli case had a lot to do with this. And yet he was amazed to learn that frozen foods are Trader Joe's biggest category, because they sell more interesting food that's inexpensive. They may drive frozen food into its fourth iteration.

Indeed, when I visited my mom in Florida recently, she set out some Trader Joe's *viennoiserie—pain au chocolat* (if I'm going to eat a stripped-carb breakfast, I choose this and a coffee) and almond croissants[104]— before going to bed, which thawed and rose overnight. Once baked the next morning, they were ethereal, an example of excellent frozen food.

No doubt my father stood in front of these cases in a rapturous wonder, his imagination so overwhelmed he would be unable to move until thirty or forty minutes had gone by. But he would be certain, in his giddy naiveté, that his choices could bring the same pleasures as meals served to him at a restaurant.

---

103 "I no longer cook for myself but microwave widower food, mostly Stouffer's," wrote one of America's preeminent poets, Donald Hall, in an essay on aging ("Out the Window," *New Yorker*, January 23, 2012).

104 This preparation is France's ingenious method for turning day-old croissants, bread that didn't sell, into something more delicious than what it was to begin with—and then charging more for it. Well, these *are* the people who convinced Americans to pay three or four bucks a bottle for what was already coming out of our kitchen faucets.

PART V

WHERE WE ARE HEADED

20.

AMERICA'S CULINARY HERITAGE

Refrigerating or freezing food is of course America's primary form of food preservation. For the past decade I've explored ancient techniques of food preservation from other countries that continue to give us some of the most exquisite food we know. Prosciutto and the many great cured hams of Europe. Korean kimchi. The fish sauce of southeast Asia. Japanese fish packed in raw rice bran and salt. The smoked and cured salmon in so many northern climes. The salt cod of Portugal. Cheese (without refrigeration, milk will sour in days). Hawaii's poi, which tastes pretty awful, as I mentioned, but in this regard is the exception; most preserved foods are delicious, which is why they stick around in a world where refrigeration is everywhere.

Cured pork, cheese, and salted and dried fish all were available at country stores and grocery stores through the 1920s. But as refrigerators and freezers became ubiquitous, these products dwindled. What cured products were available had been taken over by major manufacturers. We got mass-produced bacon, and the rest we simply turned into a blanket category, lunch meats, including facsimiles of salami (which no Italian would have equated to *real* salami) and baloney (which no one from Bologna, famed for the mortadella we renamed baloney, would even recognize).

Indeed, our governmental health agencies make it difficult for chefs to practice many ancient preservation techniques because food safety requirements rely almost exclusively on keeping food really cold. At low temperatures, fermentation (the bacterial activity that preserves food and makes it so tasty) happens very slowly if at all.

I fell in love with duck confit, a preparation fundamental to the Gascony region of France, when it began appearing widely on restaurant menus about twenty years ago. Rich, fatty duck legs are poached in duck fat for hours, then left submerged in that fat to "ripen" for a year, or two, or three. It became my favorite food to eat, and I eventually recognized, in studying it, that duck confit was not created for our pleasure by a chef who had labored lovingly over it to bring it to such exquisiteness; it was, rather, an ingenious method of preservation people depended on so that they didn't starve during the winter. My respect for preserved foods took on a new dimension once I understood duck confit.

What were America's food traditions and preservation methods, though? We didn't seem to have many. Yes, we have Virginia hams. Salmon has long been dried and smoked in the Pacific Northwest. Tasso ham—salted, seasoned, smoked pork shoulder—remains a Cajun staple ingredient. In the north, pork loin was salted and smoked and called Canadian bacon or, if rolled in cornmeal (as was common in Canada, presumably to protect the meat from drying out and from insects), called pea meal bacon. American bacon, preserved pork belly, was smoked; it was not, and still is not, smoked in France or Italy, only salted. These items remain in production for their deliciousness, not for keeping us alive. We have the grocery store to take care of that.

The ethos of America was defined by rugged individualism and self-reliance. So our preservation methods and our cuisine were individualistic as well, as settlers moved west across our vast country. The best description I've read about food preservation in nineteenth-century America comes from a children's book, *Little House in the Big Woods*, the first of the multi-volume autobiographical series by Laura Ingalls Wilder about life then on the Great Plains. Food was so important that Wilder describes at length how her family would prepare for winter early.

Her father hunted deer in the fall, then cut the venison into strips and salted them. He would find a hollow tree and hang the strips of meat inside it; he would then build a fire of green wood and moss within the hollow tree so that the venison strips would smoke and dry. Laura's mother would wrap the stiff strips in paper and store them in the attic for a meat source that would last all winter. They also salted freshwater fish and kept it in barrels. They stored root vegetables and gourds in the attic, braided onions and hung them on the wall or from rafters. Importantly, they fattened a pig with the abundance of summer so that in the fall, when the weather was cold enough, they had a hefty pig for slaughter. Its hams were salted and smoked. Its lard was rendered and stored in jars; a byproduct of making lard was cracklings, which were reserved to flavor johnnycakes. Her father blew up the pig's bladder to make a balloon to play with. They boiled the head till all the skin and meat were falling-off tender, then packed it in a mold with some of the cooking liquor; when it cooled it was a sliceable "headcheese." The abundant shoulder meat was cut into chunks, heavily salted, and kept in a keg in the shed where it would stay good indefinitely. When meat was needed, it was soaked in water to leach out the salt that had kept the spoilage bacteria from growing, or cooked in a stew that was naturally seasoned by the salt. The abundant scraps from the pig would be finely chopped, mixed with sage, and rolled into balls; they would stay frozen in a pan outside all winter, ready whenever the family wanted sausage.

Early settlers learned and practiced these techniques as a matter of course; if they didn't, they selected themselves out of the population.

We tend to forget how fundamental preserved food was to civilization. It allowed communities to develop a food surplus. It gave merchants goods for trade. It allowed for the Age of Exploration, as preserved food was the only way a ship's crew could be fed during voyages of unknown duration.

But the advent of commercially chilled and frozen food made more difficult forms of food preservation unnecessary. Milk keeps in the fridge for longer than it takes to drink, so there's no real need to make cheese. Have more pork shoulder than you need? Wrap it in plastic and freeze it—no need to cure it. The sheer size of America, and the diverse geography and climates, resulted in regional cuisines, like New England clam chowder, flavored with salt pork, and the jambalaya of Louisiana, which features tasso ham. California doesn't really have examples of these kinds of food, though I'm not sure why; but the juice of the grapes that grew so well in that climate and that soil is some of the best fermented and preserved "food" I know of.

Our country was relatively young—only a dozen decades or so—when refrigeration came along, so perhaps that's why we don't have as wide a range of cheeses as they do in Europe. In 1823, a Vermont dairyman began making Colby cheese. Swiss dairy farmers in northern Oregon found that their milk spoiled by the time it reached Portland, so, in 1909, they turned that milk into Cheddar. But the cheese we are famous for is one we named after ourselves, American cheese, which used a process that actually killed the bacteria that are so beneficial to cheeses. It was created by James Kraft in 1915 by mixing bits of pasteurized Cheddar and other cheeses with an emulsifier into a fluid. It was introduced in foil-wrapped five-pound loaves packed in boxes. It was so popular that Kraft was soon making fifteen thousand loaves a day. Kraft singles wouldn't appear until 1947, winning over an initially skeptical public that couldn't see that it was actually sliced. But Kraft Mac & Cheese had been around for a decade, advertised in 1937 as "a meal for four in 9 minutes for an everyday price of 19 cents."[105] The marketing of convenience had begun. And thus did this substance become our national cheese. Proud to be an American.

Beer, cheese, and wine are interesting examples of our emerging culinary traditions and also reflect the changing tastes of America. The development of these products even followed similar trajectories.

Until the mid-1990s, America was famous for the poor quality of its beer. Beer making has been a part of the culture since the 1600s, but it really came of age only after the Civil War. This was when the big brewers, such as Pabst, Anheuser-Busch, and Schlitz, came into their own and began to dominate the industry.

I don't think I'm going too far out on a limb to suggest that much of our food was treated like any other manufactured product in a thriving

---

105 James Trager, *The Food Chronology: A Food Lover's Compendium of Events and Anecdotes, from Prehistory to the Present.*

capitalism, with the effects of the Industrial Revolution fully engaged. Branded products weren't common (A&P, recall, introduced a branded tea in 1870, one of the first), so almost all manufacturers of any product (and the storekeepers selling them) could differentiate only on the basis of cost. Therefore, whoever sold the most for the least won, a fact that would of course lead to increased productivity all the way through the concept of the assembly line in the early twentieth century and beyond. So we brewed and bought a lot of "commodity" (mass-market) beer, and these beers continue to dominate the industry (Bud Light is by far the biggest selling brand in this country).

And Kraft made cheese. Others followed, leading to a system today in which a handful of billion-dollar companies make the majority of the ten billion pounds of cheese Americans consume annually, whether used on pizza, grilled cheese sandwiches, or Big Macs, or sold in blocks or sliced by the pound at the deli section of your grocery store.

One of those companies, Great Lakes Cheese, is based in Hiram, Ohio, not far from Cleveland, and has enormous factories throughout the country. It both makes cheese and buys cheese from other makers. It sells "block cheese" to retailers and sells bulk cheeses to companies such as McDonald's. Great Lakes makes their Cheddar cheese in a few months, although a true Cheddar cheese takes at least a year to age properly. But you can't have that much inventory sitting around for a year, so we sacrifice flavor for speed and cheapness. Up until the 1960s and '70s, we weren't aware of the sacrifice because it was all we knew—we'd never tasted a properly aged Cheddar, let alone an actual Cheddar from its birthplace in Somerset, England.

It wasn't until international travel became easy and popular (giving increasing numbers of Americans tastes of other traditions) and imports began to flow into the country that we discovered real cheese. Brie was the gourmet cheese in our house in the 1970s, though the Parmesan that I shook onto Mom's "spaghetti sauce" (today we'd call it Bolognese, even when spiked with Open Pit barbecue sauce as was her inclination) still came out of a green can.

As we got a taste of better and better cheeses, we came to demand them based on quality rather than price. As demand grew, so did cheese making in this country, as did the craft beer movement, and even wine making, which began to give French wines a run for their money starting in the 1970s. All are huge growth industries, from a percentage standpoint. Jeff Heinen estimates that commodity beer is down a percentage point or two or flat at best, whereas craft beer sales are "through the roof," up 30 to 40 percent.

Heinen's sells about $10 million of commodity cheese, growing by about 2 percent a year. It now sells $11 million in specialty cheeses, with consistent annual growth of 5 percent. Of course neither of these categories is where the growth is. That would be shredded cheeses, along with another relatively new category of cheeses: "The cheese companies got smart and started marketing it as a snack," Jeff said. This would put all commodity cheeses at more than $20 million in sales.

Happily, the non-commodity cheese, beer, and wine industries are thriving in this country, and I was lucky enough to tag along with Chris Foltz, head cheese buyer Shannon Welsh, and manager Joe Calori on a trip to the Napa and Sonoma Valleys for a wine and cheese exploration. I had a feeling this was going to be a hell of a lot more fun than Expo West.

On arrival we were greeted outside the baggage terminal at the San Francisco airport by Ed Thompkins, Heinen's head wine buyer. Ed, age fifty-one, dressed in cargo shorts and psychedelic shades, held out his long arms when he saw us, grinned, and shouted, "Aloha!" Ed is tall and lanky, with bright blue eyes, short dark blond hair, and a prominent beak. This, combined with his unflappably cheerful demeanor, brought Big Bird to my mind. Only more enthusiastic, not to mention expert in the ways of wines.

As Ed put the minivan in gear, Chris popped the first bottle of champagne (Ed had brought a selection of grower champagnes because he wanted us to taste the difference between premier cru and grand cru champagnes). Ed drove south toward our first stop, Scheid Vineyards in Greenfield, while we slathered crusty bread with Cowgirl Creamery

Mt. Tam—Ed calls this cheese his "bubbles love slave" because it pairs so well with sparkling wine.

From the backseat, Shannon, a sprite of a young woman with straight brown hair, moaned, "Oh my God, this Tam is like eating butter!"

At Scheid, which produces a range of wines under many labels, we toured the plant, viewing its floor-to-ceiling tanks of wine. Ed was there to approve a blend they were creating specifically for a Heinen's private label offering drinkable wines for under ten bucks. We all sat around a table with people from the company tasting a variety of blends so that Ed could choose the balance he wanted.[106] Scheid would bottle it, label it, and ship it to Heinen's. Because of the volume—Heinen's buys four thousand cases a year—Scheid can offer good deals on these wines.

As we pulled away, on either side of the highway workers picked seemingly endless fields of broccoli and lettuces. We then headed back north to Glen Ellen for a tour and a tasting at Benziger Family Winery, a gorgeous biodynamic farm that was among the first to bring green farming mainstream.

Next we stopped in Calistoga to explore the caves of Schramsberg Vineyards, which makes some of my favorite sparkling wines. We had lunch in the woods and watched Schramsberg CEO Hugh Davies saber a bottle—that is, take the top off a sparkling wine bottle using nothing more than a butter knife.[107] Heinen's buys a few hundred of the eighty thousand cases Schramsberg releases each year. (I drank one of Davies's blanc de blanc champagnes just the other day—it turned a trip on the Long Island Rail Road to Penn Station into a festive occasion! Amazing what bubbles can do.)

....

106 You can try this at home; at the end of a dinner party, gather all the almost-empty bottles of red wine, combine them in varying portions, and see what tastes best. That, though in a very crude and unscientific way, is how many inexpensive wine blends are created and labeled.

107 Davies explained how: Find the seam on the bottle, and rub the knife up and down the neck of the bottle rapidly, sort of winding up to hit the lip of the bottle top, then bring the knife right through that lip. It took him seven or eight tries, but off came that top, still squeezing the cork. It was strangely thrilling.

"To be taken seriously as a wine shop, you have to have a Duckhorn merlot," Ed told me as we pulled into Duckhorn Vineyards, in St. Helena. Seated for a tasting with the owner, Dan Duckhorn, I asked for his take on grocery stores and wine. "You are the vanguard out there now," he replied, directing his words to Ed and Chris. "You're changing the whole experience. Wine is part of the experience, and it's fun," he said, and added that the grocery store "has replaced the independent store and the wine shops."

Cheese is the same story. We had lunch at and toured the dairy farm of Point Reyes Farmstead, begun in 1959 by Bob Giacomini. They raise their own cows, which produce enough milk[108] to make more than a million pounds of cheese a year, including a relatively new cheese they call Bay Blue, a densely creamy, earthy blue cheese that Shannon loves so much she asked for her own personal stash to get her through our trip.

We also visited Marin French Cheese, which bills itself as the oldest continuously operating cheese maker in the country, dating to 1865. They make European-style soft cheeses, including a line called American Originals. (Wisconsin's Carr Valley Cheese has been making cheese for more than a hundred years as well, but it wasn't until the late 1990s that Sid Cook took over there. He was the first to use the term American Originals—these cheeses became so renowned that he's now considered a celebrity in the industry.) But again, until the 1990s there really wasn't a national market for handcrafted cheeses, certainly not one that could generate $11 million for a small Midwestern grocery chain, which is what Heinen's does today. Indeed, Point Reyes only started making cheese in 2000, and Sue Conley and Peggy Smith began their famed Cowgirl Creamery in the mid-1990s.

"The American cheese movement is always evolving, and we want to stay relevant," Shannon told me—which is why (twist her arm) these trips to cheese-making regions are important. "American cheeses are ready for the world stage. They're really works of art." And as with Ed in the wine department, her buying power gives her leverage over smaller

---

108 Ten million pounds, or 8.3 million gallons.

specialty stores. What a small shop or specialty store would have to sell for $18.99 a pound, she said, she can sell for under ten dollars and still maintain margins of 48 percent, one of the highest in the store. Moreover, she said, because Heinen's is small relative to the Krogers of the industry, "we can work around our margins, charging a lower retail, and therefore making a smaller margin, for certain, very special cheeses where it's just important to get it in the customers' mouths." For example: Challerhocker, an Alpine-style cheese from Switzerland that she considers a "cheese-making masterpiece."

The bigger chains spread out over multiple states have a harder time developing relationships with individual cheese makers and instead rely on merchants to come to them. Kroger, the biggest traditional chain, chose a different strategy: It made a deal with Rob Kaufelt, New York City's famous cheese monger, owner of Murray's Cheese, and worked with him to open hundreds of Murray's Cheese shops within Kroger supermarkets.

The next day, mid-morning on our way to visit a dairy, Chris Foltz turned around in the passenger seat. Holding up a glass of champagne and a hunk of bread smeared with a triple-cream cheese, he said, "How many grocery store executives are doing *this* this morning?"

Probably none. I can only imagine the Heinen's team doing it—they really love their food and wine. I raised my glass to Chris.

Regardless of the recent hunger for handcrafted foods, they remain a niche market within the grocery store. America simply didn't have many centuries during which a unique food heritage created by small pre-industrial farms might take hold. Add to that the evolving technology to process food on a commercial scale, and the large buildings we created to store and distribute these goods—the American supermarket—and you end up with a culinary tradition that consists of Mrs. Paul's fish sticks, Swanson's TV dinners, Birds Eye frozen peas, and Kraft Singles.

And yet this is changing, as Americans slowly but surely move away from processed foods and buy more fruits and vegetables, organic foods, and, as they become increasingly available in grocery stores, the handcrafted foods that younger generations are creating and marketing. These are slowly but inexorably filling up our supermarkets. When these products are shelved, something inferior is removed. Where it will end is anyone's guess. Jeff Heinen's final words to me addressed this directly, and I found it sort of thrillingly hopeful.

On my last walk through the grocery store with him, he wondered aloud at what the future of the grocery store was. To his back was the gigantic center of the store, loaded primarily with commodity products, the packaged goods that are the same at pretty much any grocery store in America. Before him was the meat case that would soon be filled with Lava Lakes lamb and the fish case with its yellowfin tuna that had been off-loaded at the Honolulu fish auction the day before, to his left the cheese case filled with unique American cheeses, and beyond that the wines and beers.

"I think stores are going to get smaller," Jeff said. "If Amazon has its way, that stuff in the center of the store will all be delivered to your door. And we'll go back to the old days, where it's all specialty stores. We'll be prepared food and specialty products and everything else will be so commoditized that we won't be able to compete from a price perspective."

21.

THE CLEVELAND TRUST

On a warm day, August 13, 2013, a fifty-three-year-old architect named John Williams entered a derelict building at 900 Euclid Avenue on the corner of East Ninth Street, a few blocks from Public Square, in the center of downtown Cleveland. Dressed in worn Levi's that contrasted with his offbeat designer shoes, stylish shirt, and retro eyeglasses, Williams wore a full, neatly trimmed beard and his hair was mussed from the breeze off Lake Erie several blocks north. He passed through a makeshift office area and entered the main building, which had been more or less vacant for twenty-four years. He beheld a grand rotunda sixty-one feet in diameter and did what any sentient human would do: He stepped onto the intact rotunda with its beautiful pale terrazzo paving and looked up at the extraordinary dome of Tiffany-style stained glass eighty-five feet above him, breathtaking blues and reds and yellows that glowed from the sunlight.

The building was designed in 1905 by George Browne Post, the architect of the neoclassical New York City Stock Exchange, which had opened two years earlier. This Cleveland building was smaller in scale but no less ornate, with granite facades graced by fluted Corinthian columns, exterior sculpture by Viennese artist Karl Bitter, and the majestic dome of leaded colored glass, made by D'Ascenzo Studios in Philadelphia. Below the dome, a mural of the city's beginnings—the first settlers greeting Native Americans in the eighteenth century, a Native American and a settler sharing a canoe on the Cuyahoga River, Cuyahoga being the Iroquois word for "crooked river"—circled the entire third-floor balcony, painted by Francis Millet, who would die on the *Titanic*. A second-story balcony with a bronze railing extended out farther.

The Beaux Arts structure became the home to the Cleveland Trust Company bank in 1908. Steven Litt, architecture critic for the *Plain*

Dealer, the city's primary newspaper (now reduced to publishing four days a week, but still one of the best-*named* papers in the country, in my opinion), described the structure as embodying "the chest-thumping opulence of the late Gilded Age," and a fitting paean to Cleveland's rise as an industrial powerhouse in the first half of the twentieth century. Noting that the building recalls the ancient Greek and Roman temples on which it was modeled, Litt quotes a city building expert who called it "a temple to money."

Indeed, it was built as the city was ascending toward its eventual status in the 1950s as the country's sixth largest city and Cleveland Trust the country's sixth largest bank. East Ninth Street and Euclid became an architecturally significant corner in a relatively small city, a ten-minute walk from Public Square, the city's epicenter, near where John D. Rockefeller set up his Standard Oil Company in 1870.

But the city would decline in the 1960s, along with its Rust Belt neighbors, thanks to the declining iron and auto industries. Its river caught fire from pollution. So many people fled this decay, begun in the white-flight 1950s, that the city soon had fewer people than when the bank was constructed. My father could see it all happening as he strode daily along Euclid Avenue, briefcase in hand, watching a grand thoroughfare grow dark. It had been the main shopping district through the 1950s, where moms would take their daughters to the department stores followed by afternoon tea. The industrial sector of the city lost tens of thousands of jobs, and as we moved into the troubled 1970s with our boy mayor, Dennis Kucinich, the city eventually defaulted on $14 million in loans.

Cleveland Trust merged with another bank to become Ameritrust in the 1980s. When Ameritrust sold to Society bank and relocated, only a few office spaces remained in the original building. The county took over the property but did nothing with it. The grand structure remained vacant for two decades as the avenue on which it sat crumbled. Once the city's prime shopping venue, with grand department stores and fancy boutiques, Euclid saw stores going out of business and window fronts emptying out or being boarded up. Few people travel that once-busy avenue today, beyond the homeless. I wouldn't have felt comfortable walking it after dark.

Yet by the time my father retired in 2004, a Cleveland developer had begun to buy up property a few blocks west of the Cleveland Trust Company Building on East Fourth Street. I remember the block from my own time at the agency as being a decrepit, grimy stretch of cheap retail stores. But Rick Maron saw potential in developing the entire street, designated "historic" in the 1980s for its buildings, which dated from 1876 to 1935. He had a vision of restaurants and entertainment venues, topped by floors and floors of residential space. In order to make it so, he needed a powerful anchor to lure enough people from the suburbs to this street, so he looked to food. In this case it was a chef, Michael Symon, who had risen to national prominence with his restaurant Lola in a nearby area called Tremont, itself a sketchy part of town until the success of Lola brought other restaurants to the area. Maron convinced Symon to open a new Lola on this redesigned street. He had his anchor and his draw.

As had happened in Tremont, other restaurants followed, thirteen more on a stretch one city block long. As did eight bars, a comedy club, a bowling alley, and a House of Blues. And, by 2009, more than three hundred residential apartments.

The city's decision in the 1990s to build new homes for each of its professional sports teams now seemed to be paying off, as the ballpark, basketball arena, and football stadium were within walking distance of East Fourth. And in 2003 the Cleveland Cavaliers recruited LeBron James, instantly turning the team into a contender and ultimately bringing the city tens of millions of dollars, if not more.[109] East Fourth Street continued to thrive as developers began to turn all the vacated office space they could get their hands on into residences. Then, in February

....

109 Figures are squishy, but *Bloomberg News* estimates that when LeBron returned to Cleveland in 2014 after his ignominious departure in 2010, it translated to an annual windfall of $215 million for the city. "LeBron $21 Million a Year Bringing Cleveland $215 Million," *Bloomberg News*, October 27, 2014.

2013, the Ohio-based Geis Companies purchased the three buildings on the corner of East Ninth and Euclid.

John Williams opened Process Creative Studios in Cleveland in 1994, and since then had become known for, in addition to standard design work, repurposing old structures and creating minimalist, modern interpretations within older buildings—turning a former brick transformer station into a sleek, spare gallery space and offices for the Cleveland Museum of Art, for instance.

Inside the rotunda on that warm August day, he waited for an architectural intern for the real estate developer who'd bought the building and the adjacent tower connected to it, a Brutalist structure by Marcel Breuer, considered something of a monstrosity now, towering over Post's ornate, classical dome. The architect was here on what he at first had thought was a joke. For the past decade he had been working with Tom and Jeff Heinen—he designed whole stores, created more efficient loading docks and in-store signage, and figured out the best place to put the rows of nesting shopping carts in store entryways. (As Williams explained to me, "When you enter a grocery store, what's the first thing you don't want to see? Rows of shopping carts. You want to see a bountiful display of apples. But what's the first thing you *need*? A shopping cart.") Jeff had asked him to stop by to see if he thought they could put a grocery store in this former bank. Williams actually laughed, though he knew that Jeff rarely joked.

Jeff explained that the Geis brothers had purchased the old Cleveland Trust Company Building. They wanted to know if Tom and Jeff would consider opening a Heinen's in their new property. They also intended to turn the monstrous Ameritrust tower into a 156-room hotel complex with 106 apartments as part of the $250 million project. Steven Litt noted that if Greg and Fred Geis's plans were successful, "the brothers could go down in history as heroes who rescued an important Cleveland legacy while fueling a downtown residential boom and making a bundle doing it."

Such a residential boom hinged on their decision to put a grocery store on part of their property. If they were going to ask people to move to downtown Cleveland, these people would need a place to buy food, certainly better food than was available at the nearby CVS, about the only food retail outlet within comfortable walking distance. So they contacted Tom and Jeff Heinen to ask if they would consider putting a Heinen's in the bank building.

Tom and Jeff had fielded such offers before, and they still weren't interested. There simply weren't enough residents to make a grocery store a viable business. They'd already been approached to open a store on the west side of downtown, in the warehouse district that saw some of the first new residential building in the city. They turned it down. A small family grocery store called Constantino's, with most of the departments of a traditional grocery store though with a limited selection, opened there instead.[110]

But the Geis offer intrigued Jeff enough, due to the building itself, that he called his architect to ask what he thought. When Williams realized that Jeff was serious, he said he'd have a look and tour the property with a Geis representative, but he was not hopeful.

So here he stood in the rotunda of a Beaux Arts building considered by most to be an architectural masterpiece.

It's round, he thought. *I'm a rectilinear guy*. And grocery stores aren't round. "I thought, there's just no way," Williams told me, recalling his first visit that summer. "I'm not thinking design or, oh, this sacred space. I'm thinking how do we get food in? How do we get trash out? How do we do any of the normal daily infrastructure stuff? How do you get semis in here? Where are you going to park?" He'd been working with the brothers for long enough to know what the grocery business entailed.

He didn't even get into questions with Jeff that weren't his concern, such as *Does this even make sense from a business standpoint?* The city proper has only about 350,000 residents, roughly the same number it

110 I should note also that Dave's Market, a full-scale, family-owned chain, has opened supermarkets in underserved communities in Cleveland, notably one a mile and a half from the Cleveland Trust building, and the owners, Burton, Dan, and Steve Saltzman, deserve admiration and thanks for doing so.

did when the Cleveland Trust was built, but more critically, only thirteen thousand residents in the core of the city could be counted on to need a grocery store there. Most retail economists suggest that the magic number a store needs to be viable is twenty thousand people. And while residential space was near capacity, with construction on new condominiums and apartments happening, how long it would take downtown Cleveland to reach that number was anybody's guess.

When Williams entered the Cleveland Trust on that hot summer day, he not only beheld the near-perfect terrazzo flooring and breathtaking dome, but he also saw years of careless refurbishing. The high windows below the dome had been partially covered, drop-ceilings and awkward soffits had been installed, and office carpeting covered the upstairs mezzanine. But more worrisome than what he called the "crap" that covered the building's interior was his suspicion that the Geis brothers had little idea what a modern grocery store required in terms of space and infrastructure.

Standing on the bronze medallion emblazoned with the words THE CLEVELAND TRUST COMPANY in the center of the rotunda, gazing up at the stained glass dome above, turning slowly around as sweat due to the hot enclosed space dripped from his sideburns, Williams thought, *No fucking way*.

However, when he met with the Geis representative, he learned that they themselves had considered building the grocery store. They had already considered the major possible hurdles to opening such a place— most notably, how to get trucks in and out and what to do about the lack of customer parking (only limited metered street parking and not-inexpensive parking garages are available in the area)—and so had already drawn up traffic plans to assess the kind of access trucks would have to the back loading area in the center of this urban block.

"They had predicted every question I asked," Williams recalled, and he left with the feeling that the project was at least *possible*. But that was not enough to convince the conservative Jeff.

Then came a day in early fall that Tom Heinen described as a kind of "karma and sign from the gods" day—a spectacular, cloudless afternoon, 75 degrees and no humidity, the city alive, people eating at out-door tables, the kind of day that makes you love a place. It happened to be the day Ari Maron, Rick Maron's son and partner in the East Fourth Street development, had scheduled to take Tom and Jeff on a tour of the city on foot. Maron was able to point to each building, name the owner, and recite how many residential units were going in.

There was no doubting what Maron was up to. During the walk, Ari said to Tom, "The day you guys open, I can raise my rents 10 percent. That's how important a grocery store is to the development of downtown Cleveland." Tom thought, *That's good for you, but what about us?* Still, he was impressed by the extent of the development and what was coming.

Jeff remained skeptical. He'd come along out of curiosity and due diligence and because of the Cleveland Trust building. "I remembered it from when I was a kid," he said. "I figured I'd at least get to see the building again."

And see it they did. Here was the power of architecture at work. They marveled at the dome, the columns. They couldn't help but try to imagine it. One of Tom's colleagues who'd joined them whispered, "Do you think we're going to do this?"

Tom said, "I don't know if we can make money, but it sure is going to be a pretty damn cool store if we do."

Jeff, too, was transfixed by the building and the idea that it could, possibly, become a grocery store.

A conversation with Greg Geis followed; looking back on the con-versation, Jeff said, "The one thing the Geis brothers recognized was that we would not make money for a very long time, if ever. And if we were not going to make money, they couldn't make money on the property. Most developers would have given up on us right there. They didn't."

The Geis brothers instead structured a deal that would be "painful" for Heinen's, Jeff said, but would it be so painful that they'd have to turn down the chance to build a Heinen's in this extraordinary building in the center of their city?

"Tom and I looked at each other," Jeff told me, "and said, 'You know, we're lifelong Clevelanders. This is a cool building. Cleveland's been good to us, let's pay back. Cleveland needs a grocery store. It might as well be Heinen's. We'll take one for the team, so to speak,' and we did it."

Tom and Jeff signed a lease that November, and Jeff gave Williams the go-ahead to take the winter to draw up plans for what would become a $10 million renovation of the Cleveland Trust Company Building and the 1010 Euclid Avenue building.

That Williams had been working for the Heinens for a decade, learning all that went into creating and running an efficient grocery store, and that his expertise and passion lay in recasting historic structures, combined to give him an uncommonly fortuitous set of skills for turning a building he considered a masterpiece of Beaux Arts architecture into a contemporary supermarket.

He knew from the beginning he would not do what he normally did with other historic structures he'd worked on, which was to remake the structure. Here his main work would be to strip away all that had been added in the 1960s and 1970s, undo a lot of bad decisions that seemed good during those turbulent years, and return the structure to the original architect's vision. Williams, a modernist at heart, didn't consider it a design project of his own; he felt more the curator of the building, its steward.

Turn-of-the-twentieth-century bank buildings, however, weren't suited to contemporary building codes, the need for sprinkler systems, heating, ventilation, and air-conditioning systems, let alone air ducts and above-stove ventilation hoods for restaurant-caliber cooking. These would require a good deal of ingenuity to build into the structure without ruining what he sought to restore, such as using one of the elevator shafts as a main exhaust duct. Another significant issue was blowing a hole through the eastern wall of the building in order to connect the 1010 Building with the Cleveland Trust, so that the large rotunda could lead to a rectangular space better suited to shelves of groceries, bins of vegetables, and stand-alone refrigerator and freezer multi-decks. But the wall was three feet thick, the buildings were on different levels, and supporting the two buildings would be tricky. He would also have to install a fire shutter that would come down to prevent a fire in one of the buildings from spreading to the other.

The basement, where so much of the prepared food would be made, would be a nightmare: fitting the freezers, coolers, material lift, and full kitchen into that space, with all the required HVAC, sprinklers, exhaust ducts, lighting, and electrical.

The main emotional undercurrent coursing through Williams as he struggled with these issues was not excitement, but rather fear. "I was terrified," he said. "Terrified of being responsible. When somebody writes about this building fifty or seventy-five years from now, they're going to write about the original architect, they're going to write about Marcel Breuer, and they're going to write about me. And that's terrifying. It's a lot of responsibility, to know that this building will not only be scrutinized by the general public but by every historic preservationist, every architect, every retailer. I didn't want to fuck it up!"

The project was so unusual, and so important, that Steven Litt begged Williams for a year for renderings, for some clue as to what Williams's plans were. Williams had to say, "Steven, look, I'm not spending time making pretty pictures. I don't have to present this to anyone. I'm not designing the space. The space was designed a hundred years ago. My goal is to tear out all the shit that's been added and then reintroduce what we need as sensitively as possible." And finally he had to ensure that all design and construction complied with the Secretary of the Interior's standards for historic preservation and have the space still work functionally and aesthetically as a grocery store.

Construction began in August 2014, and as Williams wrestled with concealing sprinkler lines and ducts and drilling as few holes as possible in original surfaces, Tom and Jeff Heinen worked on store layout, so much of which focused on the rotunda. A rotunda topped with a glorious stained glass dome may be a wonder to behold, but a circle is a spectacularly inefficient space for retail aisles and shelving. The original plans called for striating this space with packaged and canned goods, which later changed to beer and wine as they hoped to do a good business in this category and thought to make them central. During initial planning for the project, many options were studied, including making the rotunda the main grocery area. But due to the rotunda's unique geometric and dimensional characteristics, the rigid linearity of grocery aisles, and the inability to place lighting and sprinkler heads within the historic dome, it was quickly determined that the most practical option was to leave this area open for seating. This would allow customers the best area in which to appreciate the dome, which reinforced Williams's main design principle of respecting the space, not imposing themselves or the business on it.[111]

The brothers decided to rim the rotunda with the butcher, seafood, and prepared foods cases and, opposite these, the bakery case, with checkout counters near both exits, and to leave the central space open with tables only. They expected to do a substantial business in prepared foods and lunches for all the office workers downtown, and conceived a "Global Grill" for serving hot bowls of chicken curry and Argentinian beef and Korean barbecue wraps, as well as a big salad bar featuring Dr. Todd's super-salads, a sushi station, and a poke bar. They even found space for a Fair Exchange Coffee Shop, which would offer pastries and fruit in addition to coffees and teas.

Lighting in the rotunda was another issue. "The dome, as beautiful as it is," Williams explained, "and the lights around the outside, as nice as they are, give very little light. Before we got all our lighting in it was dim, with very yellowish-green light, which is horrible for food. So I've got this gorgeous dome that's completely working against me in presenting food."

One leaves the rotunda, passing meat cases, prepared meats and condiments, and a small area where Shannon's cheeses would be cut and sold, through the archway into the 1010 Building, where the produce lies in bins and on anodized misting racks, where the upright multi-

111 Anyone who would like to see what happens when you don't respect the space can have a look at the bank building at the corner of West Fourteenth Street and Eighth Avenue in Manhattan, which has been turned into a CVS pharmacy. Even though this is a rectangular space, the shelving, dropped fluorescent lighting, and garish "Grab and Go" signage are a horrible mismatch for the old bank, akin to putting a General Motors Saturn engine in the body of a Rolls-Royce.

decks are filled with ice cream and frozen food and eggs and milk, as well as four rows for groceries—the packaged, shelf-stable foods in boxes, bags, and cans—and where Dr. Todd's maca and cat's claw can be found.

The Heinens chose to devote the second floor of the rotunda exclusively to beer and wine. Beer and wine typically account for about 8 percent of their sales, but here they expected to do double that, as there were few places to buy beer and wine downtown, and nowhere with the kind of selection Heinen's would be able to carry. Not only could they be the city's main destination for beers and wines from around the world, they could also create a space designed specifically to double as a bar, restaurant, and social gathering place. On the second-floor mezzanine, green marble tables would line the balcony, made from the original bank teller counters. A Cruvinet system would dispense forty different wines, and eight beers would be available on tap. After work, people could meet for a glass of wine or a beer, and appetizers, such as flatbreads and salads and charcuterie platters and mussels with chorizo, or turn it into dinner from the Global Grill. This grocery store might even have a regular happy hour, as supermarkets increasingly mimic bars and restaurants, with many stores throughout the country—from Wegmans to Whole Foods—angling to become a social hub for a community.

Opening day was set for February 25, 2015, smack in the middle of a frigid Cleveland winter. In the days leading up to its opening, the store felt not unlike a restaurant readying to open, with food deliveries, cases of wine being unpacked, and men in Carhartt pants walking purposefully through the cluttered space with power drills or standing on ladders cutting holes in drywall to install fixtures. The first shelves to be filled were those in grocery, along with equally shelf-stable wine and beer, then frozen and dairy came in, followed in the final days by produce, meat, and fish, filling the store truckload by truckload. Joe Calori, one the store's two lead managers, walked the floor the night before till three thirty a.m. making sure all the shelves were set, all the cases in order, for opening day.

On the cold, slushy morning of the opening, the store teemed with Clevelanders eager to celebrate a historic moment for the city. Spectators and employees lined the second-floor mezzanine long before the ten a.m. ceremony, hovering over the railing and looking down into the rotunda and up at the dome. Behind them, Ed Thompkins, wine buyer, readied pink champagne on ice.

I found Jeff Heinen examining the produce aisles and asked him if everyone was in good shape.

"If we're not, it's too late now," he said breezily, without the slightest hint of opening day jitters. "And we're going to be here for fifty years, so whatever is not right, we'll get right."

The rotunda was cordoned off with red velvet roping, in preparation for the ribbon-cutting ceremony with the mayor, city councilmen, the Geis brothers, and the Heinen brothers.

Steven Litt arrived, reporter's pad in hand. He spotted John Williams in the crowd by the roping and said, simply, "I love it. It's the work of George Post." He especially appreciated how even the cases around the perimeter maintained the roundness of the building. Of the 1010 Building, where grocery and produce are, he told me, "It's very urban." He loved that they left the flooring as they found it, patches of its original black and white tile interspersed with patches of gray concrete filler wherever the tile had been damaged. "It feels like you're walking in a Roman ruin," he said. He sounded almost giddy. The air was charged with energy and excitement.

Mayor Frank Jackson arrived and joined the ten other men gathered around the Cleveland Trust brass medallion in the center of the rotunda. All but Tom and Jeff Heinen had scissors for the ribbon cutting; they instead held cleavers in honor of their grandfather.

The first person to take the microphone was John Burns, the general manager, who thanked everyone for being at "this historic moment for Cleveland and for Heinen's."

Mayor Jackson, dressed in a dark pinstriped suit, told the crowd, "Our philosophy and our goal is to have a twenty-four-hour city, where Cleveland is alive twenty-four/seven. . . . And that's why I'm going to say thank you to Heinen's, because they have moved that vision further ahead than anyone else, along with the Geis brothers. They've helped us to say to the world that if you come to downtown Cleveland, if you make downtown Cleveland your neighborhood, where you live, work, play, and do business, that the amenities will be here. They have invested in Cleveland's future, and they've done so in a way that will encourage others to do the same."

Jeff Heinen spoke on behalf of himself and his brother. Both were dressed in Heinen's blue shirts and Heinen's dark fleece vests, common attire for grocers in winter and for walking in and out of coolers.

"I'm not sure anyone would have imagined that this venerable Cleveland Trust building would be turned into a grocery store," he began. "I'm thankful that the Geis brothers did have that imagination and also grateful that they thought of Heinen's. Thank you very much for giving us this opportunity. People probably realize that this building is over a hundred years old, and while Heinen's as a company is not quite that old—we're a little over eighty-six years old—the reason we have endured, just like this building has, is because we have great people. And if you look a little bit around the second floor"—he gestured to the balcony, the railing jammed with people looking down at the ceremony— "it's because of all of our people, who made this happen. So I thank all of them for turning this gem of a building into a grocery store."

The ribbon was cut, the six-minute ceremony complete, and the former bank building officially opened for the business of selling groceries.

22.

CATHEDRAL

I walked through the milling crowd at the new Heinen's in downtown Cleveland, in this former temple of commerce, now filled with all the goods we expect from a grocery store, a place locked and loaded with food. The energy in the building seemed to underscore the fact that we shoppers, collectively, have the power to shape our stores, and they in turn have the scale and influence to change the way we grow and distribute food in this country and throughout the world, particularly small chains such as Heinen's—and Lunds & Byerlys and Festival Foods and Bristol Farms—chains that are small enough to respond rapidly to our wishes but large enough to force actual change among those growing and manufacturing our food—twenty such chains alone have a combined buying power of $10 billion annually. As Whole Foods proved, the grocery store, perhaps more than any other mechanism of change (the Farm Bill, say, or the restaurant industry, or food activists), has the power to shape how we raise and produce food in America. But only if we, the consumer, ask for it. Because the fact is that most grocery stores are led by business executives, not visionaries, so change won't come from them—their business is responding to our desires.

One of the most jolting and illuminating comments on the nature of the American grocer came from Jim Whalen, who had been in the grocery business for forty-two years—most of it with big chains owned by multinationals, such as Tops. He was now one of four market managers for Heinen's, overseeing three stores in Cleveland and the four new Chicago stores.

Jim had joined Tom Heinen and Chris Foltz on a trip to the Chicago suburbs to indoctrinate the employees of the newest Heinen's, and I'd asked to come along. Tom and Chris are lovers of great food and wine and, knowing that I had friends at the world-renowned restaurant Alinea, asked if I could finagle a reservation.

Jim had never experienced four-star cuisine, certainly not cuisine as modernist as chef Grant Achatz's. We talked about the food we were served, of course, but I think food was *all* we talked about that night. Midway through dinner, Jim turned to me and said, "You know, in all the years of meetings and dinners I had with the leaders of Tops, we never talked about *food*. They *sold* food but didn't ever talk about it. Never. All we talked about was widgets and sales."

A moment of silence followed, then Chris said, "Can you believe it? Grocers don't give a shit about food. What does that mean for the *future* of food?"

Whatever that future becomes, change is in our hands, as we are the ones who shop for food for our families. We're the ones with the cash, and money doesn't talk—it screams. But this will require our not being confused about our food, not being swayed by the billions of marketing dollars spent on selling us food that makes sick, and thinking sensibly for ourselves. There is hope, too, in people like Tom and Jeff Heinen and their counterparts from Boston to LA. Jeff had told me outright that he *did* feel it was his duty not to sell shitty peaches in winter, even though customers complained they'd seen them at Giant Eagle so why didn't he have them? There's hope in the straight-shooting Norman Mayne in Dayton, Ohio, who has only three Dorothy Lane stores, but they are renowned. He was among the dozen family grocers I'd joined during their gathering in Philadelphia.

"Grocers are our greatest friends on earth," he told the group in the Ritz-Carlton conference room where they met for several days. "You want to talk about the money? Screw it. Screw the money. . . . Bring in products that you want to sell, and care about your associates, and the money will take care of itself."

To bring in great products, though, you've got to care about the food.

There's hope in Wegmans, widely considered one of the best, if not the best, grocery chain in America. And there's hope in Whole Foods still, which fulfilled a desire most Americans didn't even know they were about to have.

And there was hope flooding through the Cleveland Trust Company Building the morning of February 25, 2015, and it was hope not only for food but for the city itself and for what it meant to have a full-scale grocery store of this caliber in the heart of it.

After the ceremony I got in line for coffee at the new coffee shop and heard a thirtyish woman in front of me say to her friend, "This blows me away." We struck up a conversation, and she told me that though she worked in a distant suburb, she'd lived downtown for seven years, many blocks west of here. She recently moved to the 1010 Euclid Building, into a condo directly above the groceries. I asked her if she was glad to have a Heinen's downtown. "It's why I moved to this building," she said, almost giddy. "This is a game-changer."

After my father died in 2008, I found among his possessions date books filled with entries of daily events. These turned out to be almost exclusively descriptions of what he served for dinner when he entertained, years and years outlined entirely by food bought at a grocery store and cooked for his friends and family. And not just a menu list but also how much this leg of lamb or that roast pork weighed, how long he cooked it, the people in attendance, and if he was feeling ebullient, a critical comment or two on the quality of the meal.

September 24, 1996: *Stu here for a drink, Peter & Henry here for scampies on grill and kung pao chicken.* January 10, 1997: *Barb & Jon here with M, D, & R for M's classic French dinner of consommé, squash ravioli, potatoes, pork tenderloin & crème caramel.* April 26, 2004: *David Ryan, David White, & Henry here for marinated steak, cauliflower, onions/tomatoes.* May 9, 2004: *C, A, & J here for swordfish on grill (8 mins/side). Great!* February 5, 2006: *To M & D's for dinner—my chile-spiced pork and potato stew.*

I have thirty of these books, thirty years, ending the year before his cancer, and they are filled with thousands of such entries.

Richard "Rip" Ruhlman was a lot of things beyond a father. He was a devoted husband; a Little League coach who loved working with kids so much that he continued to coach long after I, his only child, stopped playing; a friend to countless people; a lifelong ad man; and a mentor to more young copywriters than I ever knew (many of them wrote to me after he died). And a lover of food, as I mentioned at the outset. But the love I realize now wasn't in the *eating* of food (though he did love that), it was rather in the giving of it. It was not coincidental, I think now, that I dedicated my first book on food and cooking to him, adding the phrase "Provider of the Feast." He *was* the great provider, and food was the symbol of his love and care and joy. And it was in the *offering* that he was most himself. He was never happier than when he was serving food and drink to the people he loved most in the world.

One of his oldest and dearest friends, Stu Eilers, noted in his memorial remarks how angry he would get when he arrived at our house for one of Rip's dinners to find that the grill hadn't even been lit yet, meaning dinner was a long way off, especially if Rip's split broilers with the tarragon-butter baste were on the menu. Stu realized only on writing his remarks that my father wasn't being negligent or thoughtless; it was rather that "Rip knew that the sooner he started that fire, the sooner people would leave, and he wanted to delay this as long as possible." Till dawn, preferably.

My father felt that he had led a pedestrian life. He believed he had accomplished nothing uncommon. Late in his life, at a New Year's dinner party, the host went around the table asking guests for resolutions. When the host got to my father, my father said, "I want to do something *remarkable*."

He didn't—at least not as far as he could tell.

But he cooked for people, and poured them wine, and made them happy. He entertained twenty people for a Fourth of July cookout—I carried his oxygen tank as we walked to watch the fireworks afterward—just four weeks before he was confined to a hospice bed in my dining room. He *died* in the dining room. He carried the deep, intuitive understanding of the power of food to connect people, knew that food was not simply a device for entertaining or filling our bodies and pleasing our senses but rather that it served as a direct channel to the greater pleasures of being alive, and that it could be so only when that food was shared with friends and lovers and family. Whether it was the Vienna Beef hot dogs charred from the grill and eaten in the backyard on a summer evening with Lay's potato chips or a grand rack of lamb at the center of the holiday table, the food assured us that in this uncertain world, we were loved, cared for, nourished, together, and that, for this night at least, all was well.

I'm certain that I came to embrace food as I have in large measure because of my father's love of food and its power to connect us all, and why I would, after thirty-three years of dinners with my father, dinners both routine and celebratory, begin to write about food and cooking for a living.

I left the new coffee shop and reentered the Cleveland Trust rotunda. The first thing I did, as is the all-but-inevitable response when entering this space, was to look up at the stained glass dome high overhead, such a bright and commanding focal point, and then down along the balconies, to the ornate columns, the shined marble floor. I scanned the meat counter and the seafood on ice, a case filled with prepared food lining the circular back wall. The former derelict bank building remained a kind of temple, a cathedral of food.

I felt a strange, sad-sweet elation that didn't seem commensurate with the occasion, something deep and quiet and powerful. I couldn't quite place where it came from until it dawned on me that the last time I had been in this space had been as a small boy when, one day, I accompanied my dad to work. The Cleveland Trust was where he deposited his paychecks, but it was also his client—he wrote ads for this bank. He handed over his deposit and then we left the bank, my hand in his, and walked next door to the 1010 Building, where we took the elevator to his office on the twelfth floor.

How joyful my father would have been to know that the building where he spent most of his adult life earning the money to feed his family and friends in the city he loved had become a grocery store.

And I understood why I felt so strongly about grocery stores: because my father was somehow *here*. He perched on my shoulder when

I walked a grocery store's aisles. He haunted grocery stores for me. How I wanted him here today, how I wanted to take his hand and say, *Dad, look at this!*

Remember how amazed you were by the arrival of kiwis? Look what they have now—passion fruit and Meyer lemons and Buddha's hands and jackfruit. Here, taste these grapes—just like cotton candy, I know. Yes, they still have our old Wish-Bone salad dressing—but they now have an amazing selection of olive oils from the Mediterranean and fabulous aged balsamic vinegars—we'll make our own "Italian" dressing. Look at the meat counter, the beautifully marbled, hormone-free rib steaks you love, but check out those astonishing, gigantic bison rib steaks. And this acorn-fed ham and these amazing salamis. They've even brought in Magret duck breasts from a company called D'Artagnan—better than the best strip steak you've ever tasted. I'll grill them for us. And these moonfish, pulled out of the Pacific Ocean just yesterday and here they are now in Cleveland. And those scallops. Remember how you loved coquilles St. Jacques decades ago? Look at these scallops, alive and in the shell—you've never seen that before, a live scallop, anywhere, let alone at your grocery store. I'll make you the best coquilles St. Jacques ever with these, served in the shell it came from.

Over here, taste this kombucha—it's all the rage. What do you think? And look at these weird milks they have now—I'll bet we could create some great after-dinner cocktails with cashew or almond milk. And try this funky turmeric drink—I want to make a great pork curry with it.

Over here—remember how the fanciest cheese we'd serve in the 1970s was Brie or Boursin? America is making some of the best cheeses in the world now. Taste this Bay Blue from Point Reyes Farmstead, this triple-cream Mt. Tam from Cowgirl Creamery—it's like eating butter.

Even the shopping cart has evolved—they now come with drink holders! You can have a glass of wine (or two!) while you're shopping, and taste this incredible Parmigiano-Reggiano with it. Or we can get a bite to eat right now at the Global Grill—James makes an amazing Korean BBQ wrap.

Remember when you used to buy big jugs of Gallo and boxes of wine with spigots? You lived long enough to see wine come of age in America, but you never saw this in the grocery store—the Cruvinet. You can taste *forty different wines if you want—even the Vérité Le Désir, a bottle that sells for $453, something you'd never splurge on but now you can taste an ounce of it. We can taste that, but we'll buy the Long Valley Ranch pinot noir—Ed found it, a great bargain, $9.99. And let's splurge on the Round Pond Estate cabernet sauvignon, fifty bucks—it's brawny, with cherries and earth and tobacco, a classic cab. We can spend all day here, Dad. And this 3 Floyds Zombie Dust IPA—after all those years of Miller beer, taste this hop bomb. Amazing things are happening in America's food world. What should we get? What should we have for dinner tonight, what should we cook, who should we invite? What do you want? You can have anything. Anything. We'll cook it together.*

I stepped into the rotunda and I looked up at the colorful leaded-glass dome overhead. I felt bereft and elated at the same time. The space felt grand and church-like. I wanted to take his hand and simply regard it with him, this grocery store, this America, this cathedral of food. It is the house of my father.

SELECTED BIBLIOGRAPHY

Barber, Dan. *The Third Plate: Field Notes on the Future of Food.* New York: The Penguin Press, 2014.

Deutsch, Tracey. *Building a Housewife's Paradise: Gender, Politics, and American Grocery Stores in the Twentieth Century.* Chapel Hill: The University of North Carolina Press, 2011.

Estabrook, Barry. *Pig Tales: An Omnivore's Quest for Sustainable Meat.* New York: W. W. Norton, 2016.

Estabrook, Barry. *Tomatoland: How Modern Industrial Agriculture Destroyed Our Most Alluring Fruit.* Kansas City, MO: Andrews McMeel Publishing, 2011.

Fromartz, Samuel. *Organics, Inc.: Natural Foods and How They Grew.* New York: Harcourt Inc., 2006.

The Future of Food. Directed by Deborah Koons Garcia. Burbank: Cinema Libre Studio, 2004.

Genoways, Ted. *The Chain: Farm, Factory, and the Fate of Our Food.* New York: HarperCollins, 2014.

Glassner, Barry. *The Gospel of Food: Everything You Think You Know About Food Is Wrong.* New York: HarperCollins, 2007.

Greenberg, Paul. *Four Fish: The Future of the Last Wild Food.* New York: The Penguin Press, 2010.

Grescoe, Taras. *Bottomfeeder: How to Eat Ethically in a World of Vanishing Seafood.* New York: Bloomsbury, 2008.

Handler, Julian H., ed. *The Food Industry Executive's Pleasure Reader.* New York: Media Books, 1969.

Johnson, Laurence A. *Over the Counter and On the Shelf: Country Storekeeping in America, 1620–1920.* Rutland, VT: Charles E. Tuttle Company, 1961.

Kamp, David. *The United States of Arugula: The Sun-Dried, Cold-Pressed, Dark-Roasted, Extra Virgin Story of the American Food Revolution.* New York: Broadway Books, 2006.

Keaggy, Bill. *Milk Eggs Vodka: Grocery Lists Lost and Found.* Cincinnati: How Books, 2007.

Kurlansky, Mark. *Birdseye: The Adventures of a Curious Man.* New York: Doubleday, 2012.

Levenstein, Harvey. *Paradox of Plenty: A Social History of Eating in Modern America.* London: Oxford University Press, 1993.

Levinson, Marc. *The Great A&P and the Struggle for Small Business In America.* New York: Hill and Wang, 2011.

Marshall, Alex. *How Cities Work: Suburbs, Sprawl, and the Roads Not Taken.* Austin: University of Texas Press, 2000.

McGee, Harold. *On Food and Cooking: The Science and Lore of the Kitchen.* New York: Scribner, 2004.

McMillan, Tracie. *The American Way of Eating: Undercover at Walmart, Applebee's, Farm Fields and the Dinner Table.* New York: Scribner, 2012.

McPhee, John. *Giving Good Weight.* New York: Farrar, Straus and Giroux, 1979.

Moss, Michael. *Salt Sugar Fat: How the Food Giants Hooked Us.* New York: Random House, 2013.

Nestle, Marion. *Food Politics: How the Food Industry Influences Nutrition and Health.* Berkeley: University of California Press, 2013.

Nestle, Marion. *What to Eat.* New York: North Point Press, 2006.

Packard, Vance. *The Hidden Persuaders.* New York: Random House, 1957.

Pollan, Michael. *Cooked: A Natural History of Transformation.* New York: The Penguin Press, 2013.

Pollan, Michael. *The Omnivore's Dilemma: A Natural History of Four Meals.* New York: The Penguin Press, 2006.

Roberts, Paul. *The End of Food.* New York: Houghton Mifflin Harcourt, 2008.

Schlosser, Eric. *Fast Food Nation: The Dark Side of the All-American Meal.* Boston: Houghton Mifflin, 2001.

Trager, James. *The Food Chronology: A Food Lover's Compendium of Events and Anecdotes, from Prehistory to the Present.* New York: Henry Holt and Company, 1995.

Trillin, Calvin. *Messages from My Father: A Memoir.* New York: Farrar, Straus and Giroux, 1996.

Wrangham, Richard. *Catching Fire: How Cooking Made Us Human.* New York: Basic Books, 2009.

ACKNOWLEDGMENTS

My first and foremost thanks go to the people in this book, most notably Jeff Heinen, Tom Heinen, and Chris Foltz. Thanks to Chris for his initial enthusiasm for the project, the inception of which dates to 2009. He told Jeff and Tom that my intended book could be of value. Once Tom and Jeff agreed, they agreed 100 percent, and gave me complete access to anything I needed. They were, all three of them, extraordinarily generous with their time and candor, and always made themselves available when I needed them.

I spoke with scores of people in the company. They, too, were enormously generous with their time, with interviews, and in responding to countless follow-up emails. To all of those with whom I spoke and corresponded, whether they are mentioned by name or not in these pages, I thank you. A special shout-out and thanks to Dr. Todd, who suggested that we meet not in his offices, or in a grocery store, but, rather, in the woods.

Thanks to all those in the larger community of food thinkers and writers for their time and willingness to talk to me, including Marion Nestle, Michael Pollan, Harry Balzer, Calvin Trillin, Ruth Reichl, and Mike Lee, who has created a fascinating project, thefuturemarket.com, that hopes to imagine grocery stores of the future. And, at the Food Marketing Institute, Dagmar Farr and Sue Wilkinson. And thanks to the woman who bought the fat-free half-and-half, wherever you are. You really got me thinking.

Highest thanks of all go to Michael Sand, who acquired this book when he moved to Abrams. He is a great editor, reader, and friend—a pro—and I'm lucky to be able to work with him.

Karen Wise didn't just copyedit this book, she served as a secondary editor at my request. Not only did she eliminate dangling modifiers and correct me on any number of spellings and facts, she was also vocal about editorial issues (such as the book's structure) and helped ensure that my rants remained on the rails. She, too, is a friend and I'm grateful to work with her.

Thank you, John Gall, Abrams's creative director, for producing what seemed to be a thousand different cover ideas in the very difficult task of presenting such a simple-seeming, but complex, subject as groceries on a book jacket.

Also at Abrams, thank you to Gabriel Levinson, managing editor; Melissa Esner in marketing; and Claire Bamundo and Gabby Fisher in publicity.

Thank you to the wonderful Cait Hoyt, my agent at Creative Artists Agency.

Thank you, Caryn and Henry Foltz, and J.D. and Catherine Sullivan, for giving me a home in my hometown when I needed to be there to report and write. I will never be able to tell you how much it has meant to me.

Special thanks to Miss S. for the many reads of the early pages and drafts, and for your ever-astute comments, invaluable suggestions, and unfailing encouragement—for all of this I'm more grateful than I can say in words.

Finally, I'd like to thank all the grocers out there, those who truly care about the food they sell; and also the customers they serve, those who likewise recognize the fundamental importance of our food.

INDEX

Farley, Thomas, 82
farmer's markets
    in America, 88
    grocery stores and, 21
farming. *See* meat; produce
Fast Food Nation (Schlosser), 127, 247
fat (dietary)
    health and, 30, 80–82, 114–15
    in meat, 185, 185n73
FDA. *See* Food and Drug Administration
Ferdman, Roberto A., 125
fish. *See* seafood
Foltz, Chris, 24–26, 29, 155–59, 287
    on business, 59–61, 71–74, 151–52,
        167
food. *See specific topics*
Food and Drug Administration (FDA),
    83
    labels and, 100–101
food deserts, 1, 19–20
food production. *See also* produce
    in America, 57–58
    of chicken, 193–94
    grocery stores and, 11–12, 14–15,
        18–19, 25–26, 30
    health and, 80–82
    labels for, 31, 31n13
    of meat, 49–50, 57, 102, 184–88,
        192–94, 201–2
    transparency in, 25–26
France, 83, 260n104
Frazier, Ian, 96–98, 97nn45–46
frozen food
    in America, 257–60
    business of, 254–60
    in grocery stores, 253–60
    packaging of, 256–57
    produce as, 253–54
fruit, 218–22

Gair, Robert, 37–38
Gaul, Marty, 110–14
Geis, Fred, 276–79, 284–85
Geis, Greg, 276–79, 284–85
genetically modified organisms (GMOs),

105–8, 107n49
Gericke, William Frederick, 225
Giant Eagle, 16, 23, 23n9, 72, 145
Gilman, George, 34–35
glyphosate. *See* genetically modified
    organisms
GMOs. *See* genetically modified
    organisms
Goldman, Sylvan, 40
Gonzalez, Rick, 137
Grazia, Mario, 206, 213–14, 216–22, 225
Great American Tea Company, 34
Great Atlantic & Pacific Tea Company
    (A&P)
    as corporation, 36–39, 44–46, 48
    Gilman for, 34–35
    Hartford for, 35–37
    history of, 32–39, 42
The Great Depression, 44–46
Great Plains (Frazier), 96–98, 97n45
Green, Connie, 151
greenhouses, 223–28
grocery stores. *See also* corporations;
    Heinen's; prepared food; produce
    in America, 9–11, 27–28, 51–52,
        286–92
    A&P, 32–39, 42, 44–46, 48
    bagging in, 129–37
    business of, 4–5, 24–26, 29–30, 36–39,
        39n18, 59–61, 65–67, 74–75,
        135–37, 153–55, 153n63, 205–6,
        218n86, 229, 244–45, 286–88
    butchers in, 48
    by corporations, 15–17, 52, 55–58, 66
    carrots for, 209–13
    cars for, 13, 41, 51
    coupons for, 35
    culture of, 116–17
    customer service in, 48–49
    departments in, 3, 69–70
    design of, 276–83
    distribution for, 53–55
    farmer's markets and, 21
    food production and, 11–12, 14–15,
        18–19, 25–26, 30

ABOUT THE AUTHOR

MICHAEL RUHLMAN is an award-winning and bestselling author. He has collaborated on several leading cookbooks, including *The French Laundry Cookbook, Bouchon, Ad Hoc at Home*, and *Bouchon Bakery* with Thomas Keller; *A Return to Cooking* with Eric Ripert; *Michael Symon's Live to Cook* with Michael Symon; and *Salumi* and *Charcuterie* with Brian Polcyn. He is the author of critically acclaimed books including *The Elements of Cooking, Ratio, Egg*, and *Ruhlman's Twenty*, which won the 2012 James Beard Foundation Award in the General Cooking category and the International Association of Culinary Professionals Cookbook Award in the Food and Beverage Reference/Technical category. He also wrote a trio of beloved nonfiction books covering the culinary world: *The Making of a Chef, The Soul of a Chef*, and *The Reach of a Chef*. Ruhlman has written about food and cooking for the *New York Times, Gourmet, Food Arts*, the *Los Angeles Times*, and other publications. He was born in Cleveland, Ohio, and divides his time between Providence, Rhode Island, and New York City.